A clash of cults
A murder myst
And a Christian's
journey of Faith
All wrapped within
the slice of history
between the Arab Spring
of 2011 and 2014.

www.thenewcrusades.ca
www.ballsfalls.info

Waldemar Guenter
aka John Hartig

MW01688742

amazon.ca
chapters.indigo.ca

The New Crusades

Waldemar Guenter

Copyright © 2015 by Waldemar Guenter

All rights reserved.

No part of this publication may be reproduced, distributed, or transmitted in any form or by any means, including photocopying, recording, or other electronic or mechanical methods, without the prior written permission of the publisher, except in the case of brief quotations embodied in critical reviews and certain other noncommercial uses permitted by copyright law.

Wholesale discounts for book orders are available through Ingram or Spring Arbor Distributors.

ISBN

978-0-9947753-0-6 (paperback)

978-0-9947753-2-0 (ebook)

978-0-9947753-1-3 (Hard cover)

Published in Canada.

First Edition

CAST OF MAIN CHARACTERS:

Wally Guenter, 68, photographer and web designer.

Wally's wife, 57, prefers anonymity, especially from the internet.

Leonard Webb, 42, Wally's brother-in-law, a computer nerd.

Charlie, "dad," 80, Leonard and Wally's wife's father.

Karl de Jong, 60, Wally's counselor.

Pastor Greg, 30, Tuesday evening Prayer Meetings.

Sam Clemens, 66, Wally's photography pal.

Aamir Ibrahim, 26, Muslim extremist; his name means "civilized."

a.k.a.: Hafiz Bashir, Aamir's false identity in Syria and Iraq.

a.k.a.: Jorin Aslan, disguised as a Turk, to get back to Canada.

Amy St. Clair, 26, violinist, Aamir's former Canadian girlfriend.

Hazirah Ibrahim, 25, Aamir's sister; her name means "chaste."

Alexander Kucharski, 25, Hazirah's Canadian boyfriend.

Abqurah Ibrahim, 21, younger sister; her name means "genius."

Adl Ibrahim, 60, father; his name means "justice."

Yaminah Ibrahim, 55, mother; her name means "right and proper."

Detective Jake Klassen, 60, police detective, Niagara Region.

Detective Ed Spencer, 32, police detective, Hamilton District.

Ramona Szewczuk, 55, aka "Baryon," computer nerd.

Abdul Ali al-Sayed: Hafiz's [Aamir's] immediate commander in ISIS.

Umar Wahidi, 30, Toronto contact in terrorist cell.

Mike Feeney, 45, pilot of the Cessna.

Jerome Lavigne, 26, security guard at Wilfrid Laurier University.

Last, but not least, God and/or Allah, "The Alpha and The Omega of Everything."

CHAPTER 1

27 HOURS EARLIER, 11:00 A.M.
MONDAY, OCTOBER 10, 2011

"Please don't!"

"You have shamed the family!"

Aamir stabbed his sister without remorse. He was performing a duty motivated by an old law. Hazirah's scream was stifled as Aamir's hand clutched her mouth, turned her body around, and with a quick motion... She sagged to the ground as her life blood drained onto the path. Aamir dragged her into the bushes and kicked dirt over the bloody leaves.

It was such a lovely day. Sunshine bathed the stream coming down from Lower Ball's Falls. The woods shone with bright autumn colours. It was a picture perfect day along Niagara's Bruce Trail.

26 HOURS EARLIER, NOON
MONDAY, OCTOBER 10, 2011

Wally bicycled into the Ball's Falls Conservation Area. That way he could save the entry fee by not bringing his car all the way in. He parked on a farmer's property nearby, a friend who gave him an open invitation to leave the car there, along the grape vines. That made it easy for Wally to unload his bicycle from the car, and then pedal into the Conservation Area with his camera. Saving the entry fee meant extra change, later, for Tim Horton's coffee and maybe a doughnut!

Penny-pinching had always been a trait practiced in his family since his grandmother's time. She was Jewish, and Wally often wondered if that trait was part of the Jewish DNA, or part of a background of poverty from those depression days in Europe. Wally considered frugality a blessing, not a fault.

If there were a "Jewishness" to looks, then Wally had it. A bulbous nose went ahead of his face, with a slight hook in it. If there were one thing Wally might change about his appearance, it might be his nose. But then, he believed that, "prominent noses make for prominent people."

Wally thought about "his people," even though he had renounced his Jewishness some time ago. In regard to the Holocaust, he found it ironic that the Old Testament acknowledged genocide in its own history, "... and when the Lord your God delivers them over to you [for example, the Hittites], you shall conquer them and utterly destroy them." [Deut. 7:1-7] Some of the words smacked of the same proclamations which came out of Islamic mouths in the modern day. "No covenant, no mercy, no inter-marriages."

Wally understood how the Israelis might draw up defensive walls of self-preservation, in the modern world, surrounded by Arab nations. Maybe the Muslims feel the same way about "the Western world?" Wally was convinced that genocide was a kind of paranoia for self-preservation exercised by the nation that is afraid of losing its identity. Wally chuckled at a joke he heard on TV: "Jewish imagination is paranoia confirmed by history!" Maybe the Muslims and even the Christians think the same way about themselves? What about others, the Buddhists and the Hindus? Everybody is paranoid because there is, in fact, something to be paranoid about! Start inter-marrying, for example, and soon sons or daughters will turn away from following your own culture and your own God! There has to be some truth in that! Deuteronomy wants to keep the Jews separate, "for you are a holy people to the Lord your God... a special treasure above all the peoples on the face of the earth." Hmm, Muhammad must have felt the same way about his Muslims when his religion took over the Arabian Peninsula during the 7th century A.D.

All of these thoughts rushed through Wally's mind. He reflected upon his own heritage. "Jewish or nothing?" he asked himself. "Why make it so absolute?" Since he got married, he gravitated towards his wife's religion, which was Mennonite Christian. Was he kicking dirt in the face of the God of Deuteronomy? He scratched his bulbous nose.

He adjusted his black baseball cap which covered his balding head. It had red words in the front: "St. Catharines, 65 Plus, Hockey Group."

Wally showed all of his 65+ years, with silver grey hair, and a face, which sported a stylish grey mustache and goatee. He looked like an elderly professor, who happened to play hockey in an old-timer's league. He stopped playing since he'd pulled two tendons in his shoulder last year, but he still liked wearing the cap.

Wally could have passed for a double of Eli Wallach without the meanness of the Mexican hombre in "The Good, The Bad and The Ugly." His face was weather-beaten but friendly. His eyes were small which squinted from behind brown horn-rimmed glasses. He always wore a smile on his face, and those squinty eyes twinkled with amusement.

Wally liked people and took delight in the quirks of human nature. He walked with a slight stoop. After all, he was 68 years old! Just another senior with a camera! But he was still robust enough to tackle the woods along "The Bruce Trail" for his annual collection of autumn photos. After he got his pictures, he intended to relax in the evening. He wanted to see, "The Story of the Jews," narrated by Simon Schama on a PBS special. Wally liked history, all kinds, almost as much as scenery photography.

A family was picnicking at one of the tables, a Mid-Eastern family, from the looks of it. An older bearded man, and his wife, wearing the traditional "hijab" or head covering, which to Wally's eyes seemed out of place in Canada. But his own family had been immigrants, coming years ago from Austria back in 1954. Wally wouldn't know what to do in Austria, now that he was Canadian.

He rode his bicycle to the public washroom. After all, if he were gone most of the day slogging through the woods for pretty pictures, he needed to use the facilities. As he entered, a swarthy young man with a heavy black beard exited. He flashed a cursory smile, exposing nice white teeth. A gold necklace hung around his neck. Wally read the words on it, large and written in English! Maybe it was blatant advertisement. "Muhammad is his prophet."

"Really strange," thought Wally. "There seems to be half a saying missing!" Wally wondered how Muslim men grew those lush black beards. Must be something in the DNA?

After he was finished, Wally parked his bicycle against a post, locked it up and swung his Nikon D700 over his shoulder, along side his small backpack in which he had stashed an apple, a sandwich, some cookies and a Pepsi.

"Well, let's get to it, Alice," he said. He was speaking to his camera, of course, a nickname he gave it, somehow giving his D700 a personality of its own. When he looked through the lens, he always imagined he was Alice in Wonderland, looking *Through the Looking Glass*, at all kinds of marvelous things in nature and in people, which were normally hidden to the human eye.

He walked past the Muslim family, nodding to them with a friendly smile. The young man did not smile back this time.

There was a mosque in St. Catharines and Wally tried to accept this as part of the Canadian Mosaic, enriching and expanding the multicultural identity of Canada. The large words emblazoned on the side of the building read, "None to be worshipped but God, Muhammad is His Prophet." Wally noticed that the statement said God, not Allah. Perhaps that was to accommodate words familiar to the English speaking community.

Wally tried to think of his attitude as accepting and enlightened. After all, the French took the land from the Aboriginals and the British from the French and then the floodgates were opened to all the Europeans with a promise of more land and a new life. And now, the floodgates seemed to open up for people from Middle East and Indonesia, enlarging Canada's Mosaic, hopefully making it more colourful and richer in the mix of cultures and nationalities. Wally's own dad had to get used to hockey, a stupid game, which he eventually grew to love.

Wally found the first marker to the Bruce Trail, called a "Blaze," by a "Private Driveway, Authorized Vehicles Only." The path led along farmers' fields and orchards, along the west side of Ball's Falls. He breathed in the scenery and took some choice photos with his camera. Such lovely colours and intricate patterns! There was even a clear lookout at one point towards the other side of the gorge where trees created a patchwork of reds, yellows and greens, covering the landscape with nature's own brilliant quilt. A nice calendar shot! Wally took two. He compared all the colours in the scene to the Canadian Mosaic, how lovely with all its differences.

A couple of joggers thumped out of the woods along the path. Young guys, about 30 years of age, strongly built and kicking up a good pace. Wally thought "ouch," a reminder that his orthotics couldn't stand that kind of punishment anymore. "Ah, the days of our youth!" he thought. The joggers nodded at Wally and threw him a brief "Hi." Whoosh! They were gone! Meantime, Wally let his fingers move at their own pace, snapping pictures. Paul Simon's lyrics floated through his mind:

> "Slow down, you're movin' too fast,
>
> you gotta make the mornin' last!"

Wally looked for the turn-off going down to Twenty Mile Creek. Surely there must be a fork somewhere which would lead down to the bottom of the Niagara Escarpment! He kept going and going and going! His mind tuned in to lyrics from songs that he loved, Golden Oldies and Musicals. He only recalled snippets but they pleased him. The sun and sky seemed to bring melodies out in him. Patches of blue poked through the hazy sky. Somehow Andrew Lloyd Webber's lines from "Cats" crept into his mind:

"Memory

All alone in the moonlight

I can smile at the old days

I was beautiful then"

His eyes lit up. "Ah! A gravel road that leads down! Maybe this is it?" He followed it and when it led into an orchard, he turned around and headed back the way he'd come, wondering where he had gone wrong?

He was convinced he hadn't lost the Bruce Trail markers. But there was nothing evident which would lead him down the gorge to Twenty Mile Creek. The tune kept on going through his head: "Memory, all alone in the moonlight."

"I hope I won't be stuck out here in the moonlight. Where *was* that path to get to the bottom of Ball's Falls?"

Wally forded a little stream over which the Parks people had built a wooden bridge. There was a maintenance building off to the side and eventually the path itself opened up again... but, this time, to a flat gravel road with houses nestled along side with lovely gardens and trees. Speaking of a wrong turn!

He was on Fifth Avenue and could see Hwy #24 in the distance with cars and trucks whizzing by. What could he do? He headed for Hwy #24, knowing that he'd gone in a huge circle and that the entrance to Ball's Falls was just a couple of kilometers ahead, off the highway. Yep, he zigged when he should have zagged!

As trucks whooshed by on the highway, he took pictures of the weeds in the ditch. He trekked back into the Ball's Falls entrance, took a photo of a couple of signs, and thought about words in another song: "Feelin' like a fool."

His back now ached and he stooped more as he trudged along, pulling himself past the Tourist Bureau. He took a breather and then headed down to the parking lot where his bicycle waited patiently for him. The family had finished their picnic by now and were gone. "Folding their tents, like Arabs, stealing silently away." Wally reprimanded himself, "I shouldn't stereotype people! I'm an immigrant, myself." Little did he know they had left without one member of their family!

He told a park attendant about his wayward trek. "I zigged when I should have zagged." The park attendant was amused. Actually, he laughed!

Wally was determined to get the direction right the next day, if the weather held out. More leaves were falling each day, and the brilliant colour in the trees was slowly fading. He hoped it wouldn't rain in the next week or so! He decided, "Tuesday, will have to be 'the day'!"

CHAPTER 2

4 HOURS EARLIER, 10:00 A.M.
TUESDAY, OCTOBER 11, 2011

THE SUN POPPED IN AND OUT. THE SKY ALTERNATED between bright blue and overcast gray. It looked like Wally might catch a break, provided he could find the right path this time! Robert Frost's poem came to mind, "The Road Not Taken" [first published in 1916]. Movies, Music, and Poems, that's how Wally's mind worked!

He snagged two typical pictures of Lower Ball's Falls from the top, leaning against the retaining wall to steady his hand. White clouds floated across a blue sky. Things looked good for picture taking. He'd better find his way to the bottom of the gorge this time.

There was one other photographer at the wall snapping away but Wally was in no mood for shoptalk. He moved on. The guy's camera looked like an amateur Powershot mounted on a light-weight tripod. Wally preferred not to drag his Manfrotto tripod into the woods. He liked to steady his hand on a rock or a stump. "Do it naturally," he said to himself!

He crossed the bridge and looked at the grassy field that stretched along the west side of Twenty Mile Creek. He could see a white rectangle there, way at the end of the field, marking the Bruce Trail. He crossed to the end of the field, where somebody, sometime, had dislocated a brace in the fence which overlooked the very top of Ball's Falls.

He straddled the sagging fence and hopped onto the rocky ledge which hung over the Falls. He took two more pictures from the top, with the distant gorge stretched out below, beyond the loud, cascading water.

It was a long way down and Wally didn't tempt fate, so he retreated back over the fence, the way he'd come. He felt satisfied that he'd find the way down to the gorge this time, besides jumping or falling over the cliff! He would take the road, "not typically taken."

He found it! He'd just gone a little too far the other day. There was a split in the trail by a retaining wall, the one bearing left marking the Bruce Trail with the white rectangle, the other bearing right, not marked, but running along the retaining wall to a short drop, which led to a small path, going down to the bottom of the gorge.

Except for the immediate drop, the rest of the "trail" looked navigable. Small trees, roots and rocks were spread along the drop at strategic locations, which made descent possible, so he slung his camera strap into a safer position behind his back; and down he went, grabbing a hand hold on this root or that, and edging footholds against this rock or that.

After this drop of about 20 feet, the slope lessened and Wally felt like he had done something great, like he did when he was, well... 20! He didn't feel 68 at all, now that he caught his second wind. Wally looked back every once in a while to memorize the looks of the slope and the trees for when he'd return. He thought, "Maybe I should have thrown out bread crumbs?"

He looked up and behind, feasting his eyes on the huge white clouds which floated across a deep blue sky. It was breathtaking above the great terrain of rocks, trees and roots. This rough scenery characterized the Niagara Escarpment. The rugged hillside afforded some very impressive pictures.

The closer he got to the Falls, the more intense the spray became. He kept wiping his lens dry before each picture he took. Tendrils and branches snagged his legs, until he finally gave up and backtracked, satisfied with his shots, considering the circumstances. He had no pretense about any of his shots being "the definitive picture" of Ball's Falls. "Everybody, I guess, tries to get that or thinks they got it."

Wally was content for the moment in what his eyes saw. He knew most of his pictures were decent. Some photos he had already deleted were probably better than a lot of people's best shots. So, time to call it quits! It was getting too wet out here and the rocks too slippery. Wally backtracked past familiar trees. The uphill climb to that 20 foot drop was straight ahead. He huffed and puffed like a 68 year-old, bending over once in a while to catch his breath.

He finally got to the drop which was now a very steep rise... but it was only 20 feet up and he had to make a choice, right side or left side, for the best hand-hold on trees and rocks? Hiking boots would have helped, but he managed, with minimal slipping and sliding, despite wearing running shoes.

Poor shoes! They were new, only two months old! Now, they looked like something he'd worn for 68 years! Up he went over the ridge and faced the retaining wall once more which was there to keep fools like him out. He took a deep breath and plodded on beyond the wall, and the wire fence, getting back on the legitimate trail.

There was another Bruce Trail trekker off to the side of the path taking pictures through the trees of Lower Ball's Falls. Wally thought that the Falls were too blocked to make a good photo, not through all those trees. You have to get down below to an unobstructed view but he wasn't going to encourage any foolhardiness.

The stranger was a young man wearing a blue toque and jacket who used ski poles to assist his walk over the rough terrain. He had a Black Lab dog with him, named Lila, which sported a red bandana around its neck. A friendly pooch that didn't bark when Wally approached. The dog and its owner were mild-mannered and gentle.

Wally introduced himself and offered to take a picture of both of them by the fence with the Falls in the background. The Bruce Trail trekker wanted Wally to e-mail him the shot with his lovely Black Lab in it. He said he was on the trail on a fundraiser project for a school in Welland. It's amazing the people you run into!

CHAPTER 3

PRESENT TIME, 2:00 P.M.
TUESDAY, OCTOBER 11, 2011

PHOTOGRAPHY WAS A PASSION FOR WALLY. IT'S NOT THAT he was obsessed with it, but at times, he felt a gentle tug, just a nudge on certain days, to grab his camera and take what he called, "a photographic jaunt" to collect pretty pictures, like a gardener picking pretty flowers.

He liked scenery. In fact he loved it. Weddings had been slow this summer and nothing was moving for him in October, so he put his energies into scenery. There was something religious about the experience. When he took his jaunts, it wasn't that he was looking for pictures. It seemed like pictures were looking for him. He'd turn his head and there they were... just for the taking!

Wally was happy that he'd made it to the bottom of the Falls that morning. He came back in the afternoon to take advantage of the different light, but he never got down to the gorge. Fate stepped in to change his life forever.

He was at the fork in the road by the retaining wall. Wally reached up to grab an orange leaf hanging down from a branch. The delicate veins reminded him of human blood vessels branching out to keep the body of the leaf alive. The colours were vibrant in each and every leaf; and yet, Wally knew that was the sign that the leaves were dying. He swiveled his camera forward and took a photo of the tops of the trees which were like hands reaching for the sky. What a lovely day! He tried another angle and backed up into the bush. He tripped over Hazirah's body!

She had been dead for two days and raccoons and squirrels had already been at her. Hazirah's *hijab* still covered her head.

Wally slung his camera behind his back and got out of there. He reported the gruesome discovery to parks maintenance and got them to phone the police. He was a bit of a Luddite and didn't carry a cell phone.

. . . . .

"Did you take any pictures of the body?" the sergeant asked.

"No," said Wally, "I take pictures of scenery, not bodies."

"We'll need the memory card to make sure. You'll get it back." He paused, "Now then, can I have your name?"

"Waldemar Guenter. People call me, Wally... uh, less confusing, more Canadian," he added. He spelled Guenter, "that's with an 'e'." He hoped they wouldn't make that mistake someday on his gravestone! Wally handed over the memory card which was put it into a bag and labeled. A homicide detective from the precinct walked in.

Detective Jake Klassen looked serious. Maybe that was the look he was born with. Maybe he was always 60 years old. He wore a crumpled suit and tie, something out of the 1950s, or something he might have slept in. His hair was still black. Maybe dyed for vanity? Wally expected him to come out with the line, "Now, let's have the facts, sir, only the facts!" Unexpectedly, his faced broke into a friendly smile; and he extended his hand, "Hi, I'm Detective Klassen. Now tell me when and how you discovered the body."

"Well, I kind of backed up off the trail to get a better angle of the trees and I stumbled on something. That was her leg. She was all bloody. Wore a *hijab*... and the face was cut up and her clothes disheveled. I got out of there fast and called you folks from the maintenance shed at The Falls at about 3:00 o'clock."

"Did you see anybody at the park that looked suspicious, somebody who might have done that?"

"Well, two days ago, there was a Muslim family having a picnic. A mom, dad and a young bearded guy. I went to the washroom and ran into him. He had a gold chain around his neck that said in glaring letters, *Muhammad is his prophet*. Afterwards I went on past their picnic table and continued on my trek to the Bruce Trail for my scenery photos."

"We've got just a few more questions. We'll also have to get your fingerprints and a sample of your DNA, just to rule you out as a suspect."

"What?" Wally thought, "Rule me out as a suspect? Here I'm fingerprinted and DNA taken, so I won't be a possible suspect? I sure feel like a suspect!"

After half an hour of questioning and re-questioning, Wally walked out with his brain swimming and his emotions still in shock from all the blood he had seen. He could understand how people don't want to get involved as witnesses. But not saying anything would have made him feel worse... and guilty.

CHAPTER 4

"The victim of culture and upbringing can be retaught; the psychopath is a hard-wired tragedy."

[DET. JAKE KLASSEN]

.....

AUTOPSY REPORT
THURSDAY, OCTOBER 13, 2011

DETECTIVE KLASSEN READ THE M.E.'S REPORT. THE AUTOPSY confirmed the details of Hazirah's killing. "Stabbed, throat cut... nothing sexual!" She was evidently Muslim because of the *hijab*. Could it be an "honour killing?" Could culture or religion make somebody not criminally responsible? What would a lawyer do with that?

Klassen recalled that the photographer, who stumbled across the body, said the family "picnicking" in the

Conservation Area was Muslim. Klassen said out loud, "So, how do we find the guy who did this?"

He didn't want to reveal the more delicate details to the media. So, he kept it simple, saying that a body of a young female had been found in the bushes at Ball's Falls, murdered, stabbed to death, and that she might have been Muslim because she was wearing a *hijab*.

He did release the fact that bloody fingerprints were lifted from a smooth rock at the scene. They were run through the national database known as Criminal Record Check managed by the RCMP in Ottawa; but no match was found. A man's shoe impressions were found near the body, size 12. The guess was that the man was probably more than 6 feet tall. Despite some clues, the police felt they had hit a brick wall on this one, unless they caught a lucky break.

Klassen was hopeful, "Well, at least we have fingerprints and a possible height. Maybe something will turn up but who knows when?"

.....

Wally was called into the police station to pick up his memory card. He put it back into his camera and checked that all 72 of his Ball's Falls images were still there. Whew! They were!

"Nice pictures," said the desk sergeant, who had viewed them with Detective Klassen. It seemed like everybody at the cop shop had seen them. Wally smiled and said, "Thanks... Oh, by the way, will they ever identify the body or find the guy?"

"Probably not," said the desk sergeant. "We took a DNA sample and dental records of the girl. But she was so slashed up; we have trouble reconstructing her features... unless somebody comes in to report a missing person. But so far, there's nothing. Nobody to claim the body."

"Really sad," commented Wally.

Detective Klassen entered the room. "Ah, just the man I want to see!"

He shook hands with Wally and said, "In a case like this, a witness who discovers a body is often traumatized. Maybe you don't always feel it right away, but things have a way of catching up with you. It can be unnerving. I remember when I shot a thug threatening me with a knife... well, that's another story... but here's my card. I can give you the name of a very good counselor, just in case."

"No thanks," said Wally. "I just want to get back to my computer and my pictures." He slipped the detective's card in his pocket anyway.

Wally was itching to head out the door to "his safe place," which was his computer and his pictures. That was his refuge and, you might say, his strength. He was a master photographer who loved bringing out highlights and enhancing details in his pictures. He loved what Photoshop and Lightroom could do.

"I guess the cops, including that desk sergeant, had a good look at my pictures," he said to himself. "Well, I don't really mind... I do take nice pictures!"

A skeptical afterthought flashed through his mind, "Too bad there's no market for nice pictures!"

Wally had always felt an urge, some kind of push to take scenery photos. He thought, "Well, it was a good day! Too bad the body spoiled it!" He reprimanded himself for the stupid thought.

Wally stored a little thought in his mind about seeing a counselor sometime down the road.

.....

Nothing had come of the murder at Ball's Falls, no victim ID, no suspect, no trial and no justice. Just a little write-up on the front page of a local paper:

> **Body Found at Ball's Falls**
>
> Police discovered the body of a young woman, between the ages of 20-30, this past Tuesday, October 11, 2011. She was the victim of foul play. Police confirmed that she had been stabbed several times.
>
> Authorities say she was probably Muslim because of her head covering. No evidence was found at the scene to assist the police in finding the killer. It is hoped that someone will come forward if he or she has seen anything suspicious around Ball's Falls on or about October 6. Or knows of a missing person.

Police Detective Klassen, heading the investigation, commented to the media, "There has been no report of anybody missing and nothing we can really go on in this case. The police are at a loss, as to who did this or why?"

He added, "The body had been in the woods for several days. The poor girl was knifed. We cannot imagine why somebody would do something horrendous like this, especially in a rural community."

He said that this is the first murder he'd come across in 30 years as a police officer in Jordan, with such a small population of 3,000 people, an area characterized by farms and nice suburban houses. "We've got things like tourism, wineries and orchards. Things like this just don't happen here!"

CHAPTER 5

"If you're over 21, the brain shuts down to new things. That's all a big lie, just like, 'You can't teach an old dog new tricks'!"

[LEONARD WEBB TO HIS OLDER BROTHER-IN-LAW, WALLY]

. . . . .

2012 JANUARY @MOHAWK COLLEGE
WINTER SESSION WEB DESIGN I

LEONARD WAS WALLY'S NERDY BROTHER-IN-LAW. HE WAS A web designer, musician, singer and painter, all rolled into one. A real "Renaissance Man." His gangly 6' 2" frame looked like it should belong on a basketball court, not hunched over a computer keyboard. He was all angles and energy. He was 42 years old; and should have been born two decades earlier, during the days of the hippies, because he had shoulder-length hair and a triangular tuft of goatee under his lower lip.

He often walked around the house with a headphone stuck to his ear, talking to clients about tweaking their websites.

Leonard flipped his hair back, "Why don't you take some design courses at Mohawk College?" He gave Wally a compliment, "Your pictures are too nice to hide in your computer. You should show them off. So make a website!"

Leonard was always the bright spark when he entered a room. He habitually cradled a large Timmy's coffee in one hand, while he grabbed the mouse with the other and quickly clicked this or that on the screen. Relatives got his expertise free of charge. He'd come over to the house with his coffee. He'd put it down, take the mouse and within minutes, the problem was solved! How'd he do that?

Wally took Leonard's advice when the January Winter Term 2012 rolled along. Winter months usually meant no weddings anyway, and if any requests came in, then Wally could just refer them to a colleague.

Wally enrolled in "Web Page Design Part I," "Fireworks," and "An Introduction to Dreamweaver." All heavy courses. Classes went from 7 to 10 p.m., three nights a week. Often, he didn't get home until 11 p.m.

The drive was only 40 minutes from his home, down the QEW, off at Burlington Street, past all the steel factories, what Wally called the roller coaster ride, and then up the mountain to Fennell Avenue and Mohawk College.

Wally often popped in Gerry Rafferty's *City to City* or *Snakes and Ladders* and grooved to songs like," Baker Street," "Right Down The Line," and "Stuck in the Middle With You": *"I got the feeling that something ain't right, / I'm so scared in case I fall off my chair, /* And *I'm wondering how I'll get down the stairs, / Clowns to the left of me, / Jokers to the right,* here I am, / Stuck in the middle with you."

Gerry Rafferty died on January 4, 2011. Years of alcoholism took Gerry's life at the age of 63, leaving the music world, and in fact the whole world, a lesser place. And here, a few days later, Wally was driving with determination up to Mohawk College for night school, so he could advertise his photos on the internet. He sometimes wondered what that unknown Muslim girl's future might have been, had she not been murdered.

In the meantime, the earth rotated on its axis and time went on, whether people died or not. Gerry Rafferty's own death seemed like such a little thing, compared to huge changes in the Arab world. Wally occasionally switched on the radio to catch up on news, which sparked a good deal of cynicism in him, as he recalled the the initial hopes of "The Arab Spring," not so long ago. Promise of rebirth and new freedoms in Arab countries? "The Arab Spring. Just last year!" Wally recalled.

.....

On January 4, 2011, the same day that Gerry Rafferty died, a Tunisian street vendor, Mohamed Bouzzizi, also died from his injuries, after setting himself on fire a month earlier. The act incited anti-government protests in Tunisia and later unrest in other Arab nations. By mid-January Tunisian President, Zine El Abidine Ben Ali, fled to Saudi Arabia after 23 years in power. The movement was dubbed, "The Arab Spring," and the world, Muslims and non-Muslims alike, hoped that Muslim nations would embrace reforms which would lead to more freedoms and possibly democracy. Wally was convinced that access to modern technology had a lot to do with social protests. Sort of breaking down some medieval doors through the use of cyber space.

In February 2011, Egyptian President, Hosni Mubarak, resigned after widespread protests calling for his departure, putting control of Egypt in the hands of the military, until a general election could be held. Things were looking "good" in Arab countries, but Wally didn't hold his breath for democratic reforms.

Things changed for the worse in "The Arab Spring," within half a year, by autumn 2011, October 9 to be precise, three days before Wally discovered Hazirah's body at Ball's Falls. Two armoured vehicles were caught on video, deliberately driving through a throng of Coptic Christians, protesting in Cairo's Tahrir Square, killing and maiming a bunch of people.

When the final tally came in, 24 people lay dead and more than 200 were wounded. Egypt's new Prime Minister, Essam Sharaf, appealed to Egyptians in a public address to stem the violence. "What is taking place are not clashes between Muslims and Christians but attempts to provoke chaos and dissent," he said. Coptic Christians made up 10% of Egypt's population.

Wally saw the video on the news and couldn't believe that the Arab Spring took such a sour turn from peaceful protests! He recalled the video of the lone "tank man" in Tiananmen Square in Beijing, China, way back in June 1989, facing down a tank which refused to drive over him. His identity was never known. Maybe the government found him and "made him disappear?" Yet hundreds, maybe thousands, of protesters died that summer, repressed by martial law. People demanded reform against inflation, limited career prospects and corruption of the party elite. They wanted job opportunities and a better life. What's wrong with that?

A force of 300,000 troops moved in on Beijing and made arrests, beat people up, shot them and used any means necessary to dispel the crowds. Foreign journalists were expelled from China. International condemnation was ignored and economic sanctions seemed innocuous.

Wally wondered what had been accomplished? He was convinced that the powerful elite and the military in those countries were too corrupt to ever change and introduce a more benign government. So much for democracy and reform there! Too many factions and too many power hungry egos at the top, a lot of them entrenched old cronies in suits and ties, no better than mafia bosses!

Wally had a more benign attitude about Canada, but he was less forgiving toward the United States. He couldn't help but think of Lee Iacocca's book, in which the elderly businessman, then an author at the age of 82, blasted the leadership of corporate America and Congress:

> We've got a gang of clueless bozos steering our ship of state right over a cliff, we've got corporate gangsters stealing us blind, and we can't even clean up after a hurricane much less build a hybrid car. But instead of getting mad, everyone sits around and nods their heads when the politicians say, "Stay the course."
>
> *Stay the course?* You've got to be kidding. This is America, not the damned *Titanic.* I'll give you a sound bite: *Throw the bums out!*
>
> [LEE IACOCCA , *Where Have All The Leaders Gone?* 2007]

Wally praised Iacocca for being an outspoken senior. He thought, "Nice sounding advice, admirable... but how do you get rid of the powers that be?"

He felt that the bureaucracy in the United States was too monstrous to unseat. As far as China and Egypt were concerned, forget it!

There was no magic wand, no Aladdin's lamp and no amount of courage from protesters that could root out entrenched power groups. Somehow large crowds still managed to gather and protest. Cell phones and the internet were a great tool, and an awareness that the world was indeed a, "Global Village."

.....

Wally shared the same sentiments as Lee Iacocca. The public gets frustrated with politicians who legislate stupid laws and spend public money heedlessly. Human nature, understandably, lowers itself to verbal abuse against politicians who do stupid things. Iacocca was not above calling Congress "a gang of clueless bozos" and "bums" who should be thrown out of office.

Wally couldn't help but associate them with "lawyers and liars" who manipulate words to get themselves elected into positions of power. He felt that Iacocca would also appreciate the sentiments of Jonathan Swift who, three centuries earlier, wrote *Gulliver's Travels*, which depicted the depravity of human nature.

Wally was reminded of the country of the Houyhnhnms, who were civilized talking horses, graced with manners and reason. Their name meant "the perfection of nature." They were the rulers of the island, while the deformed humanoids, called Yahoos, were savages which flung poop at Gulliver. The Houyhnhnms had trouble conceiving of "the thing that is not," which means they had no concept of lies, [and probably no lawyers or politicians, as such, in their sensible equine society].

Wally chuckled at the rife political implications. He thought of his own Members of Parliament, supposedly the best brains in the country, who often behaved like long-winded jackasses in the House, without enough horse sense to pass understandable laws which spent public money sensibly and did not favour corporations with huge tax breaks and incentive packages. "Throw the bums out!" But what would replace them? Wally hoped that there were yahoos in government with enough of a brain, a heart and courage to do the right thing.

CHAPTER 6

"I cannot see myself becoming a couch potato after 65. Who made that the law? There is so much to learn in the world, and even beyond it! Who knows what lies in the light at the end of the tunnel!"

[WALDEMAR GUENTER TO A FRIEND]

• • • • •

RAMONA SZEWCZUK
A.K.A. "BARYON"

EVERY TIME WALLY TOOK HIS ROLLER COASTER RIDE ALONG the ups and downs of Burlington Street, and then up the hill to Mohawk College during those winter months, he was glad he was in Canada.

Wally felt that international politics were just beyond his grasp. He preferred to sit at home in front of his computer, figuring out the Hyper Text Markup Language [HTML] to create a Website. It was also preferable to be driving to Mohawk College inside his warm little Hyundai during the Winter Session of 2012, than to be stuck in a chaotic crowd in Tahrir Square, protesting against a corrupt government, which he could do nothing about.

Thank God for the car radio and his CD player! He felt that his little *Accent* was his private little bubble, a safe haven from the world, his own Starship Enterprise guided by Captain Kirk, "to the Final Frontier." For him, his "final frontier" was Mohawk College and launching a website.

His mind was at peace when he listened to Gerry Rafferty songs or symphony music from his favourite radio station, Classical 96.3 FM: "Beautiful music for a crazy world," where he might catch Beethoven's "Moonlight Sonata" or Rimsky-Korsakov's "Scheherazade." He was starting to get miffed with the news anyway, and when it came on, he turned it off more often than not, and breathed in the glorious silence inside his Starship.

Wally made new friends at Mohawk in the nippy winter of 2012. There was a 15 minute coffee break at 8:30 just before Tim Horton's closed up for the night. Wally would always order a French Vanilla and a Boston Cream doughnut.

Ramona Szewczuk was a crotchety senior, very overweight and hampered by arthritis in her knees! She took forever walking to the coffee shop. In fact, when she walked down the hallway her huge breasts bobbled back and forth like a pendulum. Wally thought this was funny and yet so sad because of her infirmity. He couldn't help thinking of the Roger Miller song from way back, "England swings like a pendulum do, Bobbies on bicycles, two by two."

Ramona liked stylish clothes though, gaudy scarves or pearl necklaces. She liked her hair short but natural, which meant grey, a dead give-away for her real age, which was 60. Next to Wally, she was the oldest member in night school.

Her car was stylish too. She drove a 1967 Chevy Camaro, a red one, which she parked in the handicapped spot close to the Mohawk back entrance. It seemed odd to see an elderly lady who could hardly walk drive up in this hot car.

Since Web Page Design was held in the basement, some of the class headed for the elevator at break-time. Ramona lagged behind in the hallway. Wally waited in the elevator and held the door open for her until she got in. They introduced themselves. Ramona sat beside Wally during class and had helped him navigate through the tutorial. She was a whiz.

Nestled in at Timmy's, Wally asked her about her background. Her parents came from Poland and stressed high academic achievement for their little girl. She had always been interested in computers and technology. In fact, when she was in her 20s, she built her own colour TV set from what was then called a Heath-kit and it worked! She became a high-school Physics teacher.

She asked Wally, "Do you know what a baryon is?"

"Some sub-atomic particle, I think."

"I'm impressed. You're in my good books!"

They laughed. Wally explained that he was taking night courses, so he could create his own website to show off his photographs. Maybe he'd also get some wedding gigs out of it. She said she was retired and bored silly at home. She liked learning and wanted to keep her brain active. They exchanged e-mail addresses. Wally confessed he might need help in the assignments and Ramona was more than willing to be an "unofficial tutor" for Wally. She said technology seemed to come naturally to her.

"My wife doesn't care about computers," Wally confessed. "As far as she's concerned, she'd just rather remain anonymous and off the internet. She doesn't trust all the stuff people are putting out there on the internet."

Ramona agreed, "Actually she's right. Hackers are getting more and more sophisticated in getting into people's bank accounts; and coming up with scams, especially to relieve seniors of their hard-earned savings. The computer is a blessing and a curse."

Wally eyed the clock behind Timmy's, "Ramona, it's time to get back to class, though I feel like I could use another coffee break!"

She laughed. "Me too. By the way, just call me Baryon. That's my nickname." Wally waited and held the elevator door open for her.

Coffee breaks at the college were always a relief and a highlight. Wally confided in Baryon that he'd stumbled upon a murder victim a few months back, in the autumn, out in the woods around Ball's Falls. "It sure shook me up!" he commented. "I wonder how anybody, in his right mind, could do such a thing to a young girl?"

"I think she was Muslim because of her head-dress," Wally added.

"Girls get killed in Muslim countries all the time, if they get modern ideas, like boyfriends and education," Baryon interjected. "And now, some of that has migrated over here to this country."

Baryon said unequivocally, "I have no tolerance for religious fanatics and stupid people. The world would be better off without God."

She figured that the Inquisition was no better than the Taliban. She had no tolerance for a religion that practiced torture or forbade women to get an education. As far as Baryon was concerned, John Lennon was right when he sang, "Imagine there's no heaven!"

Wally disagreed because Faith in God had bolstered him up in many tough spots during his lifetime, even though he had a Faith that did not follow typical church lines.

CHAPTER 7

"The reasoning behind honour killings is that it 'cleanses' the honour of the person or family whose honour has been wounded. Killing the suspected offender is supposed to restore the integrity of the family name. Actually, one alleged bad sin is followed by the worst sin of murder. The old saying is true: two wrongs don't make a right. Murder is murder."

[*Is there honour in honour killings?* BY DALLAS M. ROARK, PH.D. – INTERNET ARTICLE]

There is no historical background in Islam for "honour killing." No verse in the holy Quran and no saying of Prophet Mohammad (pbuh) sanctions such crimes. There were no cases of "honour killing" during the early period of Islam. This is a concept that seems to have appeared only recently, and is based only upon ignorance of the true teachings of Islam, and perhaps some ancient customs that pre-date Islam.

[HTTP://WWW.QUESTIONSABOUTISLAM.COM/WOMEN-IN-ISLAM/ISLAM-HONOUR KILLING.PHP]

.....

SHAFIA HONOUR KILLING TRIAL

JANUARY 29, 2012

Baryon's strict views about Islam became even stricter, that winter, because of the Shafia murder trial in Montreal. An online article featured this headline on CBC News, January 29, 2012:

> **Shafia jury finds all guilty of 1st-degree murder,**
>
> **Verdict sends message, prosecutor says.**
>
> Mohammad Shafia, his wife Tooba Yahya and their son Hamed, who had pleaded not guilty, were each handed an automatic life sentence with no chance of parole for 25 years. They were accused of killing Hamed's three sisters and his father's childless first wife in a polygamous marriage.
>
> The bodies of Zainab, 19, Sahar, 17, and Geeti Shafia, 13, along with Rona Mohammad Amir, 50, were found in the family's Nissan, submerged in a lock on the Rideau Canal on June 30, 2009.
>
> The judge called this "honour killing" despicable and heinous. And yet the family declared that they did not commit murder.
>
> [POSTED: JAN 29, 2012 ONLINE, CBC NEWS]

> "The apparent reason behind these cold-blooded, shameful murders was that the four completely innocent victims offended your completely twisted concept of honour... that has absolutely no place in any civilized society," said the judge.
>
> [POSTED: JAN 29, 2012 ONLINE, CBC NEWS]

Baryon and Wally discussed the case over coffee, the next evening, during the break in the Web Design class. Wally reiterated that he needed a Faith which gave him emotional support during tough times. He didn't care about intellectual integrity and committing intellectual suicide! He just needed something outside of this crazy world to believe in! He saw prayer and music as ways of speaking to God. He loved classical FM 96.3 which advertised the slogan: "Beautiful music for a crazy world."

Baryon dismissed religion. Maybe God was all of space and time; maybe He or She was all of the particles in the universe. Maybe God was some dumb energy which permeated Everything. She didn't care. She did agree with Richard Dawkins that religion was a kind of mass hysteria, some mass insanity which made people fabricate a religion because they were insecure. That's why the author chose the title, "The God Delusion."

Baryon stooped to a bit of "sacrilege" at Wally's expense. "Now, I know what the 'H' stands for when people swear by Jesus H. Christ!" she said. Wally played the game. "What?"

Baryon answered the six million dollar question, "What was Jesus' middle name?" "Why, Jesus H. Christ, means Jesus Higgs Christ, of course!" she said, pleased with herself. "Oh!" said Wally, blushing. His eyes reflected a sudden understanding, making the connection with Baryon's playful, scientific mind. He had always been an amateur science buff, himself.

Peter Higgs was one of the physicists who, in 1964, proposed the existence of "the god particle," now also named, "the Higgs boson." Baryon enjoyed embarrassing Wally, but she couldn't shake his Faith.

Wally and Baryon agreed to disagree. They both, however, did agree that the world still hadn't learned any lessons from wars, and that it seemed like the Crusades from the Middle Ages were still going on, but this time, with greater weapons and a wider spread of violence over a global scale.

Wally thought back to a Tuesday morning, September 11, 2001. He was sitting in his living room when the first plane flew into the Twin Towers in New York. Just that week, he had put his name on the supply teaching list but hadn't been called yet, so he made himself two pieces of buttered toast and an instant coffee. He turned on the TV, shy of about 8:45 a.m. and saw a report that a hijacked passenger jet, Flight 11, out of Boston had crashed into the north tower of the World Trade Center. At 9:03 a.m., a second hijacked airliner, United Airlines Flight 175, also out of Boston, crashed into the second, south tower and exploded.

That was broadcast on TV as it happened and Wally thought it was staged, maybe a movie. Nothing could be that perverse in real life! At 10:05 a.m., the south tower plummeted into the streets below. A massive cloud of dust and debris drifted away from the building. The 9/11 attacks killed nearly 3,000 people.

Later that evening at the college, Wally told Baryon about what he'd seen on TV and about the Muslim terrorists suspected of forcing the planes into the Twin Towers. Baryon remained firm about her doubts that the values of Arab countries could not be changed, where politics were so intermingled with religion. She couldn't see old horses learning new tricks, unless a two by four was used!

"And now we're expected to straighten out their mess, to make them adopt democracy, and give their poor a better standard of living, and their women a fair share in education and politics, after centuries of a culture based on male domination and an intolerant religion?" Baryon was wound up, "al-Qaeda, the Taliban, suicide bombers, burning of schools for girls, female mutilations... that's all nuts. How do you weed out all the crazies?"

Baryon concluded, "No, religion is not for me! When I die, I will give myself up to the void, without any expectation of Heaven or Hell, or a reward or punishment. That's what I believe! Just be a moral person here on earth, do the best you can, and don't do anyone any harm. I don't expect anything once I'm dead and gone!" Wally accepted what she said with a nod of respect, even if he didn't quite have the same view.

Time came to get rid of their coffee cups and head back to Web Design. They solved nothing over coffee! Wally had a passing thought, "If we're going to blame somebody, maybe we should blame God!"

CHAPTER 8

Mediocre people don't like high achievers, and high achievers don't like mediocre people.

[NICK SABAN – FOOTBALL COACH]

. . . . .

APRIL 2012
FINAL EXAMS @MOHAWK

SPRINGTIME 2012 WAS ON ITS WAY. FINAL EXAMS ARRIVED... as if marks mattered! Half the class were retired folks, with no intention of making computers a career. Wally scored in the low 80s. Baryon was in the high 90s. Wally was glad he had achieved his goal. Finally, a workable website! Next year, he intended to get his Webmaster Certificate, a proud piece of paper to hang on his office wall, so he'd have something to show for his achievement and hard work!

Baryon argued with a prof in the Flash course over 1%. She had 99 and would have gotten 100%. She demanded to know where she had made the one mistake. The prof couldn't find it. He just said, "Nobody ever gets a perfect score in my exams. You should be happy with a 99." She put in an official complaint with the administration and was given the extra mark. Simply put: she had a perfect score and the prof was simply wrong!

Wally nearly lost Baryon's friendship. He forwarded an e-mail she had sent him, not removing her contact info from the missive. She was royally pissed off, when she found out Wally was forwarding her Maxine cartoons, without removing her e-mail address. It was something she didn't want other people to see because she cherished her privacy. Wally promised to delete the "From: line" before forwarding anything else of hers.

Baryon kept away from Facebook and Twitter as a rule. People were revealing too much on the internet! She loved the wonder of technology but hated the abuses within it. Wally, himself, trusted the internet less and less, so he quit Facebook. This reduced his time by half when it came to going through his e-mails. He became convinced that reading other people's opinions on social media was a huge waste of time!

Wally felt the tug of springtime. Photographers who'd been hiding in their cozy corners over the winter popped their heads out like little prairie dogs. Orchards were blossoming all over the Niagara Peninsula. The Niagara Fruit Belt was coming to life with farmers getting cherry, peach and apple orchards ready. Tourists just needed to take the time to drive off the QEW highway to discover the beauty within the Niagara Fruit Belt.

Wally was getting antsy when he saw pink and white blossoms along so many side roads! Pictures for the taking!

He always found the back roads especially rewarding for his camera. He loved "roads less traveled," especially around Jordan and Niagara-on-the-Lake. The Niagara Parkway drive up to the *Niagara Botanical Gardens* was also a feast of colour for a photographer's eyes.

It was a good way to forget ugly things. Wally hardly ever thought about the dead Muslim girl anymore.

CHAPTER 9

Like the pine trees lining the winding road
I've got a name
I've got a name
Like the singing bird and the croaking toad
I've got a name
I've got a name
And I carry it with me like my daddy did
But I'm living the dream that he kept hid
Moving me down the highway
Rolling me down the highway
Moving ahead so life won't pass me by

I Got A Name, [JIM CROCE, BEFORE HE DIED 1973]

. . . . .

self-employed, paying the bills, and who would take care of his wife and two kids, should the biopsy be bad?

His biggest fear came true at the end of the week. Leonard had been diagnosed with "*poorly differentiated non-small cell adenocarcinoma*" [one of the more aggressive forms of lung cancer]. His official 'prognosis' was approximately 3 months, possibly 6 months with chemotherapy and radiation. That summer of 2012 became the family's, "Summer of our Discontent!"

Leonard chose to forego the traditional treatment of "slash, burn and poison." He and his wife chose the homeopathic route instead. He knew that the curtain was coming down on his life anyway; and he didn't want to face the last few months, with radiation and chemotherapy and their terrible side-effects. Dr. R., his oncologist, was not too happy about his decision because she wanted Leonard to take part in one of her trials. She refused to sign the form that would subsidize the cost of Leonard's morphine. He and his buddies organized a fundraiser, the funds of which were soon absorbed by the pain meds.

By the end of the summer, it was noticeable that Leonard had lost a lot of weight. Through the autumn, he was taking his meds with pudding and subsisting on Coffee Crisp chocolate bars. He couldn't keep anything else down. There was a bitter irony in eating chocolate bars because cancer apparently feeds on sugars.

Leonard requested bacon and eggs one evening, so Wally eagerly made some. Leonard took one forkful and shoved the food to the side. The hunger came more from a memory of bacon and eggs, than from what his body could handle, which unfortunately meant it rebelled at the consumption of solid food.

Leonard continued to lose weight and continued to subsist on Coffee Crisp chocolate bars and puddings throughout the autumn. He kept busy with his Wellness Blog where he expressed his opinion that people should have a say if they wanted to go the natural route for cancer treatment or the accepted chemo-radiation route.

He also contacted the Princess Margaret Hospital, in Toronto, wanting a second opinion about his situation. He received a phone-call, one day, from a doctor at the Princess Margaret Hospital, saying that an appointment was being set up for him because, "we don't want you to fall through the cracks." His local oncologist found out about this and asserted her domain over Leonard's treatment. The Princess Margaret Hospital let Leonard know that they had cancelled his appointment.

Leonard was very angry with God. He told the family that he'd like to take God by the scruff of the neck and punch Him right in the nose! "Why was this happening? What did he ever do to God?"

Leonard's father, Charlie, tried to make sense of it all. He was the patriarch of the family, 80 years old, and was affectionately called, "dad." He pointed out that God gave us free will and made a free universe. This was one time in which Wally questioned the older man's wisdom. "And that's why shit happens?"

Leonard also questioned his father's wisdom and picking up on Wally's thread, sarcastically interjected, "Well, God should have pooped on somebody else!" Leonard sat down at the kitchen table and cried.

CHAPTER 10

"Doctors can see Leonard's cancer in their tests, but they can't see the growing cancer in his mind. He's so depressed, Wally, I don't know what to do? How will we cope, and how will we get through it all?

[LEONARD'S WIFE COMPLAINING TO WALLY]

.....

OCTOBER 2012
LEONARD'S CANCER

EVERYBODY WAS DEPRESSED. LEONARD'S TRAGEDY AFFLICTED the whole family. Wally's own mind brought back memories of the dead girl's gruesome murder from a year ago. After he stumbled across the bloody body, he lost the ability to see beauty; and he started having terrible nightmares. The young woman's body was fixed in his mind, lifeless and bloody. At home in bed in the days and weeks that followed, he tried to convince himself that things like that just didn't happen, never happened, that people couldn't do things like that!

These mental meanderings slowly became fewer as the months rolled by, and in fact, seemed manageable by the time Wally registered for the 2012 winter session at Mohawk College. Wally had taken Leonard's suggestion seriously about taking Web Design. But now, almost a year after the girl's murder, Wally's spirits sagged once more, along with Leonard's failing health.

Finally, October had come again! The whole family was in the doldrums. One evening, Leonard was preparing his ugly tasting tea in the kitchen, while talking with members of his extended family. The husbands, wives and Charlie, Leonard's dad, were sitting around the table while Leonard leaned on the counter. He insisted that even family didn't know what he was going through! He uttered in anguish: "You don't understand. It's not you! It's me!" Leonard said he felt like screaming at the Heavens, especially in the dark at night! He felt so alone!

Wally was struggling with his own demons. The image of that unknown Muslim girl recurred, with all the blood! The sleepless nights came back! Wally became more agitated as October 11th, the very anniversary day of his gruesome discovery, came up. He decided to face his demons; maybe something would happen, if he actually went out there on that day. He wanted desperately to free his mind, to see beauty again in the trees and in the sky, through the lens of his beloved camera. All this time, after a whole year, the police still had not found the killer!

Wally parked his car at his friend's place. He unloaded his bicycle for his jaunt. He stroked "Alice" and said, "Let's go, girl." His camera was his "special gal" with whom he shared visual secrets which most people couldn't see.

Wally retraced his steps on the Bruce Trail. He found the retaining wall in front of the 20 foot embankment, leading down to Twenty Mile Creek. Normally, he loved autumn for obvious reasons. Spring and summer meant blossoms and flowers, but autumn? Autumn meant magnificent splendour, despite the fact that the leaves were dying! He shuddered to think it was like a glorious last Hurrah, before the blanket of death covered the ground and killed all the foliage in the trees. Wally was near the exact spot where it had happened, just off to the side of the trail. He picked up a straight branch which he figured would serve as a good walking stick.

He looked at where the body had lain and tears ran down his cheek. Why? What would make someone do such an act? Even if you don't believe in God, wouldn't you naturally feel that life was sacred? Wally had never investigated his Jewish lineage, nor his Christian side. There was a stretch in his life when he didn't consider himself anything! But a need had crept in, drawing him into Christianity, the side on which he was raised. So, he said a quiet prayer over the spot.

He scraped a cross into the soil with his stick. Something was unearthed; an edge glistened in the sun. A piece of jewelry, partly black and oxidized, maybe part of a silver necklace. Wally picked it up. It looked like a crescent shaped moon, with some Arabic script on it. He later found out, it meant Allah. Wally brushed it off. On the back was some small etching which he couldn't quite discern but it looked English.

Wally pocketed this evidence. The police could wait. His impulse dragged him to the embankment which led to the bottom of Ball's Falls. Maybe he should have headed to the police station instead?

He scampered down the 20 foot slope when a root he was holding gave way; and he crashed down to a ledge, where he broke his ankle. The lens of his camera was broken too; and he muttered in a grimace of pain, a line from an old movie, "Well, here's another nice mess you've gotten me into!" [Laurel and Hardy 1930]

How could he get himself out of this predicament, with a bum ankle? Especially up a steep embankment! He wished he could reverse time to about 10 minutes ago. He should have gone to the police station right away with the new evidence!

He didn't even have a cell phone. He yelled up for help at several minute intervals. He felt an irony in all this, as he thought of John the Baptist from the Bible, "a voice crying in the wilderness." Chances were good though, this time of year, that other Bruce Trail trekkers had come out of the woodwork on this fine day. Within half an hour other people, indeed, did appear above the 20 foot embankment.

"Hello down there. Are you hurt?"

"I broke my ankle. Alice is broke too."

"Alice? How bad is she?"

"Oh, that's my camera. I call her Alice! I just call her that, like Alice in Wonderland. Oh never mind!"

He grumbled to himself, "So much for the looking glass!" He yelled up once more, "My camera lens is smashed... and my ankle doesn't feel too good either!"

"We called 911 on our cell phone. The paramedics will be here shortly."

As it was, they were there within 30 minutes and hauled Wally and "Alice" up with ropes and a sling after stabilizing Wally's ankle. The ambulance was waiting along the road at Ball's Falls and headed to the emergency ward at St. Catharines' General Hospital right away.

The paramedics waited there with him for about an hour, seeing that he was properly registered with his OHIP number. They put Wally on a gurney in the hallway. He had to wait another hour for X-rays and then a doctor's assessment.

"You've got two breaks in that ankle. The tibia and fibula. You'll need surgery, maybe a plate, some screws and a pin."

Wally frowned, with this passing thought, "Well, here's another nice mess you've gotten me into!"

CHAPTER 11

Pins and needles, needles and pins

One by one I feel them at my heart again

I think I'm getting over you and then

Pins and needles, needles and pins

[THE SEARCHERS-1964]

.....

WALLY'S ORDEAL
OCTOBER 12, 2012

WALLY WAS PUT ON MORPHINE AND ON THE WAITING LIST for surgery. There was no room available, so he found himself lying on a gurney in the hallway. It seemed the doctors were inundated with patients that week. Maybe that was the case every week? He wasn't given breakfast for two days, just in case a doctor was available with an operating room. He asked for ice chips which came rarely because the nurses seemed so busy. At least, he got his morphine. He dozed in fits between those numbing stretches of constant pain.

Wally's wife had picked up his broken camera and his torn clothes from the hospital and brought him a new change of clothes for when he'd be released. He didn't feel good about having to order a new lens for Alice since he and his wife were on a tight budget from year to year. It wasn't like his phone was ringing off the hook with wedding gigs. "Oh well, maybe a new lens will give me a new perspective on life, 'through the looking glass'," he sighed. "Maybe I'll see things more clearly now."

He made sure that his wife had also picked up the silver necklace he'd found at the scene of the crime. He instructed her to get the evidence to Detective Klassen. Wally was not too surprised to get a visit from the detective while still waiting for surgery in the hospital.

"I hope you're not going to arrest me," Wally quipped dreamily. "I've been taking morphine." The detective smiled. "We're good. You've got the government's permission!"

"Now," he said, "let's hear about this silver necklace your wife brought in."

"I was scratching around in the dirt with my walking stick, when I unearthed the thing," Wally confessed. He didn't mention that he was making a sign of the cross with it.

"But it doesn't mean I'm the criminal going back to the scene of the crime, you know!"

The detective chuckled. "We know. Your fingerprints didn't match the bloody prints on that smooth rock. We had the silver necklace cleaned at our lab and it's bringing us closer to some kind of ID on the killer. The front of the necklace had the word, Allah, and the little etching on the back, said: 'To Hazirah, Love Alexander'."

Wally wondered if "the perp" was Alexander and the occasion of the killing was some kind of crime of passion. Star-crossed lovers from different cultures? It could have happened.

"Thanks for visiting me detective. I hope you'll catch the guy. A lover's spat or not, it's an ugly thing to do to that girl." Wally confessed. "I went back there just to say a little prayer at the spot." He closed his eyes momentarily as if saying another prayer. The nurse came in to readjust the meds in his IV. Wally was tired and licked his lips.

"This necklace you turned in may just break the case," acknowledged the detective. "We're grateful you found it and that your wife came in with it."

"Yeah," Wally said, "I hope you catch the son-of-a-bitch." He closed his eyes in sleep, a deeply needed sleep.

On the fourth day, his wife and father-in-law were fed up with waiting. They demanded to see the CEO of the hospital.

"My husband has been on morphine for 4 days and is still waiting on surgery for his broken ankle. The wait is ridiculous!"

"I'm sure if the surgeon thought there was any immediate danger, then your husband would get immediate attention."

"Oh come on, we're stuck in bureaucratic red-tape! He should have had surgery within a day or two from the time he was admitted."

"There's nothing I can do about it. The surgeon makes the decision based on the seriousness of each case."

"Both bones in the ankle are broken! How serious is that!"

Frustrated, the wife eyed the CEO seriously. "How much do you make just sitting there keeping books or whatever you do?"

"$333,000 a year. And I'm worth every penny of it."

"That's ridiculous. That's as much as a surgeon makes! A doctor should make more than a bureaucrat!"

Wally's wife and her dad [Charlie] couldn't believe the gall of the CEO. They had run out of patience and with a shake of the head, they left her office. Wally was operated on the next day, on a Sunday morning. That evening he finally got a meal, five days after he'd first come in!

When the surgeon came into the hospital room, Wally's wife had a few questions.

"Isn't the cast a bit crooked? The leg looks like it's turned inward."

"No, it's fine. It will straighten out. There are a plate, six screws and a pin in that ankle to hold everything in place. Everything's perfect." He turned toward the door. "Okay then, I have to move on to my next patient." He left. No smile. Charlie looked at his daughter. "He's as bad as the CEO. Where do they get these egos from?"

At the second appointment, Wally wore a "space boot" over his broken ankle. He swayed back and forth on crutches, as he made slow progress towards Doctor G's office inside the hospital. Wally had a list of 10 questions to ask him. The doctor said, "I've got no time for this. My time is too important. I'll give you 3 questions."

So Wally got his 3 questions, one of them being: "Will I walk okay after rehab?" Doctor G was abrupt and said, "You've had a serious break in both your tibia and fibula. You'll never walk right again!" With that the doctor left and told his secretary to set up a final appointment at his private clinic.

That week, Wally's wife got to the appointment at the clinic in plenty of time. They both brought books to read. They hated the glitzy *Elle* and *Canadian Gardening* magazines found in the typical doctors' offices. The receptionist asked for the Ontario Health Insurance card and then said, "Have a seat."

They waited an hour and were grateful for their own reading material. Wally glanced up at a poster on the wall, a picture of a silhouetted sculler on a lake at sunset. Light sparkled all around him. The caption read, "If you have a goal, failure is impossible!" Very inspiring! Wally smirked as he juggled the words around in his mind, "If you have failure, a goal is impossible!"

Earlier, when they had parked their car, Wally noticed a Porsche parked in a "Reserved" spot. The license plate read: *4G 4FUN.*

"Nice car," said Wally.

"Yep, that's our next one," joked the wife.

They instinctively figured it had to be Dr. G's Porsche. Who else could afford it? Wally figured that salaries couldn't have been that bad for Canadian surgeons. Dr. G was probably making in the range of $300,000 to $400,000 per year. Wally later Googled what the average salary was for orthopedic surgeons... yep, way up there in the Porsche stratosphere!

He didn't mind that they got 5 or 10 times the money ordinary people earned in a year. He had no complaint about that. He just wanted shorter waiting times in the system; and he wished more doctors, especially specialists, had a more humane bedside manner.

Did anyone remember Tommy Douglas anymore? And the concept of Universal Healthcare in Canada? Wally had an intense aversion to the system in the United States. What a mess they had with hospitals, insurance companies, medical plans and lawyers!

Wally found it ironic that a survey was e-mailed to him from the St. Catharines General Hospital, basically asking how the service was, whether the patient found the hospital clean and how the food was. Wally laughed. He hadn't been fed in five days and hadn't noticed anybody cleaning the rooms on his floor, day or night. He deleted the meaningless survey. He heard rumours that the old hospital was going to be replaced sometime in 2013 by a brand spanking new one. He hoped the quality of service to the public would be improved by then!

Wally still didn't sleep well after his ankle surgery. He awoke one night from a terrible dream. He knew his wife was already awake, close to the time for the clock radio to turn on. In the darkness, Wally told his wife about his nightmare. "I dreamt I had needles and pins in my ankle. I looked down; and there they were! Needles and pins, two potato peelers and one knife, stuck in my ankle! I started pulling them out."

Just when he said that, the clock radio came on. "Welcome to Classical 96.3 FM. Beautiful music for a crazy world!" It was 5.45 a.m. Time to roll out of bed! His wife had a long day ahead of her at school. Wally was exempted from getting her breakfast ready, as long as his ankle was on the mend. "I'm so glad I have you to support me through this," he said. He hugged his wife before she rolled out of bed. "We need to stick together," she said.

CHAPTER 12

Nobody knows the trouble I've seen

Nobody knows my sorrow

Nobody knows the trouble I've seen

Glory, Hallelujah

[SUNG BY LOUIS ARMSTRONG]

. . . . .

AUTUMN 2012
DIFFERENT DESTINIES

IN THE WEEKS THAT FOLLOWED, WALLY UNDERWENT PHYSiotherapy and soon got rid of his space boot. He bought a treadmill, so that he could train his foot to walk again, slowly at first. Within a few months, he proved the doctor wrong; though on long jaunts, he had to use a cane to steady his ankle. On damp, rainy days, it ached.

Since he was going to be a "semi-cripple," Wally thought he'd become one with distinction. He ordered a Shillelagh Walking Stick online and was thrilled with the heft and the look of it when he got it. "It'll be part of my persona from now on."

"Besides," he chuckled, "I might want to use it as a putter on the golf course!"

When he was mobile enough, Wally visited his ill brother-in-law. He shuffled into the family room downstairs where Leonard lay among the pillows trying to ease his aching joints in his ever thinning body. Lung cancer was taking its toll day by day. Wally brandished his shillelagh in the air to get Leonard's attention. "Hey, maybe you could get one of these? And then we'd be 'the two musketeers!' We'd be 'brothers from another mother', right?"

Leonard was in no mood: "If it's all the same, I'd just as soon do without! I've left a lot of clients hanging with their websites. I've got to make other arrangements for them." Wally hated to see Leonard's business disintegrate after it took so long, and so much effort, to build it up. The visit was a downer; Leonard fell asleep with his meds.

.....

The worse Leonard got during October and November 2012, the more family came around to keep him company. They knew what was coming, and so did Leonard, even though he kept up "the good fight."

Family wanted to help out any way they could. Wally's wife made Russian pancakes [ruhrei] for the family for supper. The pancakes were cut up into pieces in the pan, served on a plate in a heap and then Aunt Jemima syrup was poured on top. The kids loved it, a good Mennonite dish.

Leonard was usually drugged, asleep downstairs on the couch. He did not want to be moved to the hospital. He wanted to be at home with his wife, kids and family, as he declined into his last days. When family visited, they'd find him the same every day, asleep, ensconced in his duvet with his pillows tucked around him, so that his bony body wouldn't hurt. Whenever the family visited, his two year old son whispered: "Daddy sleeping." The family felt helpless.

Everybody was gathered in the kitchen one evening, talking about this and that, and nothing in particular. Wally's wife kept the six year-old girl out of the way downstairs, occupied in the playroom. That way the adults could talk. The boy was usually sent off to Granma's.

All of a sudden, a frightful crash resounded from downstairs. Leonard tore around the corner of the kitchen, as quick as a wink, in bare feet... to see what happened... when he stubbed his toe on the threshold. He went down with a cry and a crash, rocking back and forth in pain, holding his foot. He had broken his toe!

Wally and Charlie attended to Leonard's painful foot, while others checked out what had happened downstairs. A cabinet full of toys had come crashing down onto the floor. Nobody was hurt but the crash frightened the dickens out of Leonard's little girl. Wally's wife whispered, "That sure was a close call." She asked, "How's Leonard?"

Everybody was relieved that nothing serious had happened downstairs. The attention then shifted to Leonard and his smarting toe. Wally explained to the little girl that her daddy had fallen in his hurry to see that his precious little princess wasn't hurt. He regretted he couldn't do more in the situation because of his own broken ankle. What an irony! Everybody was breaking something!

Wally's wife said, "Let's see what we can do about getting him to the hospital."

She and her dad bundled Leonard up and headed to the emergency ward. The foot was X-rayed, the big toe was obviously broken. The doctor on call said, "Nothing can be done. Just tape it, put a cold pack on it and stay off it." Wally's wife and her dad had waited 4 hours in the emergency ward for this news.

Leonard mumbled something about the Ontario Government lying about how waiting times had improved. Charlie, and his daughter and son, didn't believe a word of it, as they came back into the house, miffed and fatigued. Leonard hobbled in on crutches. He was helped downstairs to his cushiony couch. Well, he wasn't going to go out for walks anyway once winter came. He eyed Wally's space boot and Shilelagh and sighed. Then they both chuckled. Tragedies were really funny!

.....

Leonard lost his appetite by the time Christmas arrived. He lost his strength to fight; the family still prayed.

People have a misconception about 1 Corinthians 10:13 in the New Testament, that they think God will ***not*** give them more *suffering* than they can bear. But that is not so!

What the Bible says is: "God is faithful. He will not allow the *temptation* to be more than you can stand. When you are tempted, he will show you a way out so that you can endure." So it talks about temptation and not suffering! Wally was convinced that people do get more suffering than they can handle! Of course, he believed that prayer helps to soothe the anguished soul.

Leonard, reached out to other people, in his last days, for emotional support, even with little prayers, because he felt so alone and so angry. He was looking for reassurance and peace to calm the storm raging inside. He wanted people to visit him, the presence of other human beings for company. He needed their prayers as a shelter from the storm, taking him away from the frightful fury raging inside his heart.

Friends and relatives, in fact, came in and out of the Webb home whenever they could; and that helped soothe Leonard's anxiety during those dark days and black nights when the winter snows blew outdoors, when everything that ever blossomed in Niagara seemed dead.

PRAYER FOR LEONARD

Dear God:
If you will not take a prayer,
Will You take a tear?
We are tested and often fail.
We are angry
and helpless and small.
All this has been felt before.
All this is nothing new...
We do not understand
We have no choice but to pray,
If you will not take a prayer,
Will you take a tear?

CHAPTER 13

In Irish History, when Irish workers were beset by Highwaymen on the long road home, the Shillelagh was used as a defense against cutthroats and thieves. Made of Irish Blackthorn, it was named after the Shillelagh forest in County Wicklow.

[GOOGLE HISTORY OF THE SHILLELAGH]

. . . . .

JANUARY 2013
WINTER SESSION WEB DESIGN II

JANUARY 2013 ARRIVED AND WALLY WAS GLAD TO SEE Baryon back in "Web Design II," "A Beginner's Guide to Web Scripting" and "Digital Imaging." Opinionated and irritating at times, she nevertheless had helped him through some difficult lessons in last year's curriculum.

He had not taken a Summer Session in 2012, considering all that happened to the family over the past year. The one thing he accomplished was publishing the Photo Books which he donated to the local libraries.

Wally practised doing and redoing his web sites, in the autumn of 2012, so that when the Winter Session came along, his Web Design skills remained fresh in his mind. He knew he could count on Baryon to help him through obscure parts of the course, when his unmathematical mind couldn't quite grasp the codes in Web Scripting, a new challenge for an older mind.

Baryon was older too but Wally was always amazed at how she kept her mind "so young." She understood the code and the tables in page design right away. Oh well, why be jealous? She had agreed to be his buddy and show him how things worked whenever he didn't get it. That was one thing about Wally. He was not too proud to accept help.

At coffee break, he showed off his shillelagh. He had gotten rid of most of his limp by now; but he had gone through so much over the past few months, that he could identify more personally with Baryon's handicap.

"I came by this shillelagh the hard way," he said.

"It's quite stylish," noted Baryon.

Wally talked about his yearly walks along the escarpment to get autumn photos. He said something drew him out to the spot, on the anniversary date in October when he found the dead girl's body.

"I poked around and found a necklace there, crescent moon shaped, kind of black from being there a long time. Detective Klassen had it cleaned by the lab. It had the word Allah in the front and a dedication in the back: 'To Hazirah, Love Alexander'."

Wally recounted how he intended to take the item to the police station after his jaunt down to the gorge. But when he climbed down he lost his grip and broke his ankle on a ledge.

"So much for being the athletic/photographic mountain climber type," quipped Wally. "Luckily some other nature lovers passed by and called 911."

"The hospital stay wasn't much fun," he said, "but I enjoyed picking out this shillelagh. Gives me a sense of authority."

"I suppose, if somebody doesn't listen, you can always club them with it," Baryon teased. She figured that Wally had found the very item, the necklace, which might just crack the case!

CHAPTER 14

LEONARD KEPT BUSY WITH A BLOG WHICH HE HOPED would be a book someday, once he was cured of his cancer. "Maybe I should start a Blog too," thought Wally, "just for therapy. Well, why not? Who knows maybe I'd get a book out of it too someday? I need to get things inside me out in writing! The only thing? I hate to be criticized that it's poorly written!"

.....

JANUARY 4, 2013
DEALING WITH DEATH

Leonard died on Friday, January 4th 2013, at 3:39 p.m. It was cold when the doctor came to fill out the certificate and then the undertakers carried the covered body to the hearse. Snow flakes fell lightly down outside. Leonard left behind a six year old daughter and a two year old son, now fatherless. Leonard was 42. Happy New Year!

A few weeks after Leonard was buried, his personal web sites disappeared from the internet, one by one, like lights going out, since the payments were not made to his hosting server for renewals. In the world of virtual reality, there was no proof of Leonard's existence anymore. Wally felt sad for Leonard and for the death of his websites.

May it be an evening star
Shines down upon you
May it be when darkness falls
Your heart will be true
You walk a lonely road
Oh! How far you are from home

(Enya "Lord of the Rings" 2001)

Wally wanted to keep Leonard's memory alive. He had a notion to start a book on Leonard's experiences, so helpless within the grips of the medical system. He knew that third world countries were far worse off with medical care. However, he was convinced that in a civilized society, our system in Canada could be improved immensely. The United States should be ashamed of itself!

Maybe Leonard had just fallen through the cracks and just drew the short end of the stick as far as doctors were concerned. Maybe nothing could have been done, no matter what! He wondered how he would start his book; maybe as a blog following Leonard's example, when he was first diagnosed?

.....

The First Step
The Road goes ever on and on
Down from the door where it began.
Now far ahead the Road has gone,

And I must follow, if I can,
Pursuing it with eager feet,
Until it joins some larger way
Where many paths and errands meet.
And whither then? I cannot say

(J.R.R. Tolkein "Fellowship of the Ring" Part 1 ch.1)

POST 1: THE FIRST STEP IN A PAINFUL JOURNEY

MORNING ENTRY

This first sentence is the first step. There are so many paths and only one large chore looming in the back of my mind, which says I must somehow get this done. This journal is my painful journey about one life that was lost and another that somehow missed his calling. Leonard's story and mine. I have no compass in hand, except what my eyes see straight ahead on a blank computer screen, as my fingers search for words to type. I cannot say which way to go, except to…just go! I've stepped outside the door and have looked down the Road that seems to stretch far ahead, winding ever on and on. It is a Road I must follow, if I can. My feet are not eager for this journey. But it must be done or who else will do it?

. . . . .

Wally was satisfied with his first entry. He wanted the blog to flow honestly and do honour to Leonard's memory. He tried to absorb the feelings the family had after the funeral and then he projected his mind back into the feelings Leonard had in his final days. What a painful chore. Somehow he felt driven to do it. Maybe writing things down would be a catharsis for him, a clearing out of all resentments against

God and unfairness in the world, against the disease of cancer itself, and against all the other sicknesses in people's souls and minds. Maybe Mark Twain was right that God invented the monkey because he was ashamed of mankind. Wally posted his second blog entry that evening.

.....

POST 2: LETTING GO OF LEONARD

EVENING ENTRY

We have trouble letting go of Leonard, don't we? I still think of what could have been, should have been, might have been, but wasn't. I'm sure all of Leonard's family and friends are passing through stages, just as I am, wishing to reverse the tide, to paddle backwards, in the ever flowing stream of Time, to land somewhere at a point where Leonard was still alive and with us... just so that this sad reality isn't so. I don't quite want to let go of Leonard's last hours... and I wish there were other possibilities for his mind to live on, beyond suffering and beyond coming to an earthly end. I want to look for a blessing for him and for a wondrous eternity. As a writer, I investigate possibilities when touched by a creative spark. Leonard would understand the magic. By that magic and by our memory, we keep him in our hearts.

.....

Wally seemed to be in a trance when he wrote thoughts down about his brother-in-law. How real was this situation? Leonard seemed to be so alive a little while ago. Now hidden in darkness, he was no longer with us! Leonard had lost his voice during those last few days before he faded into a coma. That was hard on everybody. He had such a beautiful singing voice.

CHAPTER 15

Sun's up, uuh huh, looks okay
The world survives into another day
And I'm thinking about eternity
Some kind of ecstasy got a hold on me.
I had another dream about lions at the door
They weren't half as frightening as they were before
But I'm thinking about eternity

[BRUCE COCKBURN SONG, 1979]

JAN. AND FEB. 2013
WALLY'S ENTRIES

LEONARD HAD INSISTED ON NOT DYING IN THE HOSPITAL. He wanted to be at home with family, so the family brought a hospital bed into the basement. That's where Leonard lay on his last day, breathing quietly and steadily in his coma. A monitor checked his breathing. Did he hear the family pray around the bed? Was he thinking at all in his stillness, with eyes closed? Wally reflected on these things and wrote another entry in his blog, taking time to make it a kind of long prayer.

.....

POST 3: COMAS AND CHOICES

ONE DAY'S WORTH OF THOUGHTS

Friday, January 4th, 2013: Leonard died at 3:39 p.m. At 3:39 p.m., he got his voice back in Heaven. Aged 43 on earth. Forever in Heaven.

The family was sad and broken, down here on earth, in the family room, beside the bed. The question, "Why?" lingered in the air unasked, unanswered. To me, it seemed like a dream. This should not have been. Leonard had been in a coma for a day and a half. He was in the hospital bed for only one night.

Home is behind, the world ahead,
And there are many paths to tread
Through shadows to the edge of night,
Until the stars are all alight.
Then world behind and home ahead,
We'll wander back to home and bed.

(J.R.R. Tolkein, "The Fellowship of the Ring," Book 1, ch.3)

Is it irreverent to ask what his mind was dreaming in that coma? Maybe this is just another way of hanging on to his being around somewhere, somehow in some parallel universe beyond the stars. We looked at his dead body but knew his soul was somewhere else without pain. Who's to say what a mind goes through in the last hours of life inside a coma?

> Still round the corner there may wait
> A new road or a secret gate,
> And though we pass them by today,
> Tomorrow we may come this way
> And take the hidden paths that run
> Towards the Moon or to the Sun.
>
> **(J.R.R. Tolkein, "The Fellowship of the Ring," Book 1, ch.3)**

Those who have come out of a coma, say they've seen a light at the end of a tunnel. Maybe Leonard saw such a light and walked toward it or into it. Those of us left behind can only speculate and if not speculate, then have Faith. Having Faith is a better choice. It's more comforting. Who cares if it's a delusion!

I've thought about these possibilities, being there with the family during Leonard's last two days alive on earth. Four possibilities crossed my mind about "the light at the end of the tunnel":

1. a person sees the light before all lights go out
2. maybe it's the door to a dream world where he or she recovers and is living out his or her entire life in that dream
3. maybe the tunnel is a wormhole to another universe
4. and my choice: the tunnel is actually a gateway to Heaven

Neurologists have explained that the end stages of life in the human brain result in synaptic short circuiting [which explains the light before all the lights go out]. That's death and there's no hope at the end of that tunnel. That's not Leonard because he was all about hope and faith, especially faith in God who holds the Universe together and who has His own reasons for everything, even the terrible things that happen in life. Let scientists keep speculating about the chemical and synaptic reasons for "lights" firing on and off in a dying brain. At the core of what matters, that speculation holds no interest for people of hope and faith, who are hurting.

> "Don't let anyone lead you astray with empty philosophy and high-sounding nonsense that come from human thinking and from the evil powers of this world, and not from Christ. For in Christ the fullness of God lives in a human body, and you are complete through your union with Christ. He is the Lord over every ruler and authority in the universe."
>
> [COL. 2:8-10]

Well, if Leonard stepped through a door into a wonderful dream world during that coma... then, that sounds like a good thing, doesn't it? Leonard said one time in one of his kitchen confessions upstairs that his illness seemed unreal and like a dream to him. Maybe in his final dream, he dreamt that he recovered after all. Right after the fundraiser would have been a good time. Can you imagine it? The Juravinski Clinic managed his pain after all [in that dream] and was able to do something about it. That should have been reality but as a dream, it still would have been a good experience [delusion?] for Leonard to have in those final hours and it would have been a blessing.

May God have granted you that dream, dear Leonard. May He have granted you the dream that you got cured and lived out your entire life as a husband and a father to your kids, as they grew up and got married in your blessed dream.

May you have had a healthy and long life in that dream. Perhaps you even squared off with the doctors when you recovered, as only you could, with that passion in your eyes, those angry words from your quick tongue, even giving God Himself a piece of your mind! Maybe you even designed a website for Heaven there with your deft fingertips.

Maybe your larynx got healed in a parallel universe and you got your Josh Grobin voice back again, so that you might even have sung your way to fame on radio and TV. You would have been brilliant, a master craftsman in publicity, to give a resonant voice towards better things in our society. Maybe in that dream you had a fruitful life to the end of your days, your long and happy days. After all, William Blake says that the poetic soul can, "Hold eternity in an hour," and you, Leonard, had a poetic soul!

Who knows? Maybe the light at the end of the tunnel was a wormhole to another universe! You and me buddy, both of us, might be captains on the star ships, Enterprise and Voyager, not just traveling at multiple light speeds to another quadrant but to another universe entirely, one that is parallel to this one, and one where we all live out our lives, the way we were meant to! There you may have recovered and are back to web-designing, landing that De Grassi contract and networking to market your creative talents, so that your career takes off like a star ship into unexplored galaxies. Well, we'd settle for family security and better vehicles anyway, wouldn't we? Hey, if the likes of Stephen Hawking, can entertain the possibility of parallel universes, why not God! After all, God is the One who created the "Big Shebang." And nothing is impossible for God!

To see a world in a grain of sand
And heaven in a wild flower

Hold infinity in the palm of your hand
And eternity in an hour.

(William Blake 1757 - 1827 'Auguries of Innocence')

.....

But God has told us to believe in His Kingdom like little children, "as one of these." So I prefer not to dwell on complicated speculations. My choice is the simple one, just to believe in The Father, in Jesus Christ, and in the eternal life in Heaven, in a transformed body as the New Testament promises. A body that is healed. This choice, I think, leads a person to a healthier and saner lifestyle here on earth. Delusion or not! Who Cares? What is Reality, anyway? Humans thrive on Hope.

Leonard would agree that it's a far, far better thought to believe that the light at the end of the tunnel is actually a gateway to Heaven, to God, to the arms of Jesus, and to the end of pain. After all, we can use a comforting thought. I don't care, Leonard, if that delusion makes me simple minded.

We are told that we will inherit different bodies when we leave this earth and pass on. Maybe the phrase "to pass on" is more appropriate than to die. In that respect, Leonard lives on in a different form in the Everlasting Arms of God. This also gives hope to all of us, that there is the possibility that we will "see" him again and that we will be with him once more.

Little lamb who made thee
Dost thou know who made thee?
Gave thee life and bid thee feed
By the stream and o'er the mead

(William Blake 1789 Songs of Innocence)

CHAPTER 16

NOT UNTIL SINS ARE REMOVED IS THE SOUL FIT TO BE admitted to what St. John of the Cross calls the "Dark Night," which consists in the passive purgation, where God by heavy trials, particularly interior ones, perfects and completes what the soul had begun of its own accord.

[HTTP://WWW.POETSEERS.ORG/SPIRITUAL-AND-DEVOTIONAL-POETS/CHRISTIAN/ST-JOHN-OF-THE-CROSS/INDEX.HTML]

JANUARY 5TH, 2013
WALLY'S PONDERINGS

Wally thought about *The God Delusion* and about what Baryon might say about his weak admissions in his blog... but he didn't care. If it all was a delusion, so be it, he would be deluded. He found some comfort in it. He made one last entry in his blog before he gave it a rest and concentrated on his Web Design courses. He needed to focus his energies on his learning if he was going to pass the exams at the end of winter. So he wrote something that expressed the depth of the despair that the family and that Leonard must have felt during those cold autumn and winter months of suffering. He posted it on the following day in January 2013, after Leonard's death.

.....

POST 4: THE DARK NIGHT OF THE SOUL

VENTING MY OTHER THOUGHTS

During those months, through autumn and winter, Leonard must have experienced many a "dark night of the soul." The term "dark night of the soul" is used in Christianity for a spiritual crisis in a journey towards union with God, like that described by Saint John of the Cross, a 16th century Spanish poet. Jesus must have felt that way too in the Garden of Gethsemane before his crucifixion, to the point of sweating droplets of blood from the stress of knowing how he was going to die. This condition is medically possible, called "*hematohidrosis*."

Maybe we all face a dark night of the soul at some point [provided Alzheimer's hasn't hit us yet]. During those nights and days, after Leonard heard the pronouncement "cancer," he must have felt so isolated downstairs on that couch, lying there captive in his own body, feeling stranded on an island with no rescue boat in sight.

Had he lived in Elizabethan England, Leonard might have become friends with John Donne or even become another John Donne, himself, because he had such poetic talents. Instead of a computer geek, he might have become a poet or a minstrel. Instead of a blog, Leonard might have penned this poem: "No man is an island; entire of itself every man is a piece of the continent...never send to know for whom the bell tolls it tolls for thee." John Donne wrote these lines looking out of his window, recuperating from tuberculosis. Some say that Donne finally died of stomach cancer. [d. 1631]

As Donne got older, he wrote works that challenged death. He wrote about the fear that it inspired in many men but he believed strongly that those who die are sent to heaven to live eternally. "Death, be not proud, though some have called thee / Mighty and dreadful, for thou art not so." [Holy Sonnet X]

Leonard had the feistiness to challenge death so many times during those months of his illness. Near the end, he gave himself more to a hope in God because fighting his illness on his own just got beyond him.

I'm split on the idea of "no man is an island." We are each of us alone at the end to face our own death. It was Leonard who had to face it, even though family had gathered around his death bed at the end for support. We each felt like an island in our own sorrow and grief; and yet, we were not alone because we also shared that grief. What a paradox!

When Leonard raged in the kitchen one evening, I went home and made a lengthy comment about Dylan Thomas, the Welsh poet, who told his dying father to rage against death. I told Leonard later that he was quite right to rage and that he showed courage in doing so and that this was a good sign for him to be so angry at God and at everything. And I left it at that.

Now, that I've witnessed Leonard's death myself, sitting by his bedside, I would add more comments about Dylan Thomas and John Donne [which would never have been said directly to Leonard's face, because words were meant to be tactful at that time and encouraging].

Thomas, like Donne [and Leonard no less], was very angry about the human condition.

> Do not go gentle into that good night
> Old age should burn and rave at close of day;
> Rage, rage against the dying of the light
>
> **(Dylan Thomas d.1953)**

Dylan Thomas, himself, died far too early at the age of 39. I don't think he raged against his own death; he was probably too drunk. When he wrote the poem, he was writing about his father's death, as I recall, identifying with him about what his own attitude would be, faced with dying. Thomas was, I think, unrealistic in his poem, fired up with a young man's ire in the face of death, picturing how he would rebel against "the dying of the light." When you're old and dying, chances are good you wouldn't have the vim and vigour anymore to rage. You would go quietly into that good night.

With Thomas's own death, it wasn't his drinking but pneumonia and morphine [poorly prescribed] which finally put him into a coma. So, Dylan Thomas just slid away into the arms of death. All his bluster, courage and rage did him no good; after all, at the end, he had no choice but "to go gently into that good night." Maybe it's different when you're still hale and hearty? But poor Leonard also slid into a coma in the last two days before he died, so meekly, so silently sinking into "the dying of the light." We go through this world with so much piss and vinegar when we are young; but when life ends, we are frail and call on God [or Something] to help us!

And you, my father, there on that sad height,

Curse, bless, me now with your fierce tears, I pray.
Do not go gentle into that good night.
Rage, rage against the dying of the light.

(Dylan Thomas d.1953)

.....

This is the way the world ends
This is the way the world ends
This is the way the world ends
Not with a bang but a whimper

(T.S. Elliot d.1965)

Leonard journeyed through rage to hope and then to acceptance. I wish I had his thoughts to share with the world… but I don't. My own weak memories and my frail insights will have to do to fill in some gaps about his last days' journey. Leonard's thoughts and his wisdom, like precious jewels, wrought through the suffering of his last days, will forever be lost. Drugged up and dreamy. That's the way the world ends!

I want to say something about Leonard as a person, so his memory is preserved. It's a difficult pursuit, maybe a solitary one on my part, because the dynamics among family and friends have changed so much since Leonard died.

It seems that everybody wants to bury memories about Leonard now, which are still too painful to exhume. Everybody in the family is already going their own way. I'll do the best to "time-freeze" some record of him. He should not be forgotten. What he thought and felt during his illness should be preserved, as worthwhile lessons about life and dying. Dying is a lonely act.

He sought comfort in sharing with family and friends when they visited. In fact, Leonard extended an open invitation when he got sick, "Please feel free to drop by anytime over this coming weekend and beyond. We would love to see you!" When troubled waters come, we all need a warm shelter from the storm.

And if I pass this way again, you can rest assured

> I'll always do my best for her, on that I give my word
>
> In a world of steel-eyed death, and men who are fighting to be warm
>
> "Come in," she said, "I'll give you shelter from the storm"
>
> [BOB DYLAN – *Blood on the Tracks* ALBUM, 1975]

CHAPTER 17

"You can never tell about people. They wear masks, you know, they're like icebergs showing only what they please, and they die full of secrets. You'll be blessed, Andrew, if you come to know-really know-just a handful of people in a lifetime."

[P.67, *Thale's Folly*, BY DOROTHY GILMAN, BALLANTINE PUBLISHING, 1999]

• • • • •

2013 WINTER SESSION @MOHAWK

AAMIR BEATS THE DEADLINE

THE NIGHT COURSES PICKED UP SPEED. WALLY FOUND IT difficult to keep up with his blog about Leonard and his studies at night school. Somehow he managed to burn the candle at both ends, maybe at three. He loved e-mailing Baryon and taking those chatty coffee breaks at the college.

A new face joined the group before the deadline... Aamir. He was tall, 6' 2," and darkly handsome, in his mid-20s, clean shaven. He had a head of rich black hair, with a strand strategically curled down on the left side of his forehead. Dark eyebrows, which looked manicured, arched above piercing lion eyes. Unusual, thought Wally.

Aamir's nose was straight, almost delicate. His teeth were also straight and white inside an expressive mouth whenever he spoke. His cheekbones and chin tapered into a gentle triangle, giving his face the appearance of a young Antonio Banderas. He could have auditioned as a double for the Zorro movie! Aamir radiated not only confidence, but arrogance. He wore a black T-shirt under a dark suit jacket. Wally didn't like the new fashions. Formal wear and sloppiness just didn't go together.

There was a hint of some Eastern accent. "Actually, it's Afghan," he corrected. He said his real interest was videography but he also wanted to create a website which explained the difference between Muslims and Western society. He felt that the West was decadent and democracies were not really democratic.

"You have to have money to get elected."

Both Baryon and Wally wouldn't argue the point. When Aamir got up to leave, he extended to his full height, hovering over Wally and Baryon. She said, "I thought people in the Middle-East were supposed to be small like Italians?" He said sarcastically, "You're like all Westerners, you stereotype."

When Aamir left, Wally nodded his head. "He's got some points. We do tend to stereotype people. He's also right we are a spoiled society, and Hollywood has a deserving reputation for decadence." Wally couldn't help but add, "Shari'ah Law, though, now that's extreme... but probably effective!"

Baryon said, "Damn religion and cultures!" She got up and headed back to the elevator. Wally got up too and thought, "This will make some interesting coffee times!" He had no clue who Aamir was! Somehow, he seemed familiar.

.....

At the next break, Wally commented, "I thought all Muslim men had to wear beards?"

"Not true!" said Aamir. "It depends on the sect or how deeply you want to emulate our Prophet, Muhammad, may peace be upon him."

Baryon kept quiet, thinking that beards were just a way to hide the real face. She finally said, "Beards or burkhas, it's all the same to me. I don't trust a culture that hides their faces."

Aamir gave her a sharp look as if his eyes would throw daggers. Then in a flash that look disappeared.

"I guess, the biggest objection I have," she added, "is that Muslims subjugate their women, make them wear head coverings and don't give them a chance to be educated and get jobs."

Aamir argued that the man should have a career and the woman should stay home with the children. "It was the proper balance," he said. He felt that this was the example set forth by the Prophet, Muhammad, "may peace be upon him."

"Sounds like a pretty good deal for the man," retorted Baryon, "I understand that the man can have four wives. Your horny Prophet, Muhammad, had 11 wives and married Aisha when she was only six years old."

That was enough for Aamir. He shot up off his chair and headed back to class, leaving his coffee unfinished. Baryon stared at Wally, with a victorious glint in her eye, "It seems I've hit a religious nerve!"

Wally had more respect for somebody else's religious convictions, maybe because of his own inclinations; Baryon was a staunch atheist who loved to goad religiously minded people on because she believed most of them were hypocrites anyway, especially extremists.

She was disappointed at the open-door policy in Canada for immigration, believing that better practices were followed in the 1980s with Prime Minister Trudeau. Now, there was too much that wasn't politically correct and too much allowed into the country from troublesome foreign religions and cultures. Baryon was aware of Canada's history and the old wounds, now scarred over, where the white man took the land away from the aboriginal peoples. Nothing was fair, but a Confederation in 1867 became a country and Baryon was happy with the outcome in terms of standard of living and medical care more than 100 years later. She saw these things threatened now by foreign influx in Muslim immigration from overseas and corporate infiltration from the United States. She respected Wally's moderation, but not Aamir's extremism.

"I'm afraid for Canada," she said. "We've made the kirpan legal for Sikhs to carry. Catered to the turban for Mounties. And now religious freedom demands that Muslim women can wear the niqab during the swearing in of Canadian Citizenship. I think the hijab is quite pretty, but the niqab where the face is covered and only the eyes are visible disrespects the values in Canada, where faces should be open to view, especially in the swearing in ceremony as a Canadian citizen."

Wally listened. Baryon was wound up.

"The line has to be drawn somewhere, and if people don't respect our values, then some people shouldn't be let into this country. Where is the line for religious freedom? Child sacrifice? Devil worship? Nudity because it's nature worship?"

Just then, Tim Horton's locked up its gates and the signal was obvious, "coffee break was over." As she got up, Baryon threw out one last thought with conviction. "We've had it good in this country. I hate to see it lose its identity. Rome had it good too for many years and then fell. The way I see it, we need to preserve our 'Pax Canadiana' for Canadians." Wally raised his eyebrows at that comment and chewed her words over carefully, maybe for a future discussion.

.....

Aamir didn't come to the next break but stayed in the class to work. There was an uneasy distance between him and Baryon for the rest of the semester. Wally and she took their coffee breaks together at Timmy's without Aamir, though the topic of Muslims was not left untouched.

"It's the extremists who scare me," said Baryon. "They're the ones who use Allah as a cudgel against women. They want to make women wear niqabs or burkhas. They believe in a Holy War and they arm themselves, with AK47s, to kill infidels." She added, "By their understanding, anybody in the West is an infidel... so much for a religion of peace!"

Baryon's heroine was the Pakistani girl, Malala Yousafzai, who wrote a blog criticizing the Taliban for banning girls from attending school. In the afternoon of October 9, 2012, Malala boarded her school bus in the northwest Pakistani district of Swat. A gunman asked for Malala by name, then pointed a Colt 45 at her and fired three shots. One bullet hit the left side of Malala's forehead, traveled under her skin, the length of her face, and then into her shoulder. Malala was 15 years old.

She was sent to the Queen Elizabeth Hospital in Birmingham, England, where she received intensive care until her recovery. The assassination attempt sparked a national and international outpouring of support for Malala Yousafzai... and admiration from Baryon for this young girl who stood up for women's rights in the Muslim world.

CHAPTER 18

THE PHILOSOPHER, JOHN LOCKE, IN THE 17TH CENTURY claimed that humans started out with a "tabula rasa," a blank slate, and acquired their behavioural traits as they grew up by "nurture" or environmental influences. Charles Darwin added to this picture of human development 100 years later in the 18th century by claiming that "nature" or heredity passed on certain predispositions. [Wikipedia]

.....

AAMIR'S SCRAPPY BACKGROUND
HIGH SCHOOL AND COLLEGE

Aamir's name was known to Hamilton Police. He had been arrested, when he was fifteen, for minor possession of pot and been let off with a warning by the judge. Unknown to the police, he graduated to crack by the time he was eighteen. Unlikely as it seemed, he cleaned up his act at that age.

Aamir had found religion... Islam! He read the Qur'an and stopped his habit of drugs by sheer will. No dope, no alcohol!

Women were an exception. The other exception was his hair-trigger temper. Somebody slurred Muslims in the high-school cafeteria one day. Aamir heard, "Damned immigrants, they'll ruin this country." The guy felt a tray come crashing down over his head, angrily applied there by Aamir from behind. Others jumped in to break up the fight. The two offenders soon found themselves sitting in the office, outside the principal's door.

The sign read, *W. Irfan, Principal.* The door remained shut. Aamir sat with his head down, trying to ignore the door. When would it open? He was meant to sweat it out a bit. Finally, the principal opened his door, and motioned Aamir to come in. The principal's face showed a clear sign of displeasure. He pointed to the seat in front of his desk. "Now, then," said Mr. Irfan, "let's hear it!" Aamir said he could not take a racial slur against immigrants. The principal said he was an immigrant himself, but there was no need to erupt in violence. Aamir could yet be charged with assault. He should have reported the slur to a teacher. Aamir rolled his eyes. The principal chose his words carefully: "I will deal with the other boy later, but you! You cannot do violence in my school! You have a three day suspension... now, I don't ever want to see you in this office again!" The incident didn't go any further. Maybe too much paperwork, too much hassle?

Aamir was glad when his picture was taken for the grade 12 yearbook. He even smiled. Two more months and he'd be out of there!

That summer meant freedom. A friend at a local mosque said Aamir could work as a drywaller for his construction company. Aamir tried it for a week and told the foreman he wasn't coming back. He didn't like bosses, nor the lifting; he had better things to do with his time.

Aamir settled into pumping gas at his father's Pioneer station. All he had to do was ring in the cash, give change and then settle back behind the counter with a book.

September rolled along. Aamir had registered at Mohawk College in videography. He liked holding a camera. It was lighter than a sheet of drywall.

Rashid, another Muslim, was the only person whom Aamir was seen with. They took breaks together and berated the West, how Islam was the only true religion and how it would rid the world of infidels. They insisted on their rights to leave class whenever their time for "salat" came, their 5 times daily prayers. They left and came back into class late.

It was understood that coffee break would last 20 minutes at the most. Just time to sit and grab a coffee and something to munch quickly. Aamir and Rashid didn't return to class one Thursday. The instructor asked the last person coming in where they were. "Oh, they're at the dean's office. They got into a fight with a guy who said Canada shouldn't allow Muslims into the country."

When they heard the racial slur, Rashid and Aamir both jumped up from their tables next to the guy. They tackled him and pummeled him with their fists. Two security guards rushed in to break up the fight. They hauled all three of them off to the Security Office and took their names.

"What a scene!' recalled the kid, when he told the story to the class. "It was just the guy's opinion. They could have walked away."

.....

The two guards ushered the three of them into the Security Office. Officer Jenkins and Adams asked if they were ready to talk.

"Now then," Officer Jenkins said to Owens, the engineering student, who had thrown out the racial slur. "You don't like Muslims?"

"Just some of them, sir. What I meant was that Canada should tighten its immigration policy against extremists."

"Do you realize that you could be charged with a hate crime?"

"No sir. I knew no such thing. It was just my opinion."

"Watch your mouth in public. I want you to appreciate what it means to be politically correct. We are a multicultural institution here at this college and in fact, in our country."

Owens rolled his eyes momentarily. He finally said, "Yes sir."

Adams the senior security officer faced Rashid and Aamir. "You could have ignored what he said and walked away."

"We cannot ignore an insult to our culture," objected Aamir. "Okay, okay," said Officer Adams, not wanting to draw things out.

Adams continued, "We're not going to make waves by bringing this to the Dean's Office. It could mean expulsion for all three of you, especially since you guys threw punches." He took a breath and then in a tolerant, paternal voice said, "Let's not have you three coming back here again." He opened the door.

Officer Jenkins walked Owens back to class and Officer Adams walked the other two back to their videography tutorial. They hoped they had heard the last of them. Owens quit school the following week.

CHAPTER 19

"Why am I writing things down?" Wally asked himself. He saw no difference between a Blog and a Diary. "There's an urge inside me, like my photography, to do it. I can't keep all my thoughts bottled up."

.....

MARCH 2013

WALLY QUITS!

WALLY DIDN'T ENJOY HIS WEB SCRIPTING COURSE THAT semester, not only because he had no interest in defining variables and scripting "IF THEN ELSE" control structures, but more than that, the learning atmosphere had degenerated since Aamir joined the group. Wally quit.

He already had accomplished what he first set out to do, which was create a photographer's website for himself. Instead, he and his wife looked for a cruise to the sunny Caribbean over the March break. After all, what was important? Nose to the grindstone or some enjoyment out of life?

.....

Now that he had nothing to study for, Wally turned his attention back to his Blog. Originally, he meant for his writings to turn into a book about Leonard, but the Blog sort of veered off into another direction, becoming instead his own Diary. He liked doing a Blog, a great way to harness his feelings and write them down. Maybe an invisible public might make him write better. Occasionally, he wondered, if sharing thoughts with total strangers was wise. For the moment, the Blog served as a way to hone his writing skills as an "author." Instead of a story about his dead brother-in-law, he wrote more and more about himself. "Maybe Leonard's story will make a separate book someday, maybe at a later date?" So, Leonard got put off.

Wally puttered around with words, talking about his daily life, his readings, or whatever he saw or heard on the news. He mused, "A blog isn't a blog; it's a diary... made public!" Oh well, he would be careful about what he put in it! He posted something about the concert he and his wife took in one Friday evening. He even talked about what he watched on his old movie station, "Antenna TV: Television the way it was meant to be!"

.....

POST 5: KEEP ME IN YOUR HEART

TAKING TIME OUT

My wife came home early enough, so we could get to that blue grass gospel concert at that little café in downtown St. Catharines for which we paid $40. *House of Doc* from Winnipeg was featured, all talented Mennonite people, fiddle, guitar, banjo, accordion and drum. I told my wife not to go to her seminar after school but to just get home quickly…because we had a life! The "theater" was set up like a beatnik coffee house, little tables with candles lit in the center. Coffee was percolating on a side counter. We sat near the back by the window. It was raining outside. The group sang a song written by Warren Zevon who died of terminal lung cancer in 2003 at the age of 56. The sentiment reminded us so much of Leonard who had died at age 42 of the same disease. Wally's wife cried during the song.

Shadows are falling and I'm running out of breath
Keep me in your heart for awhile
If I leave you it doesn't mean I love you any less
Keep me in your heart for awhile
When you get up in the morning
and you see that crazy sun
Keep me in your heart for awhile…
Hold me in your thoughts, take me to your dreams
Touch me as I fall into view
When the winter comes keep the fires lit
And I will be right next to you

(Warren Zevon died 2003)

CHAPTER 20

PEOPLE WHO WATCH OLD TIME MOVIES ARE POETS AT heart. They are harmless souls who are stuck on nostalgia, feasting their eyes on the styles of antique furniture, old buildings, and old cars recorded on the silver screen. They see morality in black and white... well, sometimes in forgiving greys. They love the simplicity of the plot, where the hero delivers classic lines to his heroine, "Here's looking at you kid."

[FROM WALLY'S BLOG: NOTE ON *Casablanca*, 1942]

. . . . .

WALLY'S TRIVIA
MARCH 2013

POST 6: DRAGNET AND PETER GUNN

INDULGING MYSELF

Hmm, I'm home. *Dragnet* is on Retro TV, starring Jack Webb, badge number 714, a 1969 rerun about a German shepherd, named Ginger, sniffing out marijuana. I was in third year university, writing essays, at that time, reading English Literature and history books and having a great time at the University Pub. Loved those all-night movies of Humphrey Bogart on Friday or Saturday nights at the Campus Centre. What a life! American kids my age were fighting in Viet Nam, while I was indulging myself in "film noir." Whoops, I'm missing *Dragnet*! Got to stop my rambling! Tomorrow is another day. Who knows when I'll get back to posting anything about Leonard? So, what's the definition of procrastination?

AFTERNOON

I watched Peter Gunn [1960] over lunch hour, munching a sandwich [leftover meats from supper at last night's Parent/Teacher interviews]. We had our air ducts cleaned this morning. At least I don't have to listen to sucking air hoses this afternoon, while I indulge myself in some writing. I've got all the doors open and the overhead fans going to air out the house. Children's voices are filtering in from next door through our open sliding doors in the Great Room. The neighbour lady runs a Day Care and has a playground set up in her backyard. She does a terrific job by giving the kids a regular play schedule. The little voices calm me. They do not disturb, while I think about what to write next. I think about Leonard's own kids. They were 6 and 2 when he died. His girl is a little starlet and his son is a little ham. We're seeing them again this coming Sunday, so the kids can light a remembrance candle at church for daddy.

It's funny seeing *Peter Gunn*, filmed in black and white, broken up by colour commercials! I guess stringing those coaxial cables along the joists in the crawlspace was worth it after all, one line for the front TV and one line for the back TV in the Great Room. I felt like a soldier in the crawlspace, scraping along on my tummy in enemy territory down there. Had to keep my butt down, otherwise lift it a little, and I'd bang it on a furnace duct or a joist. Ouch! My work down there is not good for my sciatic nerve or the arthritis in my shoulders, but hey, we can watch High Def TV without paying the cable company!

I must admit the commercials during *Peter Gunn* are pretty tacky and tell a lot about the broken health system in the United States. Obama hasn't solved anything in my opinion. There's Humana with all-in-one Medicare [if you have the money], all kinds of options, plan A, B,C and so on. Then AARP insurance pops on screen, offering to supplement your regular Medicare [which is extra money]. Then DePuy Hip Replacements, which have left people crippled, so that the Johnson Law Group is advertising for litigants on TV to get, "the compensation they deserve." And finally, there's a free book [no obligation] if you suffer from "Mesothelioma" [more lawyers looking for clients]. I googled *mesothelioma* - it's cancer from asbestos and the source says, "Compensation via asbestos funds or lawsuits is an important issue in mesothelioma [see asbestos and the law]." My plumber died of that disease at the age of 70. He worked with it when he was young and nobody told him it was dangerous.

In my opinion, Oasis Legal Finance is another example of the United States being in deep doo-doo, where people seem to dig themselves into more debt. They promise money up front, so you don't have to be kept waiting in the court system to tide you over until you actually win the compensation "you deserve." They are banking on the possibility of a buck from the courts and that's just plain stupid, in my opinion.

Drug companies have grown smart over the past few years and now, there are all sorts of disclaimers about side effects. How can the Food and Drug Administration [FDA] pass all these drugs which can make things worse than what they are supposed to cure! America, the Beautiful!

CHAPTER 21

The Big ol' City was such a lonely place to be

Hussle all day, and dream of the islands and sea...

Livin' on love and the fruits from tropical trees

[*Just Another Day in Paradise,* BERTIE HIGGINS SONG, 1982]

.....

FINAL EXAMS @MOHAWK
APRIL 2013

MEANWHILE, THE CARIBBEAN

BARYON STILL E-MAILED WALLY ABOUT HOW THINGS WERE going in the class with Aamir. Not too well! She was looking forward to the final exams in April 2013, and in the future, making sure she didn't take any more classes, "with this macho Muslim." Wally didn't think that all Muslims were like that, maybe they had just run across a bad apple?

Wally and his wife thrived during their Caribbean cruise, seven days of sun and sand. When they got to Grand Turk, his wife headed for the reclining chairs lining the beach and found one aptly positioned under a palm tree. When Wally took her picture, he thought: "Is there any place, we'd rather be? Not Canada, for sure!" His wife was content, "I sure enjoy the warmth and watching people on the beach."

Their boat, the Maasdam, floated peacefully at dock under sunny skies. Wally wandered the beach taking pictures with his wife's pocket camera, occasionally straying to the edge of the water to wiggle his toes there. Grand Turk was a restful stop. Wally was happy for the blue sky, the emerald water and the warm sand. Canada seemed so, so far away. If they had enough money, they'd be one of the "snowbirds," looking to retire in the Caribbean, a Paradise in the sun, away from it all!

Holland America listed a total of 5 stops for the 7 day cruise, including Grand Turk, Willemstad in Curacao, Oranjestad in Aruba, Colon in Panama, Tortuguero Canals in Costa Rica and finally Half Moon Cay. What was there to say? They were getting well tanned, well fed and well entertained. Mohawk College, the stress of Web Scripting and personality clashes between Aamir and Baryon seemed so far away, like the white clouds floating away in the distant sky.

POST 7: MARCH BREAK 2013

WILLEMSTAD, CURACAO

We booked a shore excursion for Willemstad, Curacao, That colourful city has a long history. One of its quarters, Punda, was originally established in 1634, when the Dutch captured Curacao from Spain. In 2010, the Netherlands relinquished ownership of the island to make it autonomous; however, still being a constituent country of the Kingdom of the Netherlands. If you want to understand that, just think of Canada's association with the United Kingdom and the British "Commonwealth of Nations."

Willemstad is the capital of Curacao with a population of 140,000 people. Portuguese Jews also have a long history in Willemstad having moved there from Amsterdam to seek religious freedom as far back as the late 1600s.

I couldn't help but have a passing thought, where would Jews look for religious freedom if Islam took over the world, or Christianity for that matter! But never mind, let's focus on this holiday in the sun! I'm writing as a tour guide to our Caribbean cruise.

We were in Willemstad on Christmas Day. We were told shops would be open, so off we went, my wife and I, not to shop but to sight-see. We crossed the "Queen Emma Bridge," also known as the "Swinging Old Lady," which is a pontoon bridge that was completed way back in 1888.

The floating fruit market along the bank of the harbour was open and busy. It's a mini boat fleet that comes in from Venezuela. Our eyes were filled with the colourful buildings along the streets, many of which were "Bling" and craft stores. Pleasantly, we were not pestered by a lot of "hustlers" on the street. I took a photo of the Mikve Israel-Emanuel Synagogue founded in 1651. It's the oldest temple in the Western Hemisphere, quite a history! I tried entering the square of the synagogue to get a better angle for my photograph but a policeman standing there said I could not enter the square in front of the building. I had to take the photograph from where I stood outside.

Shabbiness seemed to be mingled with better maintained buildings in Willemstad. There were some run-down structures which we passed. But overall, it was a lovely walk through town and certainly colourful. Buildings were painted greens, blues, reds, yellows and oranges, quite a feast for the eyes!

Had we wanted to, we could have booked a tour of the Hato Caves, out of town, which featured stalagmite formations, water pools and a waterfall. And we could have gone to an ostrich farm but we had that booked for Aruba. I was amused to see a McDonald's as we walked. There would be one in Aruba too.

When we got back to the Maasdam, we had a special dinner booked in the Pinnacle Grille. We ordered steaks, a 12 ouncer for me. I could have had a 23 oz. steak but I didn't have the appetite of a lumberjack. The "volcano cake" was delicious. I'd have to do a lot of walking on the deck to work off the desserts on this ship?

I sacrificed my movie for the evening. Instead I voted for the song and dance show in The Showroom Theatre. That night's performance was entitled, "Unforgettable," which was indeed unforgettable, a great tribute to songs "from the old days." I especially enjoyed that old Peggy Lee classic, "Fever" and Elvis Presley's popular hit, "Only Fools Rush In."

It was a great show before we headed back to our cabin for bed. There was always a towel folded to look like an animal on the bed with two chocolates for eyes.

POST 8: MARCH BREAK 2013

THE PANAMA CANAL

The French originally tried to build the Panama Canal back in 1880 but gave up after disastrous costs of money and lives.

The brochure said that 20,000 lives were lost building the canal, due to malaria, dysentery and work accidents. Panama negotiated with the U.S. in 1903 for the completion of the canal, which was finally done on August 15, 1914. At noon, December 31st, 1999, Panama took over full operation and maintenance of the canal.

Somebody told me that the toll for each ship coming through was in excess of $100,000, quite a bit of change for passing from the Atlantic to the Pacific [and vice versa]. When we got into Gatun Lake, my wife counted a total of 51 freighters and cruise liners within the range of her eyesight. The Maasdam's brochure noted that the annual transit was more than 14,000 ships and that the canal employed more than 10,000 workers. Despite all the heartache in the early years of building the canal, it's been a boon for Panama since the years of its completion. I hope that the revenues the canal reaps filters down to benefit all levels of their society.

I was impressed by how the canal operated. Guide cables were hooked up to a ship on each side, so that it could be pulled by these mini-trains, called "mules." These mini-engines guided these mammoth freighters into the locks! Amazing to watch. I photographed a freighter which according to its name, "Cosco Aqaba," must have come from the Jordanian coastal city that is situated at the northeastern tip of the Red Sea. It was loaded with gigantic boxes, ready for transport by truck or train.

We left Gatun Lake and headed back into the locks to get back into the Atlantic. The Maasdam docked at Colon. After breakfast, my wife and I went ashore to explore "the mall." Again shops, shops and more shops and taxis to take tourists on tours inland. My wife and I did our usual walk-about. We found a huge store, like a Wal-Mart or a Target and purchased a comb and a toothbrush [I had snapped mine in half by brushing my teeth too hard]. We were not exactly the last of the big-time spenders!

My wife went to "Afternoon Tea" and also took in the chocolate seminar in the Culinary Arts Center. I took in the cartoon matinee, "Despicable Me Part 2," but walked out after 20 minutes. I guess, my little niece and nephews, might have liked it better. I sank into a chair in the Library on Deck 8 and read my James Patterson murder mystery novel, *Cross My Heart*.

The show that night was "A Little Bit of Country and a Little Bit of Rock n' Roll." The singers and dancers of the Maasdam were gathered on stage in the saloon: "Roy's Road House." I liked their rendition of Roy Orbison's "Blue Bayou" and Bonnie Raitt's "Somethin' To Talk About."

What an eventful day we had! I finally got to see the Panama Canal and could prove it with a few choice pictures! What a feat of human engineering; what a lot of lives lost!

POST 9: MARCH BREAK 2013

COSTA RICA

I booked our second shore excursion in Puerto Limon, Costa Rica! The 4 hour tour of the Tortuguero Canals was very worth-while!

We had an early lunch on the Lido Deck 11. Our host, Nursaf, and maître d', Badus, brought my wife her gluten-free food. My wife had also requested two extra slices of bread with Nutella to make a sandwich for taking along on our shore excursion. Nursaf and Badus were happy to oblige. I filled the water bottle. The forecast was partly cloudy, 84

Fahrenheit [26 Celsius]. We met our tour guide, Allan, at the bus which was scheduled to leave at 11:30 a.m.

As we drove through the Costa Rican countryside, we discovered Allan had a wealth of knowledge which he shared with us, seasoned with an enjoyable sense of humour. We stopped at a banana plantation where the process of harvesting, and not bruising bananas, was explained to us. We wondered why banana bunches were covered in blue plastic bags. Costa Rica also supplies much of the tropical fruit that we, in North America, see in cans in our grocery stores, famously labeled with the brand names, *Del Monte* or *Dole*.

The houses we passed looked very poor. They were made of concrete block and often had rusty corrugated steel roofs. People applied a coating of plaster to these concrete structures and then painted them with bright colours, which eventually stained and became an eye sore. However, Allan pointed out that the state provided healthcare for everybody in his country, providing anything from aspirin to a heart transplant. Money was diverted from the military for that purpose. The bus occasionally stopped when Allan spotted a monkey or a sloth in a tree. He was excited that we had actually seen three of the monkeys indigenous to Costa Rica: the howler, the capuchin and the spider monkey. I sort of got a picture of one of the little rascals in a tree, but facing the other way. Camera shy, I guess, or just plain obstinate!

Our bus parked at the entrance to the canals near a dock; and we boarded a tour boat, for part two of our trip. Allan used a mirror to shine into the trees when he spotted bats, monkeys or iguanas. We even stopped along the shore of the canal, so that Allan and the boat driver could search for a poisonous frog to show us. Allan was immune to its touch, so he had its leg trapped in a slit in a leaf. Tiny, tiny little red creature. Who would think it was dangerous? But we were safe in Allan's immune hands!

Again as the boat cruised the canals, I was impressed by the lush vegetation all along the shore but not so impressed by the dilapidated looking domiciles which occasionally dotted the shore line. Homes looked run-down, docks looked rickety. I spotted a couple of guys working on an old rusty truck. I guess that's how people lived.

Yet, Allan told us that Costa Rica had the third highest literacy rate in the world, next to Cuba and Chile. Canada came after that. Maybe he's right. I need to Google that, and maybe it depends on which government gathers the statistics.

During the canal trip, we also saw various birds: snow herons, blue herons, krakels and the yellow-throated Euphonia. No huge billed Toucans though [like the one featured on Froot Loops cereal boxes]!

We got back to the boat in time for its departure at 3:30 p.m. We got a sort of inside scoop on the lives of Costa Ricans through Allan's tour.

We remained at sea the next day. It was partly cloudy, 88 Fahrenheit [27 Celsius]. I refrained from taking pictures. Instead I puddled in the pool and hot tub, had my ritual two scoops of ice-cream on the Lido Deck and read some of James Rollins' *Altar of Eden*.

My wife did her usual tour to discover the ins and outs of the Maasdam in the afternoon, while I sunk into another movie at 1:00 p.m.: "Elysium," starring Matt Damon and Jodie Foster. "In the year 2154, two classes of people exist: the very wealthy, who live on a pristine man-made space station called Elysium, and the rest, who live on an over-populated, ruined Earth." Anyway, the hero and villain both die at the end but there is a generally happy ending "for the rest of us." Hmm, in some ways, Elysium reminded me of the condition of the Earth in the present day, 2013. What lessons have we and will we learn? "When will they ever learn? When will they ever learn?"

We had a great time that evening in *The Showroom*. The piano concert by "Count Dimas" was an exceptional experience, highly energetic and very funny. As usual, the announcement was made "No Cameras," which I guess meant most of the audience, including me! Anyway, Count Dimas showed amazing versatility as his fingers magically travelled over the piano keyboard, playing both classical and popular selections in a scintillating style. His half-time show was "The Draculaphone" since he hailed from Transylvania. He appeared covered in a black cape, and after a brief explanation, he dropped the cape revealing, "The Draculaphone." It was a full-bodied suit with whistles attached to rubber bulbs, an outfit which must have mystified customs. The band behind him started playing and "The Count" joined in, playing his suit! To get sound out of the variously pitched rubber bulbs, he had to squeeze them, using hands, feet and sometimes a twist of his head. It was hilarious... and he was in tune! What a talented Count, straight out of Transylvania! Who would have thought? He told us not to tell his music teacher that he did this for a living!

I wondered, if Islam ever ruled the world, what would these talented show people do for a living? How would their creative energies be expressed?

.....

We were indeed lucky to have had this experience, to have been on the ship in the warm Caribbean! I felt like we were in a protected bubble, isolated from the worries of the world. When I lay down in our cabin at night, I could feel the boat's engines vibrate through the hull of the ship. I thought our captain was Captain Kirk and we were flying through space on the starship, Enterprise. If we ran into the enemy, all would be well. We had the Captain and we had Spock! The inside of the ship hummed with warm security.

CHAPTER 22

Definition: "The *American Dream*" is a national ethos of the United States, a set of ideals in which freedom includes the opportunity for prosperity and success, and an upward social mobility for the family and children, achieved through hard work in a society with few barriers.

[WIKIPEDIA]

.....

HOLLAND AMERICA AND INDONESIAN EMPLOYEES

POST 10: MARCH BREAK 2013

HARD WORKING PEOPLE

HOLLAND AMERICA TREATED US ROYALLY. MY WIFE AND I really appreciated the hard work and the cheerfulness of all the Indonesian employees on the Maasdam. Since 88% of

Indonesia is Muslim, it was not unexpected that many of the workers adhered to their Muslim Faith. They worked so hard and were so willing to please... and they were so different than that Muslim fellow, Aamir, whom I ran across at Mohawk College.

I couldn't help but notice how skinny many of these employees were. I was kind of embarrassed on behalf of the ship's passengers, who were... well, obese! There were so many wheelchairs and canes in the crowd too. I was told that some passengers booked cruises back to back because they received better care on the ship, than they did in seniors' homes in North America.

My wife thanked the Lido Manager, Eka, and Lido Supervisor, Nursaf, for their care in providing her with her gluten-free needs. They did a great job, as did the staff at the *Rotterdam Restaurant*: Afid and Kiki. Afid was very good at recommending gluten-free alternatives and brought my wife her food in a timely manner. Kiki was so cheerful, he always made us smile. His ambition was to save enough money to start a grocery business in his homeland.

Nursaf told me he was writing a children's book because he missed his child back home. Afid, as well, told us he had a 9 month old in Indonesia; and he wouldn't see his baby, until she was 15 months old. The family skypes and that makes the separation easier! I hope Holland America is paying these people well, so they can send enough money back home to support their families, because they are worth every dollar they earn!

Whenever we walked into the restaurant, the maître d', Aziz, welcomed us by name. How he remembered us out of 1,200 passengers, I'll never know? We also appreciated our beds being made every day by our room stewards, Asep and Donny, who managed to leave us those amazing folded towel animals with chocolates for eyes.

My wife and I always had something to keep us busy on the ship. I usually attended a morning and afternoon Digital Workshop given by that Microsoft guru, Trisha. Otherwise I'd puddle in the pool and hot tub or munch on popcorn in the movie theatre. My wife would enjoy the sessions in the Culinary Arts Center with Hostess Ashley. Even the Cruise Director, Michael, showed his culinary skills in one of those sessions. It's amazing that he started his cruising career as a piano player on a ship... and he's Canadian, so he knows what kind of weather we got away from!

All in all, we rated our experience with the Maasdam, a 5 star out of 5.

CHAPTER 23

"...my feet will want to walk to where you
are sleeping

but I shall go on living."

[PABLO NERUDA – CHILEAN WRITER]

• • • • •

MARCH 2013
LEONARD'S GRAVE

WALLY WASTED NO TIME POSTING HIS HOLIDAY COMMENTS to his blog after he got home. He also e-mailed Baryon about the sheer enjoyment of the cruise. The weather in Canada was still chilly, and there was a forecast of snow, when they got home, maybe winter's last stand?

The day after they got home, Wally decided to take a walk to Leonard's grave in the nearby cemetery. He put on goulashes because the streets were slushy; and snow was drifting down from an overcast sky, a last breath of winter before it died.

Wally had a pad and pencil with him because he felt like he had some kind of poetry floating around inside his head. His heart felt light and heavy at the same time. He found Leonard's gravestone; and just stood over it in the cold, while snow flakes floated gently down.

After he got home, Wally had a hot chocolate and started to rearrange the lines which came to his mind at the cemetery; and before he knew it, he had his poem, a gentle tribute to his dead brother-in-law. He e-mailed the poem to Baryon.

From: Wally
Date: March 24, 2013
To: Baryon
Subject: I Walked to Leonard's Grave Today

I haven't heard word back from you for almost two weeks. Hope you got my last missive about our trip. We got back to Canada with the snow still hanging on. I decided to walk to Leonard's grave and forged a poem, as a tribute to him. I'll put that in the blog later when I have time. Seems like we're always pressed for time here. Wish we were back in the Caribbean! Anyway here's my poem. It was a lonely walk to his gravesite.

I Walked To Leonard's Grave Today

I walked to Leonard's grave today...

Snowflakes fell down

like little kisses from Heaven.

Canada Geese honked far off,

in their flight to who knows where?

I shed a tear...

I couldn't locate the tree, Leonard,
Where your mother lay.
They all looked the same to me,
so many names along the way,
I touched the stones and brushed the snow.
Where are you, Leonard, where did you go?
I looked up as I went.
Snowflakes touched my face,
like little kisses from Heaven sent.
A dog barked in the cold air.
A sad thought came... are you really there?
A truck changed gears on a road nearby;
Sound of a jet plane headed some-
place [warm, I hope].
This death, this everything... so unfair!
These cemetery paths
reminded me of that Beatles' song
The Long and Winding Road.
which one will lead me to your door?
Snow-limned branches hung above my head;
old knots and scarred bark with moss.
A black squirrel scampered
nimbly from branch to branch.
My soul was mourning your recent loss.
Ah, here you are!
A plastic marker, no gravestone yet,
same lane as your Oma and Opa,
just a couple of doors down.

Is it comforting that you are neighbours?
Or don't those things matter anymore?
Birds chirp busily, a lonely dog barks
once more... at what?
Is there any sense to me being here,
making footprints in my fear... and anger?
No more Coffee Crisps,
no more chocolate puddings
[mixed with horrible meds]
Leonard, I hope you're eating
a big fat juicy steak right now!
My face turns upward toward the sky.
I feel an angel has brushed me by.
Snowflakes and kisses,
sent from Heaven above,
touched my face with tender love.
I feel your quiet presence, as I leave,
Kissing my face, as I grieve.
Snowflakes and kisses sent from above;
Thank you Leonard for your life,
... and all your love!
-- Your brother-in-law, Wally

CHAPTER 24

"I hate coming to dock on the cruise where I can find a café with free Wi-Fi. I hate sitting there like everybody else, frantically receiving and sending e-mails, instead of doing a tour. On the ship, Wi-Fi costs money, often with problems logging on. No, I won't be e-mailing on this cruise!"

[WALLY'S RESOLUTION]

.....

MARCH 2013
E-MAILS, CATCHING UP!

WALLY CAUGHT UP ON HIS E-MAILS WHEN HE GOT HOME, back to a nippy Canada.

From: Baryon
Date: March 14, 2013
To: Wally
Subject: Your Holidays

I wish you and your wife a lot of warmth down in the Caribbean. Meanwhile, I'm slogging away at my courses. Aamir's still unpleasant. I sat down beside him at Timmy's with my coffee and asked him if he knew the age of Muhammad's youngest wife. He said six but the marriage was not consummated until she was nine. He said that was culturally accepted in the 7th century and that he admired Muhammad's restraint. I asked him if he knew what a pedophile was. His only answer was that Western culture did not understand Islam nor the Qur'an.

I don't know, but I think there's something not right about Aamir, even for a Muslim. Every time I make eye contact with him... well, I feel I'm looking into evil. Maybe I'll take another course next semester, but not one he's in!

Final Exams are coming up by mid-April. So far, Aamir and I are neck to neck with our assignments. He seems irritated that a female can do, just as well as he can. He doesn't know how hard I work, but then I'm single, and I have nothing else to do but study at nights. I'm too old to party and I like living alone. My only vice is my Camaro. Love that car. It needs some repair. And so do the shingles on my roof. Nothing new to report, except the weather is lousy here in Ontario. Can you send some Caribbean warmth this way?

Live long and prosper,

Baryon

From: Baryon

Date: March 25, 2013

To: Wally

Subject: Your Poem

I read your poem. That's a lovely tribute to Leonard. I did find the poem a bit long though. I'm thinking of taking more courses, maybe PHP or ASP, in the summer and fall. But we'll see how my legs hold out and my money, after all it's not easy for a senior on a fixed income. My Camaro is a gas guzzler and I don't think I could fit into a Smart car. [lol]

Live long and prosper,

Baryon

CHAPTER 25

SOMETIMES IT'S EASIER TO TALK TO A STRANGER THAN TO relatives or friends. During talking therapy, a trained therapist listens to you and helps you find your own answers to problems, without judging you. The therapist will give you time to talk, cry, shout or just think. It's an opportunity to look at your problems in a different way with someone who'll respect and encourage your opinions and the decisions you make.

[GOOGLE: THE BENEFITS OF TALKING THERAPY]

.....

WALLY @THERAPY

APRIL 2013

SESSION ONE

After he wrote his poem about Leonard's grave, Wally's energy just sagged, and a huge sadness engulfed him. He experienced writer's block. He had nothing left for the Blog. He sat at the computer and stared. Just a big nothing!

Wally held the phone to his ear and sounded apologetic, "Hey Detective Klassen, it's Wally Guenter. Yeah, I know it's been a long time."

He paused, "I've been thinking about seeing a counselor. Your suggestion might not be such a bad idea, after all. Can you give me his name and phone number?"

.....

Wally parked his car in downtown St. Catharines, put money in the meter, and found the sign: "Karl de Jong, Counselor." He was amused. A simple sign. Nothing pretentious, like "World-Renowned Psychoanalyst!" He knew the man had a Ph.D. in psychology. Maybe the guy's parents chose his first name with a sense of predestination, pointing their son into his "chosen" line of work.

Anyway, a simple sign, "counselor." He didn't seem to need glitzy advertising. Word of mouth? Wally thought, "A lot of people must be screwed up. Business must be good... after all, I'm here."

No receptionist? A white haired, older guy, about 60, peered up from behind the desk. He wore a white shirt with a blue bow tie which had little bicycles on it. Cordial, smiling face, as he took his glasses off his forehead and put them back on his nose, like some eccentric university professor.

"I'm Professor Karl de Jong. You must be Wally? You can call me Karl. Let's go into my study." No couch? No desk? Several chairs around a coffee table, a Keurig Coffee Maker on the counter by the sink. A box of Tim Bits at the side. Wally thought, "Psychiatry has changed!" Wally asked him, "Do you bicycle?"

"Oh, you mean my tie? Yes, I do. I believe in keeping fit."

De Jong pulled out a pencil and notepad. He sat and crossed his legs, sipped his coffee and said, "Now then, let's get started. Get yourself a coffee but leave the doughnuts alone!" Wally thought, "Now, that's specific!" De Jong said, "So, why are you here?"

Wally unraveled his story. "I stumbled across a dead woman in the woods. That was, let's see, about a year and a half ago. I'm having nightmares again and can't get her image out of my mind. For a while, it wasn't too bad, but then, my brother-in-law died and these nightmares have come back. I can't sleep."

"Tell me when you first discovered the body, how did that make you feel?"

"I was disgusted, horrified that this could be done to a person. Her face was slashed up and there was a gaping wound along her throat. It was gruesome."

"Tell me what prompted you to be out there in the first place. What led you to stumbling across this murdered woman?"

"I'm a scenery photographer and that was supposed to be my enjoyable outing at Ball's Falls for autumn pictures. I was standing on the Bruce Trail, but it didn't give me the exact vantage point I wanted of the trees, so I backed up into the bush... and I bumped into her leg. Turned around and there she was with blood everywhere!"

Wally repeated how she lay, what she looked like, the blood on the *hijab*, the shock he felt, how his mood for picture taking had disappeared, how he stepped away from the body and out of those bushes. How he got back on the path, eager to tell somebody what he discovered. He didn't have a cell phone. Didn't believe in one. He had to let the parks people know, so they could call the police.

Wally loved computers but he couldn't be bothered with accessories, like the iPhone, iPad, and all the other "iDoDads" which made Apple rich. The same went for Microsoft, Telus and Rogers, no tablets, no nothing powered by "the Cloud." He saw no sense in texting or talking to people when he was out in the woods with his camera. He liked the isolation. So, he ignored getting a cell phone, even for emergencies.

What did people do when there was no cell phone? It would have been handy, sure! But the dead body was there. It would keep! It wasn't going anywhere. Still, he wanted to get away from the horrible scene; and report it to somebody, to let the parks people deal with it!

He explained all that to Karl de Jong. Wally recalled his state of shock. How it ruined his day. He had to spend a long time at the police station, being questioned and then finally Detective Klassen came in.

"I know Detective Klassen. He's a good guy," said de Jong. He explained that Wally was still going through what was known as post traumatic stress disorder [PTSD], which was very normal and very human. It needed to be dealt with through professional help, maybe even meds and through the support system of family. De Jong said, "You need to put the image in a safe place, sort of quarantine it in your mind, like a virus, so it won't bother you night and day!"

"You can't keep this terrible experience to yourself!" said de Jong. "I'm glad you came to see me."

The counselor reassured Wally, "Not everybody reacts the same way. Sensitive psyches like yours are deeply affected when they run across evidence of gross cruelty. Consider yourself fortunate that you have these feelings because that's your sign that you're human. Whoever did this blocked out his own humanity, otherwise he wouldn't have murdered that girl."

"Yes, but how do I sleep at nights?" asked Wally.

De Jong prescribed a regimen of Melatonine, a natural sleep inducing agent, Valerian, another natural drug, and alternating these with doctor prescribed Lorazepam.

"Now, as to those images in your head. We need to make them weaker and eventually put them in a corner of your mind where they won't just pop up to haunt you. We need to understand the criminal mind too. The Why, behind what this guy did."

Wally said, "That's been my big question, Why?"

"Maybe we'll never know. People murder for different reasons. They could be sexual, religious, getting even or just plain being cruel. You'll have to come to terms with the fact that ugliness exists in the world. The world isn't always beautiful. It doesn't hit us so much in our little communities here in Jordan or Niagara... but it's out there and sometimes it breaks into our pleasant little world here, when we least expect it. It's one thing to hear it on the news; it's another to have it happen to you in some personal way."

"The police department said the woman was probably from the Middle East," observed Wally, "maybe it was an honour killing like the Shafia family in Montreal?"

"Most likely. That's something Canada has to deal with more and more, where other people bring their values here from the old country. Some extremists want to bring into Canada what they've been raised with, like Shari'ah Law. If there are enough of them, they figure they have a right to practise it here. But that's not respecting the country you moved to. How do you filter these people out from the mainstream of immigrants, those who would make great Canadian citizens, willing to accept the law which already exists here? ... but I digress."

It sounded like a tedious lecture. But de Jong had used it as a ploy to give Wally some other "hooks to hang his hat on," so he would talk.

"Well," said de Jong, "we've got lots of food for thought here. Let's have some Tim Bits." He chuckled to himself, as they took what he called, "their doughnut break."

"So," said de Jong. "Tell me about your picture taking."

"My photography is my passion. When I look at a tree or a blue sky, I feel like all the stress in the world just drifts away."

"You're fortunate to have that outlet. I would suggest when your mind is haunted by your nightmare, pretend you're on a trail in the woods and it splits right and left. You choose the one where you know there's a calm place, a sanctuary where you can think of peace and pretty pictures which heal."

De Jong continued, "For me, it's music. I like the romance composed by Tchaikovsky, *None but the lonely heart.* Even rock 'n roll does it for me, Bob Seger or Gerry Rafferty. I'm a sucker for Doo Wop music too. There's beauty out there of all kinds, with great healing power. Strangely enough, a lot of that beauty came out of heart-break and incredible talent, which is a real gift to all of us. Find your little sanctuaries, Wally, and treasure them when you deal with your nightmares."

De Jong had mentioned Gerry Rafferty. Wally knew he was in the right hands.

De Jong got up. Time was up. Wally left the session not knowing what to think. What had he gotten out of it? Some of the conversation was... well, trite philosophy and unoriginal thought... but somehow he did feel better just talking and sharing.

CHAPTER 26

KISS is an acronym for "Keep it simple, stupid." The KISS principle states that most systems work best if they are kept simple rather than made complicated; therefore simplicity should be a key goal in design and unnecessary complexity should be avoided. The phrase has been associated with aircraft engineer Kelly Johnson (1910–1990).

[WIKIPEDIA]

. . . . .

APRIL 2013
WALLY @THERAPY

SESSION TWO

WALLY LOOKED AT THE SIGN AGAIN: "KARL DE JONG, Counselor." He walked in. Wanted to talk about his dead brother-in-law and the "Blog that died." How his own Blog had come to a sudden stop because he didn't have the heart to keep it going anymore. He didn't care if people read it or not, or if they commented. He initially cared more about his "posts," using them as a tool to vent his emotions, thinking that eventually he would scrape them together into a book someday.

"It kind of just stopped one day. But now I'm thinking I'd like it to continue. Leonard's death was painful and I wrote some thoughts about it. I'd like to preserve that. But now with this murder and my nightmares, I'm thinking of, well, about writing a murder mystery, a novel of my own. This business of honour killing is an intrusion into Canadian life which is a new concept for us. We've brought stuff into our country from overseas that we have to deal with here. Our society and our laws have to look at it. I'm trying to understand why somebody would do a killing in the name of honour, and feel justified in murdering that girl at Ball's Falls. It's like the concept of Holy War. It just doesn't make sense to me!"

De Jong frowned. "Writing a novel may and may not be healthy for you. I'm not sure right now. I guess it's like talking things out if you write about them which could be good for you. But I just don't want you to get obsessive, where you look at this murder from every angle possible... and then keep looking at it again and again. We don't want to reinforce the image in your head. In a way we want to put it, how shall I put it, "in a virus vault," where we can isolate it and eventually delete the image altogether, so you can live a normal life."

"Well," said Wally, "that's why I've got you to keep me from making it an obsession. I'll let you know how my writing is coming along. I don't think I can stop now anyway. You'll be my weathervane and my marker in the storm."

De Jong said, "These tragedies in your life must be some kind of awakening for you! Reminds me of the title of a hymn by J.S. Bach, *Sleepers Awake*! In a way, we're all sort of asleep, even when we're supposedly awake. We go along in life taking things for granted, especially the lucky ones, who have health, good jobs and pleasant lives, until something happens which shakes them awake to a new reality. And that's when they begin to live and not take things for granted. Yes, we are all sleep walkers, in a pleasant valley, until we walk through the valley of death in some way."

"I feel like I'm one of those people who have been jarred awake with Leonard's death," acknowledged Wally.

"Sometimes you may have to be jarred awake twice or three times before you really wake up!" said de Jong. "Often the people, who have suffered and died, leave something behind to make the rest of us sleep walkers wake up and really live. I think writers, painters, poets and musicians do that for society. They bring out our humanity, our soul and our ability to identify in the joys and sufferings of others."

Wally told Professor de Jong that his wife had given him a little lecture, which for her was actually a "talking to." She hated computers and she hated the social network, which she felt was a big gossip club, maybe a neurotic club.

He confessed, "I've quit Facebook. I don't Twitter. And now I don't Blog. I've put all my writings in a folder in My Documents. I've deleted the Blog from the internet, following my wife's wishes." He emphasized "*wishes.*"

"And she says, I never listen to her!" Both Wally and de Jong chuckled.

"I don't know if my writing will become worse because there's no invisible person reading it like in a blog. But, on the other hand, maybe it'll become better. Maybe I'll be more honest with myself."

"What I don't want," continued Wally, "is for it to become, what's the word, 'didactic'? In fact, I hate words like *didactic*, *exigencies* and *intrinsically*. Mark Twain hated that kind of pompous writing. He once said that's why Congress took so long to make decisions, because they went the long way around to get rid of one single idea. I don't want a Ph.D. thesis," said Wally, " I want it to be understandable."

De Jong listened, while Wally rambled on. This was Wally's moment on the soapbox, his dream, a means to cover up that stark image at Ball's Falls. De Jong didn't want to smother Wally's enthusiasm, so he smiled approvingly while Wally went on... and on.

"The novel will be about culture shock, the destruction of a family, whatever's on the news. I want to leave people with an impression about what's morally right or wrong, whether they're Catholic, Muslim or Atheist, whatever. I want people to feel that life has meaning. I've got lots of things brewing in my mind. I want to include thoughts on natural death compared to senseless violence and war. I want to get something down on paper and see if I can make some sense out of this whole cockamamie mess we live in?... But how do I start this thing?"

"Start at the beginning," suggested de Jong.

"Not so easy," said Wally. "My favourite writer, right now, is Lee Child. He appeared in an interview on Youtube recently. He was asked how he writes his novels. He said he writes the first two pages and then just goes from there!" Wally knew that some writers sketched out a storyboard, others wrote a small synopsis of each chapter and where it was going. There was one author who insisted on writing a whole novel out in long hand on a scratch pad. Wow! Very few could just start at page one and then write until it ends.

Wally thought, "It's hard to believe Lee Child just starts writing from page one and two and goes until he reaches the end!"

Wally couldn't see himself doing things the slow way, labouring over a story-line with an intricate plan. He decided to adopt Lee Child's approach. Just sit down and start writing! Things would have to come out of him naturally from whatever creative spark he had inside. At home, he sat in front of his computer and started typing... "Please don't!"

CHAPTER 27

MOST JOB INTERVIEWS WILL START WITH A PROMPT LIKE, "Tell me about yourself," or "Walk me through your résumé." Don't blow it off with boring answers, and don't approach the interview with a chip on your shoulder. Use a "Story Statement" about your life showing that you're special. Talk about your passion for learning, and about life in general.

[GOOGLE: SURPRISING JOB INTERVIEW TIPS]

.....

FINAL EXAMS @MOHAWK
APRIL 2013

THE JOB OFFER!

THE FINAL EXAMS WERE A BRUTE FOR MOST OF THE CLASS. Aamir and Baryon went through their answers with a fine-tooth comb. They walked out of their exams, second last and

two new Photo Books, featuring Niagara-On-The-Lake and The Niagara Peninsula in general.

"They are very pretty books," he wrote in his e-mail. "But they're not anything that people will necessarily spend $80 on."

Wally complained, "A woman admired the sample I left in the foyer of the local Meridian Bank. She said it would make a great gift for her husband's birthday. When she found out it cost $80, she backtracked. 'Oh I thought you were mass producing the book through a real publisher, so the book would be cheaper, like $40'."

"I couldn't help thinking, 'Is that all your husband is worth, $40?' I told the lady I was selling my books already at cost, which was $80! She walked away with, 'Well, I was just asking. Nice pictures though'."

Maybe I should have stressed that she was paying for my talent, in taking those pictures, in the first place!

Sorry about the complaint,

Wally

.....

From: Baryon

Date: April 28, 2013

To: Wally

Subject: Re. Your Photo Books

It would be great if we could celebrate together. Me with my new job and you with sales in your new photo books. Hang in there, maybe a windfall will come. I've gone by the motto, "Luck is always friendly with talent." Luck will blow your way, soon!

Live long and prosper,

Baryon

CHAPTER 28

Envy is an emotion which occurs when a person lacks another's superior quality, achievement or possession and either desires it or wishes that the other lacked it. Bertrand Russell said that envy not only rendered the envious person unhappy, but could also lead the envious person to inflict misfortune on the other person.

[WIKIPEDIA: ENVY, ONE OF THE SEVEN DEADLY SINS]

.....

MAY 2013
AAMIR'S BLOOD LUST

BARYON BEGAN HER JOB THE LAST WEEK OF APRIL. SHE WAS prompt each day in showing up and got along with the rest of the staff and her boss. She came up with a bright new revision of the front page for the Con Ed website with an impressive header done in Flash [i.e. animation]. She didn't show up the next Monday for work and the boss was worried. Phoned home and left a message. Baryon didn't show up Tuesday either. The office couldn't understand it.

.....

Aamir hid behind the bushes close to the house. It was a solitary place out in the country, late at night, perfect for assaulting his intended target, Ramona, his one-time classmate in Web Design.

"She's so smart. Baryon, sub-atomic particle!" he sneered under his breath. "I'll show her. I'll make particles out of her."

He'd launched a harassing campaign against her after she landed the job. He knocked over her mailbox and phoned her every night for seven days, hanging up when she answered. He wanted that job. He was sick of his humdrum life pumping gas at his father's station.

"I'm as every bit good as she is. I'll show her."

A cloud drifted over the moon. The air was cool, not bad for the end of April, a perfect evening for Baryon to die. He edged his way closer to the house.

"The dog, what about the dog? How to deal with that?"

Aamir kept up his contacts from his days with drugs, and was willing to pay a good dollar for certain weapons. He attached the silencer to his pistol. The dog was always kept in the unlocked shed. Two quiet shots, like little sneezes, dispatched the dog. Aamir had other things in mind for Baryon.

He knew where the phone lines ran. He cut them. He broke a window and crawled through making sure his hands remained uncut by wearing gloves.

Aamir came prepared. He had been thinking about this for days. He entered her room. She jumped from her bed and made for the phone. No dial tone.

"You?" she said, "It was you all along on the phone!"

Aamir drew his switchblade. "Yes, I've come to inflict pain."

"Why do you want to do this?"

"You are a woman and an infidel!"

He grabbed her, she screamed. The walls and the night drowned her futile cries. Easy to manhandle an old lady. He raised her chin and then...

He laughed as he looked down on the lifeless body.

"Yesterday's pain is tomorrow's joke. Where's your 98% now?"

He washed everything down and made doubly sure he left no prints.

CHAPTER 29

"You're very bitter Mr. Smith.
How'd you get that way?"

"Facts of life!"

[HUMPHREY BOGART MOVIE, *Sirocco*, 1951]

.....

AAMIR AND AMY
APRIL 2012 FLASHBACK

"IMPOSSIBLE!"

AAMIR BLINKED AND IN HIS MIND'S EYE HE TRAVELLED back over a year and recalled the word, "impossible." Amy was his girlfriend at the time. When they first met, he liked the fact that he had conquered a North American white girl.

He felt something prophetic about the similarity in their names, Aamir and Amy! His parents had disapproved.

Amy St. Clair was a lovely brunette with long straight hair which tumbled over her shoulders. She smiled a lot and used her hands expressively when she talked. Her hazel eyes radiated an inner peace, which came from her musical gift as a violinist. She hoped to be a world-class violinist someday because when she played on stage, she was a whirlwind of energy. Right now, she was content to play in local orchestras and teach the history of music at Mohawk College. Aamir had attended a noon-hour concert, after which he approached her and said, how he was touched by her playing. She was impressed with his height and dark handsome features. They agreed to meet for coffee.

His father, Adl, said, "No, I won't hear of it. A white girl, a Christian, in the family? Find someone from your own culture."

"Yes," said his mother, Yaminah. "A nice Muslim girl! Nothing good can come from this. I see black." Abqurah, the younger sister, kept quiet. And so did Hazirah, the older sister, who had been seeing Alexander secretly, a white boy, wanting to be like the other girls in North America with boyfriends of their own. Mother and father were not happy that their children were becoming "Americanized." They demanded the TV was turned off whenever "Dancing With the Stars" or "The Big Bang Theory" came on.

"What filth, these half-naked women!" rebuked Yaminah. "And those suggestive remarks on that silly comedy!"

"That is not the way of Allah, nor of our prophet, Muhammad, may peace be upon him," said Adl. "Someday justice will rain down upon this degenerate country."

The family took turns putting in hours at the Pioneer Station in Hamilton, squirreling away hard-earned savings. They hoped their son, at least, would make something of himself at college, maybe in a business degree. Aamir hated business but liked computers.

"What are you going to do, answer the phone for Bell the rest of your life? Or go out on calls and troubleshoot computers for old ladies when they press something they shouldn't?" His father couldn't be more disgruntled. "You should be a programmer or maybe a doctor. They make good money." Nothing ever seemed to be good enough for his father... and his mother always agreed.

.....

His girlfriend, Amy, was the one who had seen black. She was convinced the relationship would not work. Unknown to Aamir, she had applied at Wilfred Laurier University for graduate studies in the music department. She had worked hard at becoming an excellent performer in both the violin and the piano. She received a scholarship to continue her studies there, and so she made the decision to move to Waterloo, to terminate her relationship with Aamir, and to pursue her own future. She had already picked out an apartment.

During their walk through Montebello Park, she told Aamir that she was breaking up with him. It was a warm evening in the last week of March. The sun was setting, a big red rubber ball in the western sky.

Aamir clutched at straws, refusing to admit that their relationship was ending. He blurted out a futile proposal, "But I want to marry you!"

"Impossible!" she said. "It's over. I don't want to be tied to someone in an unequal yoke!"

"What does that mean?" asked Aamir.

"It means it won't work. It's impossible."

Aamir's attitude abruptly changed. "Well, how do know our relationship wasn't all a game anyway. That I was only using you!"

"How do you know I wasn't using you?" she countered.

"It's over then?" Aamir asked, still not believing.

"Yes," Amy said.

They did not leave on good terms. They went in opposite directions. The sun had set.

.....

Amy had read the Holy Qur'an and researched the history of the Prophet to see what she was getting into. There was more to the relationship with Aamir than just loving him and going out. She felt tendrils of control reaching out more and more, taking over her life, month after month, during the time in which they were "courting."

Deep down she sensed a two-sidedness to Aamir. She researched his religion because it meant so much to him. Amy was confronted with several startling facts. One was that Islam permitted lying, called "al-Taqiyya," which was an Islamic word for concealing one's beliefs if it would promote the cause of Islam. She wondered if he had also "fed her lines" to get her to go to bed with him.

Another startling fact was that Islam recognized the existence of angels. There were some equivalent names to Jewish or Christian angels, like Mikail [Michael], Jibril [Gabriel] and Israfil [Raphael]. What Amy did not like about that aspect of the Islamic Faith was that these "jinn" or spiritual creatures had no free will of their own. They were created to do only what God ordered them to do.

Amy wondered if this heavenly hierarchy was mirrored in the distinct roles assigned to men and to women within various Islamic societies. She did not like the idea of being "submissive" to the man and not being able to express her own free will. She also did not like the fact that the very word, "Islam," meant submission and obedience to God. Muhammad seemed more like a man of war to her and not of peace when he made non-believers submit within the Arabian Peninsula in order to "unify" it under one God, Allah.

Muhammad appealed to her sense of equality more in his earlier years. His first wife, Khadijah, was his boss, who, as a widowed woman had been a successful merchant... and this in the sixth century CE! She had hired Muhammad upon the recommendation of a distant cousin to be the agent for her caravan business. He later married Khadijah keeping a monogamous relationship with her for twenty-five years. Amy admired that part of the Prophet's life. She did not like the fact that the Prophet practised polygyny after Khadijah's death and that some sects still allowed the practice to continue to the present day.

Amy had enough criticism for Christianity as well. She knew of its horrendous history and cruelty practised by the Catholic Church under various popes. Submission of women, there too, seemed to be a major theme, much to her distaste. "Wives, submit yourselves unto your own husbands, as it is fit in the Lord." [Col. 3:18] In fact, the whole idea of religion, any kind of religion and culture, which defined a submissive role for women, repelled her. She wanted to be a woman with a career and one who was her own boss.

Amy was a liberated young woman with ambition. She had read Betty Friedan's historic *Feminine Mystique* and Germaine Greer's *The Female Eunuch*. She did not want to lose her decision making ability, and become subservient to a man caught within a medieval mind-set and worse, a repressive religion!

She not only felt stifled by Aamir's religion and culture, but also by his prospects in a dead end job at the Pioneer station. He had never shown any ambition to make something of himself, despite his skills on the computer. Sometimes, he could be a boor too socially with her friends and that bothered her.

There was no sense in arguing religion or cultural differences with Aamir. They would never come to a resolution. The thing simply would not work; she knew this in her heart. Maybe the problem was not even Islam, as much as it was Aamir himself!

Amy couldn't see converting to Islam, nor wearing the required *hijab*. "That's just not me," she thought.

She felt reborn, walking out of Montebello Park, away from Aamir. Amy had her sights set on a Ph.D., becoming a university professor, and establishing her own career and independence.

"Much more satisfying, living and being myself, than hiding behind a domineering husband and a hijab all my life! Life is too short."

.....

Aamir felt rage. He had been rejected, not only for himself, but also for his culture and his religion. Maybe it was his dark complexion? He would embrace Allah more closely and the Prophet, may peace be upon him. He would become the Muslim of Muslims! How could she refuse him? He was not good enough?

He pictured her future. She would go on to a university career and make good money. He would be destined to man his father's gas station forever. He felt like a bug inside a bottle where he could not find his way out, no escape. The world must know that he was special, that he was great. Sayings from the Qur'an burned inside him.

"The only true faith in God's sight is Islam." [Qur'an 3:19]

"Let not believers make friends with infidels" [Qur'an 3:28]

Aamir wondered what Amy had meant by, "unequal yoke." He googled it:

2 Cor. 6:14 "Be ye not *unequally yoked* together with unbelievers: for what fellowship hath righteousness with unrighteousness?"

He was unrighteous? Is that how Amy saw him? He felt unjustly compared, unequally yoked in religion and in careers! Bah! She was the unbeliever and only a woman! He would show her!

CHAPTER 30

"I want to scream sometimes, because I hate when people refer to a dead person as the 'late' so and so. I'm sorry to break that bad news, but that person isn't just late—they're not even coming!"

[JAROD KINTZ]

.....

SUMMER SESSION @MOHAWK

MAY – AUGUST 2013

BAD NEWS!

THE FIRST WEEK OF MAY 2013 WAS A WARM ONE. SPRING was looking good, but Wally doubted he'd go out "photo jaunting" like he used to with his game leg. He had gotten rid of his "space boot" last January, but he still felt uncomfortable going into the woods, now that he relied on a shillelagh to steady his walk.

He enrolled in the summer session of Web Design at Mohawk College: PHP [the Personal Home Page language]. He had e-mailed Baryon, wondering if she had enrolled in PHP or one of the other script courses like ASP [Active Server Pages] or JavaScript. For himself, Wally figured one scripting course was enough, more than enough to addle his brain. He just wanted to touch the waters in what real computer geeks dove into on a daily basis to make websites work like magic. His dead brother-in-law had recommended PHP.

He e-mailed Baryon about his new course and received nothing back, but dead silence. Usually she responded more promptly.

Wally missed Baryon. He was hoping that she'd sign up for PHP despite her day time job at the front office. At break-time, he didn't use the elevator anymore. He sidled up to the new fellow who sat beside him in the tutorials.

"Hi, my name is Alexander. If you don't mind, I'd like to partner up with you for assignments. They look tough."

"Alexander the Great? Sure, two brains are better than one. I'm Wally."

During the next class break, Wally saw Aamir who gave Wally a cursory glance, and then wandered off by himself to sit in a corner, and go over his ASP manual. "Thank God, I registered for PHP," thought Wally. "What a cold fish!"

.....

Bad news comes unbidden! Things you didn't even ask for, and things you don't want to hear!

Wally was in the kitchen, and caught snippets of news on TV, CHCH 11. "Elderly woman murdered, lived alone in the country outside of Ancaster, a dead dog." Wally's brain put two and two together, "That sounds like Baryon?" He came into the living room, and the news continued: "Ramona Szewczuk, murdered in her home, suffered multiple stab wounds. The body was also badly mutilated."

"Oh my God," Wally said to his wife, "that is Baryon, the woman I used to take Web Design courses with at Mohawk College! She e-mails me all the time, jokes, Maxines, political articles, things about computers."

Wally's heart sank. Most of his e-mails came either from Baryon or Dad.

"Baryon is gone. No more jokes. No more sarcastic Maxines." Wally told his wife more about her, and how he would miss her e-mails. "She was a perfectionist, and a very logical lady who knew the computer inside out, not letting her age get in the way. She was 73." Wally sat down. He shed a tear over supper.

.....

Word got around the office at Mohawk. That answered the question about why she hadn't shown up for work. She had a good reason! "She's dead!" her boss sighed. "Who would do such a thing?" Baryon was exactly what they had been looking for. The manager dialed a phone number, and told the young man to come in for another interview. It was not Aamir!

CHAPTER 31

"Our job is to collect and compare the evidence, so we can identify the perp and nail his ass to the wall. We cannot let evil walk, not now, not ever! Find whoever did this!"

[SPENCER'S BOSS]

.....

DETECTIVE ED SPENCER
MAY 2013

AND DETECTIVE JAKE KLASSEN

DETECTIVE ED SPENCER FILLED OUT HIS REPORT. OTHER than Baryon being stabbed multiple times and her body being mutilated [without specifics given], the news media didn't get much from the police.

"It's an ongoing investigation; and we hesitate at this time, to give out too many details about this murder case," said Spencer. "The media has the right to know, but we also have the right to go ahead with our investigation."

Detective Spencer read the M.E.'s report in his private office:

The victim was decapitated.

She was stabbed 7 times in
various parts of her torso

Her breasts were cut off

Other than that, no evi-
dence of sexual assault

Word Allah smeared on the
mirror in her blood

The dog was shot twice

The red Camaro was smashed

Only the victim's fingerprints
were found on the car

No other fingerprints evident

Phone lines were cut

No cash or valuables were taken

In all his years on the force, Detective Ed Spencer had not run across such a puzzling case. He couldn't understand this murder. Vicious stabbing! And yet, nothing was taken. He told the media, that he hadn't run across a horrific crime like this in the 10 years during which he had been a police officer.

He said the victim was knifed, and that more details would be forthcoming upon further investigation. "No, nothing to add, no further comment!"

.....

Detective Spencer had heard about the Ball's Falls case from the previous year. He phoned Detective Jake Klassen.

"You had a mutilation last year? What are the details in your report?"

Klassen read them: throat slit, vicious slashing of the face..."

"We've got something similar here, except that the Vic was also decapitated! The word Allah was smeared in blood on the old lady's mirror! Sounds like the killer is escalating in his viciousness."

"The work of an extremist."

"I agree. We better get together on this."

Klassen explained that they had a fingerprint, and one additional piece of evidence, brought in later, by the Bruce Trail trekker who found the body.

"The guy's a scenery photographer. A good one at that. He just went out there a year after he found the body to cope with some kind of mental block. Well, we got a lucky break from him poking around out there again."

"He found something?"

"Yeah, a necklace that said Allah on the one side, and a dedication on the other: 'To Hazirah, Love Alexander'."

Spencer said, "We're getting closer. Too bad there had to be another killing to make a connection to Hamilton. We're pretty sure this is where the son-of-a-bitch lives."

"I think we're both looking for the same guy, a Muslim extremist, who has one hell of a perverse streak against women! We'd better treat this case carefully. We don't want to lump in a lot of good Muslims out there with this bad apple."

Klassen faxed his report to Spencer and vice versa. Spencer was glad there was a fingerprint lifted off that bloody rock at Ball's Falls, and that "Allah" seemed to be the common thread. How could God be the common thread in a murder? Unfortunately, no fingerprints in the Hamilton case to match with the print lifted off the rock at with Ball's Falls. The killer used gloves and was getting smarter. He was also escalating in his violence.

Spencer gave a statement to the media. He said that the time could not be pinpointed when Ramona Szewczuk was last seen alive by friends or neighbours. They were appealing to the public, so they could trace her movements over the past week. Anyone with information was asked to call Crime Stoppers.

CHAPTER 32

"By indirections find directions out."

[HAMLET: ACT 2, SCENE 1, P3]

. . . . .

THE MISSING PIECE!
MAY 2013

WALLY WENT TO HIS PHP CLASS, BUT WAS IN A MINDLESS state for most of the lecture, thinking about how Baryon was too valuable a person to be killed. He was glad when time for the coffee break came. Alexander had sensed that something was wrong. He followed Wally out the door.

"You look like you need to talk."

"Yeah, that might help. A friend of mine got murdered."

Wally explained over coffee that he had hoped Baryon might register in the PHP class. They might have collaborated on assignments together. Aamir sat in a corner intent on his iPad, aloof and alone in the world. Wally was glad Aamir was in the ASP class.

"That fellow there was in our last class," Wally nodded. "He and Baryon didn't get along. He's Muslim. Used to rag on Baryon about the decadence of the West. Baryon hated the intolerance shown by religions. I guess she hated religion, period."

Alexander said, "You know, I used to go out with that guy's sister for a while. She kind of disappeared out of my life. Maybe it was the parents, and brother, who stepped in." He added, "You can't paint all Muslims with the same brush. I've met some very decent people."

"What was her name?"

"Hazirah. I think the *hijab* made her look prettier. I gave her a necklace with the word Allah in the front and an inscription in the back from me."

"What did it say?"

"To Hazirah, Love Alexander."

Wally did not need a wake up call! He glanced over at the corner, at Aamir sitting alone with his iPad.

"Could it be?" he wondered.

Wally needed proof.

.....

Wally got the idea to set a trap before he went to the police. How would he go about it? Aamir drank coffee during the break like everybody else. Wally would just lag behind and carefully collect Aamir's coffee cup, put it in his satchel, and hope that viable fingerprints were left on it.

When it came time to go back to class, Wally held back, and pretended to do something on his iPad. Aamir left Timmy's. He was the type to just leave his cup anyway for staff to clean up. Perfect. So when Aamir was gone, Wally limped over to the vacated table with his shillelagh, and picked up the cup carefully in serviettes, and placed it in his bag. He had to bring it to Detective Klassen and explain his suspicions.

Except that Aamir didn't quite leave. He hid around the corner, glanced back and saw what Wally was doing.

"Does he know? Has Alexander told him about my sister? Has he talked to the police? How much do they know? I must find out."

Aamir hatched a plan to kidnap Wally. He would waylay him outside the parking lot, force the gun on him, and have him drive to his parents' home to grill him. His parents wouldn't like it but the family had to be protected. He had to find out what Wally knew, and whether he had gone to the police. "After all, it is a Holy War!" he reasoned.

Aamir waited behind the building, just outside the exit, smoking a cigarette. An excuse for his presence there, in case somebody spotted him. He waited for Wally to come out. It was a fresh, but comfortable May evening. Very idyllic for a kidnapping! And possibly a third murder! Shooting Baryon's dog didn't count.

Wally limped out the exit, using his shillelagh to hold the door open. He had his satchel in hand. Aamir sidled up along side, pushed his gun into Wally's back and hissed, "There's a gun at your back. Do what I tell you. Or I will shoot, in the name of Allah, I will shoot."

They walked to Wally's car. Aamir settled himself in the passenger's side, and pointed the gun at Wally's kidneys. They drove to Aamir's house and parked inside the garage.

"Mother, father, we have a guest," Aamir announced as they entered the mud room.

Aamir's father, Adl Ibrahim, stood only shoulder high to his son, but his bearing demanded respect. He had short grey hair, a bit balding at the top. His forehead was furrowed with worry and his dark eyes shrewdly assessed the problem which Aamir had brought into the home. His mouth puckered into deep lines of disapproval.

Yaminah stepped closer to her husband. She was still blessed with black hair, now gathered back behind her ears in a bun. Her eyebrows lifted up with deep concern; her mouth slanted down in a frown. She was plump, in contrast to her husband's thinner form. He looked like a bantam rooster next to his plump little hen.

"Who is this, what have you done?" asked Adl. The wife and sister looked on, amazed that Aamir should dare to bring an infidel into the home.

"He knows about Hazirah and Alexander. I need to find out how much he's told the police."

Adl nodded and opened the door to the basement. That was the first real admission about what Aamir had done to his sister. Abqurah was stunned. Yaminah stepped aside.

Aamir held the gun steady, leading Wally to the basement door, "We will tie him up downstairs and question him thoroughly."

"You'll never get away with this Aamir," challenged Wally. He added a lie, hoping to unsettle Aamir, "Alexander had his suspicions about you all along and so do the police. Even without the fingerprints on the cup, you are tied to the case and they will find you."

The father and son tied Wally to a chair. Hands behind his back, legs secured below. He had no place to go. Who would miss him? Except his wife. She would report him missing when he didn't come home later that night. Aamir knew that the police wouldn't go looking right away, so Aamir and his father, Adl, drove back to the college to fetch Wally's car. They had taken Wally's keys and would drive both cars back home. They would hide Wally's car inside the garage.

Had Wally actually told the police anything? They had to find out and they had to have a plan! They could get rid of the body and the car later. There was no choice. The men agreed on their course of action. The women were hesitant. Abqurah fretted. Should she go to the police? She wanted no part of this. But if her own brother killed her older sister, then her own fate was sealed if she went to the authorities.

Wally sat in the dark in the basement, wondering when his wife would phone the police for a missing person? He had already rubbed his wrists raw from struggling with the cords. A Gerry Rafferty tune kept a rhythm in his head:

"I was lost on an endless sea

Going down, going down, going down on an endless sea

Sail with the wind, you weather the storm

You bring it all home, bring it all home, you bring it all home"

CHAPTER 33

"Allah holds all the stars in his hands. If he snuffs out one or two, or a dozen, there still are too many stars in the night sky to count. We will not notice, or miss them, if it is his will. Praise be to Allah, the cherisher and sustainer of the worlds."

[AAMIR'S THOUGHT ONE STARRY NIGHT]

• • • • •

NO WAY OUT!
MAY 2013

WHEN THE MEN GOT HOME AND HAD WALLY'S CAR SECURELY parked inside the garage, they turned on the TV before going down to grill Wally again. The news was on.

"Still no progress onthe Ramona Szewczuk death. Police continue the search for the killer or killers. Szewczuk was a 55 year old adult enrolled in Web Design in night school at Mohawk College. If anyone has any clues about this gruesome murder, you are encouraged to report it to Crime Stoppers."

Yaminah looked at Aamir. "Was it you my son?"

"Yes, mother. She spurned our religion and called our Prophet a pedophile." Both parents bowed their heads and then accepted what had been done.

The father said, "What's done is done. We are with you."

The younger sister, Abqurah, objected. "Aamir, you killed my sister! And now, this old woman too! These are not righteous acts!"

"Yes, they are!" hissed Aamir. "Hazirah meant to betray our culture by dating outside of it. The old woman called our prophet a pedophile because Aisha was promised to him when she was still a child."

Abqurah kept quiet and looked away. The mother, Yaminah, looked at her husband and said, "We will stand by our son."

.....

Aamir found himself paddling on the lake early next morning. He had loaded his canoe on the top of his car, and gone out a fair distance to drop the switchblade into the lake. He saved the gun for later. He may still have to use it.

"This knife has taken two lives. It sinks so easily to the bottom of the lake, hiding what it has done."

He smiled, "I can always replace the blade. Ordered through the internet, from the sports section, no less."

Aamir had already prepared a long distance plan. His passport was in order. He had purchased a flight out of Pearson International Airport to Pakistan. He intended to make his way to Syria to join the new group of jihadists, called ISIS. That would be Allah's answer to prayer against the Western World. Yes, it would be the beginning of "The New Crusades," and the birth of an independent Islamic State!

Adl had given Aamir a substantial portion of his life's savings for the escape. After all, it was his son who had carried out the honour killing which Adl, himself, had requested, with the approval of his wife. When Aamir was gone, the police would have a much harder case proving that they had anything to do with the honour killing.

CHAPTER 34

Humans aren't as good as we should be in our capacity to emphasize with the feelings and thoughts of others, be they humans or other animals on Earth. So maybe part of our formal education should be training in empathy. Imagine how different the world would be if, in fact, that were 'reading, writing, arithmetic, empathy.'

[NEIL DEGRASSE TYSON – ASTRONOMER]

.....

WALLY FINDS HELP

MAY 2013

AAMIR'S YOUNGER SISTER, ABQURAH, WAS 21 YEARS OLD. SHE was a beauty, with cascading black hair hidden under her hijab. Her face was beautiful, smooth with an olive skin tone. Her eyes were light brown marked with kindness and intelligence. Her lips were full, ready to break out in a friendly smile for people she liked. She was 5' 7," an amazing packet of Middle-Eastern cuteness and energy. Wally noticed her when he was first brought into the house. How could she be the product of these strange parents?

Abqurah was uneasy about keeping Wally imprisoned in the basement. She did not feel the same way her parents did, especially her fanatical brother. In fact, she toyed with the idea of marrying a white boy herself someday. The parents had said that Hazirah had run away but she knew better. They had lied. Didn't the Qur'an teach mercy? Abqurah felt sorry for Wally imprisoned in the basement. She shuddered to think what her brother might do to him when he came back?

Abqurah turned on the light to the basement, and slowly came down the stairs. She hoped her brother would be gone for a while yet.

"Have you come down to gloat? Did you not feel sorry for your sister?"

"I did not know she was killed. My parents said she ran away."

"Her throat was cut. She was murdered in cold blood. Ask your brother. She was seeing a white boyfriend."

"In the name of Allah! How could these things be happening?"

Abqurah confessed that she too was thinking Western thoughts. She liked the boys at Mohawk College. Most seemed nice, although somewhat immature."

She confessed, "I've wondered what it would be like to marry a Christian."

Wally explained that his basis for belief was a need for emotional support when life became too tough. He had no intellectual conviction about God, and didn't care about which religion was the right one. He admitted that being a Christian was the closest thing to what he was raised in, and the practice of it, at least in the Mennonite tradition, appealed to his sense of morality.

"There's nothing Holy about a Holy War," he said. All he knew was that Jesus seemed gentler than Muhammad. It was the systems which men created through the centuries afterwards that screwed things up, actually for both Faiths.

Wally recalled the story from Matthew 26:52 when Peter drew his sword and cut off somebody's ear: "Put your sword back in its place," Jesus said to him, "for all who draw the sword will die by the sword." Muhammad instead raised his sword, by raising an army, in the 7th century to unify the tribes in the Arabian Peninsula. Islam meant submission. Wally was convinced that the Prophet killed or had people killed during his wars. Wally kept his mouth shut.

Abqurah loosened Wally's bonds. She gave him the key to his car, and said he must hit her as part of a credible escape plan, so she would not be blamed by her family for helping an infidel. Wally complied, not willingly. He made his way upstairs, where he saw his shillelagh leaning against the wall. He pushed Adl and Yaminah aside.

Aamir drove into the driveway, not knowing what was going on. He had left his gun in the glove compartment. The garage door opened. Aamir's eyes blazed with fury when he saw Wally. He ran at him. Wally grabbed his shillelagh and swung at Aamir's head. Instead, Wally caught him on the shoulder. Aamir winced. Wally swung again and hit Aamir in the shins. Aamir doubled over in pain.

Wally opened the car door. Inserted the key and started the engine. Aamir clutched at the window and door handle. Wally screeched backwards out of the garage, swinging around the other car in the driveway.

"Detective Klassen will have to dust my car for prints," thought Wally, as he made his way to the QEW. He'd phone home from the police station. "Bringing in a coffee cup with Aamir's prints on it would have been much, much simpler!"

.....

Aamir grabbed his travel bag, which had been packed since Baryon's death. He drove to the Pearson International Airport for his flight, ticket already purchased on the internet for Pakistan. He had prepared well, except for Wally's damned escape. He was limping, not too badly, but he made a stop at a Shopper's Drugmart on the way, and bought a cane, kind of light-weight compared to the shillelagh which Wally used on him. The cane would come in handy to get ahead of the line at the airport, and buy him a little sympathy for being "lame." His limp was legitimate.

Too bad he couldn't deal with his sister, another betrayal by women. He got past customs with no problem. A young man going overseas to visit friends and family. Aamir landed at the Benazir Bhutto International Airport in Rawalpindi, Pakistan. He then booked another flight to Lebanon and landed at the Beirut Rafic Hariri International Airport. No problem getting to Turkey from there, as long as as he showed he was generous with his tips, handing over ready cash to the right hands. His five o'clock shadow would soon be a full black beard to honour the image of the Prophet, Muhammad, may peace be upon him. Aamir was only a hop, skip and a jump away from his eventual goal, which was Syria and then ISIS!

CHAPTER 35

DEFINITION: "CULTURE SHOCK" IS THE PERSONAL DISORIENTATION a person may feel when experiencing an unfamiliar way of life due to immigration or a visit to a new country, a move between social environment, or simply travel to another type of life.

.....

FLASHBACKS "THE SALAD DAYS"
WALLY'S OWN IMMIGRATION STORY
ROY VICKERS, ABORIGINAL ART
KERRY STRATTON, "CONDUCTOR'S CHOICE"

"HE'S PROBABLY ON HIS WAY OUT OF CANADA," SAID WALLY.

"You could have been Aamir's third murder victim!" said Klassen. "We've arrested the parents and the sister. I've passed your information on to Detective Spencer there in Hamilton who's sent out an APB on Aamir. But I think the guy got clean away. We've dusted your car, and the fingerprints do match the Hazirah murder. Hard to believe that was his sister! Honour killings must be a crazy family thing. Thank God, not in Canada."

Klassen didn't quite catch himself. This was Canada!

Wally wondered how Aamir made it through customs. He remembered his own family landing at Pier 21 in Halifax in 1954. The customs officer lifted the towel in dad's large suitcase. He saw the two bottles of home-made wine that dad was so proud of, which he had carefully packed into the suitcases in Lager Wegscheid, Austria.

The translator said, "For your personal use, right?"

Dad said, "Ja, nur für mich! Schönes klares Wein. Selbst gemacht!"

Dad beamed. "Yes, just for me. Beautiful clear wine. I made it myself." The customs officer put the towel back and waved dad through.

"Welcome to Canada."

Wally made the mistake of wearing his Lederhosen, leather pants which were obviously Austrian, to grade school one day. He was waylaid by five Polish kids who were taught to hate Nazis. At least, that's what they thought Wally was. Wally determined to learn English without a trace of an accent, which he accomplished within three years. Playing hockey in the local outdoor rink during the winter of course helped. Kids picking teams and yelling at each other to pass the puck... and of course, television, like watching Richard Green as *Robin Hood* helped.

Wally preferred the *Lone Ranger*. He had always wanted to be a cowboy, so he owned two cap pistols, and played cowboy and Indians with kids around the neighbourhood. He learned English that way, much better than at the foot of a nun, who tried to make him memorize words from "Dick and Jane."

He recalled seeing Lorne Greene on stage at the Kitchener-Memorial Auditorium in 1959 when *Bonanza* first came on Sunday nights after the *Ed Sullivan Show*. Greene was twirling his gun on stage and shot off a few rounds [blanks] into the air. Wally was 13 and yelled up, "Hey are those bullets real?" "Ben Cartwright" must have wished those bullets were in fact real, the way he glared down at young Wally. Cartwright plugged him with his eyes instead, and probably thought, "Yeah, I'd like to shoot the little smart ass!"

That's how Wally learned English and became Canadian! Neighbourhood kids and television! It was essentially easy. There was no religious component in his assimilation. So he didn't have to deprogram the sayings of a prophet. It was mainly, learn the language, and act like everyone else.

"Well," he said to Klassen. "Things sure have changed since I was a kid growing up. I want you to know that the sister, Abqurah, helped me escape, and I want to put in a good word for her."

.....

Wally wondered what would become of Abqurah? "Torn between two cultures, feelin' like a fool?" Wally somehow thought about his own future. Then he thought about his past. What could he have become? Was he happy now that the race was almost done? His mind drifted back to Chilliwack and those Grande Prairie days, his "salad days," when one decision [or indecision] might have nudged the tiller in his future into a completely different direction.

He recalled meeting a young native Indian in Chilliwack, Roy Vickers. Wally was a reporter for *The Chilliwack Progress* at the time. He needed to get a feature article on this up and coming painter and sculptor of Tsimshian Art. Vickers had already claimed some minor fame by making several appearances on the popular TV show, *The Beachcombers*, starring Bruno Gerussi.

Wally wrote the article and then got to know the artist a little bit. The man needed a car; Wally had a Renault 10 for sale. As an "up and coming artist," Vickers had little money. He offered a trade. "I'm going to be famous someday. I'll give you two of my prints for the car." They were two 16x20 frames, head and shoulder prints of an "Indian Maiden" and a "Tsimshian Chief." Wally thought they looked too blocky, but he went ahead and shook hands on the deal.

Years later, Wally's brother inherited the prints, stored them forgotten in the basement somewhere. Wally never liked them. But when Wally googled Roy Vickers, he discovered that the artist did indeed become famous, and owned the *Eagle Aerie Gallery* in Tofino, British Columbia. He also had a feature write-up on the *Kickass Canadians* website, posted March 4, 2014. Wally liked his new stuff. Maybe the artist improved! Or was it just a matter of taste and bad luck, that those were the two prints the artist had available in those "salad days"? The Renault was only worth $150 anyway.

Wally moved to Grande Prairie, Alberta, for his next newspaper job, and eventually an editorship at *Grande Prairie This Week*. He wrote a feature on the President of the Regional College. They chatted over a coffee while Wally took copious notes. At the end of the interview, the College President turned to him and said, "You are an under-achiever. You should have a better job."

Wally thought quietly, "Yeah, then why don't you hire me?" Out loud, he kept quiet. Could this have been the moment he missed? Should he have challenged the president to hire him for a teaching job? He had his MA. Wally closed the door to the president's office; the chance was gone forever.

It's amazing how paths can cross in the ripples of time and space. Wally played violin in the *Grande Prairie Regional Orchestra*, during those "salad days" in the early 1980s. He recalled a charming, and sometimes facetious, young conductor, not to overuse the phrase, "up and coming." His name was memorable, Kerry Stratton. Wally enjoyed his repartée during rehearsals, and his ability to bring the best out in amateur musicians.

Years later, Wally moved to Jordan, Ontario, and on a Sunday afternoon, tuned into Classical FM 96.3, a radio program called, "Conductor's Choice." Wally heard something very recognizable, the deep and resonant voice of Kerry Stratton. Wally was amazed, but not so amazed, that Kerry's orchestral performances were now featured on some of the world's top labels. Kerry had become a specialist in Dvorak. His international career took him to orchestras all over Europe, North America and Asia.

A momentary regret stole into Wally's heart. Could he really have swung his ship around had the college president hired him to teach an English course, if his talent seemed so obvious? Wally headed instead for a nervous breakdown; and then, a search for God in Winnipeg at the "Canadian Mennonite Bible College" [CMBC].

Well, all in all, in 50 years, what would it matter?... Still?

Wally's mind swung back to the present, to Abqurah, so young at the age of 21, and torn between two cultures, "a stranger in a strange land," and "feelin' like a fool."

CHAPTER 36

Surah 4, An-Nisā' (The Women), verses 34-35 state that men are in charge of women, being their protectors and maintainers. The pressure of the Muslim community is on men to control the wives and daughters entrusted to them. In order to keep the honour of the family, the strain could become so great that murder seems to be the only answer.

[HTTP://WWW.ANSWERING-ISLAM.ORG/AUTHORS/OSKAR/HONOUR_KILLINGS.HTML]

.....

IBRAHIMS ARRESTED

MAY 2013

BUREAUCRACY IS SLOW!

MAY 2014

IN MAY 2013, AAMIR'S PARENTS WERE ARRESTED AT THEIR home and led away in handcuffs. Adl and Yaminah Ibrahim were charged in the conspiracy to commit murder of their daughter, Hazirah Ibrahim. Abqurah Ibrahim was also arrested, and held in a separate charge for aiding and abetting, which was later dropped, with a condition of probation.

The Hamilton Court of Justice was in a buzz over this sensational crime. The deadly combination of murder and religion made for spicy head-lines. ISIS made the international news with its Holy War in Syria and Iraq. The killings by Aamir, a local Hamiltonian, made the news on the home front. Lawyers and the media had a field day with this. Two murders from the same family, with religion at the heart of it! The younger sister cooperated with the police. She was assured of probation, with a good word put in by Wally for helping him escape. She would have talked to the police anyway.

The wheels of the legal system ground slowly in Ontario, especially on a capital crime. The trial was postponed for a whole year, so that both the prosecution and the defense could prepare their cases. The Ibrahims, in the meantime, were housed and fed at the government's expense in jail.

Finally April 2014 arrived. The season showed signs of new life in Niagara. Orchards were blossoming and southern Ontario was awash with pinks, yellows and greens. News of the trial was on everyone's tongue. The favourite topic of conversation in coffee shops was the death of Hazirah and Baryon, two lives snuffed out by a crazy jihadist, who had fled the country. The parents had allegedly incited their son, Aamir, in the willful murder of his sister, Hazirah, as an "honour killing." The younger sister had been lied to, that Hazirah had apparently run away and abandoned the family, infatuated with a white boy.

The prosecution had a precedent in the Shafia family who were found guilty of first degree murder in Montreal for their honour killing of four family members. In that trial, the prosecution accused Mohammad Shafia, his second wife, Tooba Yahya, and their son Hamed, in a conspiracy to drown their three daughters, Zainab, 19, Sahar, 17, and Geeti Shafia, 13, along with Mohammad Shafia's first wife, Rona Mohammad Amir, 50, in the Rideau Canal.

Detective Spencer and Detective Klassen were amazed at the bizarre nature of the Montreal case. Their own murder cases of Hazirah and Ramona Szewczuk [Baryon] also came about because of a wrong headed notion rationalized within the Muslim religion. The two detectives had trouble understanding a God who approved of murder.

The Ibrahims pleaded "not guilty." Their lawyers launched a three-pronged approach for the defence. The parents kept saying over and over again, "We are not guilty of murder!"

1. "Let what is right be right," said the father. "It was an honour killing, not a murder, as Allah is our witness." The parents demanded to be tried under Shari'ah Law. They did not recognize Canadian Law. They would appeal the court decision if found guilty.

2. The lawyers tried to talk the Ibrahims into "an insanity plea." The justification? They would reference the book written by the respected author, Richard Dawkins, who maintained that a belief in God was a sort of "mass hysteria" encouraged by churches, a kind of insanity that feeds people in a common belief in God. Dawkins went so far as to call it a delusion, *The God Delusion*. The Ibrahims rejected this plea outright. Islam was not crazy!

3. The defense lawyers then put their thinking caps on. After all, their job was to get the Ibrahims off by any means possible, or to delay the wheels of justice or grind it to a halt. They demanded that the Ibrahims be judged by their own peers under Shari'ah Law. This would be an expression of the freedom of religion. The prosecution rejected this approach outright! This was Canada!

The prosecution made their case that Shari'ah Law was not recognized within the established history and Constitution of Canada. Freedom of religion, yes, but honour killing and Shari'ah Law, outrageous! The system did not need to revert back to the Dark Ages.

The Ibrahims were found guilty for conspiring to have their daughter, Hazirah, killed by her brother, Aamir. Federal Justice Minister, Michael Roberts, said, "I find you guilty of conspiracy to murder. I sentence you both to 25 years imprisonment!" He added, "It is too bad we do not have the actual perpetrator of this terrible act within our custody, namely your son, Aamir Ibrahim." He addressed the court with these words, "Murder in the name of honour killing is a heinous crime, not acceptable in Canada." He quoted the same words used in the Shafia trial in Montreal: "This verdict sends a very clear message about our Canadian values and core principles in a free, democratic society that all Canadians enjoy and even visitors to Canada enjoy."

The Federal Justice Minister went on to say that the government is committed to protecting the rights of women against any forms of violence. "We need to hold perpetrators accountable for violent actions," he said.

Omar Noorani, the family lawyer told the media that the family will appeal the verdict. He had no comment to make on the deal struck by the defense on behalf of the younger Ibrahim daughter. He did acknowledge that Aamir Ibrahim, who allegedly committed the actual honour killing, was still free somewhere in the Middle-East.

Wally was relieved that Adl and Yaminah Ibrahim were put in jail. He was glad that the younger daughter, Abqurah, received probation. She had saved his life. Wally still couldn't believe the family's take on "honour." He saw how extreme religion could destroy a family. What a shame, what craziness!

Wally wanted to understand the Why behind it. He took his Christianity for granted, not that he was a Bible thumper, but he went to church, agreed with some parts of the sermon, disagreed with other parts in his own mind, and generally enjoyed the easy going fellowship. He liked Bible study on Tuesday evenings with his little group and then coffee and cookies afterwards. He felt like he could at least talk about his doubts and ask questions within his "religion."

CHAPTER 37

I have measured out my life
with coffee spoons;

[*Love Song of J. Alfred Prufrock* - T.S. ELIOT, 1920]

.....

IBRAHIM VERDICT
JUNE 2014

SPENCER AND KLASSEN
@WILLIAMS FRESH CAFÉ

"THIS THING COULD DRAG ON FOR YEARS YET," SAID Detective Spencer. He and Klassen were having coffee at the *Williams Fresh Café* across from McMaster University. It was just after the verdict was read, finally at the end of June 2014, over a year after the Ibrahims had been arrested! The defense lawyers, of course, said there would be an appeal.

Spencer and Klassen sat comfortably at the café to talk about this, on their own time and their own dime!

"Yeah," said Klassen, "look at how that Magnotta case dragged on!"

Sitting at the opposite ends of the Café table, Spencer and Klassen made the most unlikely duo of detectives, you'd ever want to see, working on the same case. They were Mutt and Jeff! They were Sgt. Joe Friday and Dirty Harry!

Klassen, older, close to retirement, looked like he stepped out of the old police series, *Dragnet*, from the 1950s, a series probably collecting dust within the archives of black and white TV from years ago. At least, Klassen didn't put the police force to shame [completely], wearing his crumpled suit and tie. He was intelligent and competent in his work and he closed cases to the department's satisfaction.

Spencer sat a head taller than Klassen at the other side of the table. He wore an open collared golf shirt, with a light sport jacket over top. Spencer was what Clint Eastwood must have looked like at the age of 32. A huge shock of healthy hair, rising above a weathered face that a cowboy could be proud of. Spencer looked like he'd be comfortable on a horse, riding the range. Spencer stood 6' 2," more than 6' 4" in his cowboy boots. Sgt. Joe Friday and Dirty Harry were ready to order.

The waitress was a pretty black girl. They both ordered coffee.

"How do you take your coffee?" she asked Spencer.

"Like my women... black."

"Humph," she eyed Spencer skeptically. But there was an amused twinkle in her eye.

"And you sir?" she asked Klassen, the older of the two gentlemen... and obviously less brash.

"Oh, with double cream... and bring me a slice of pie, whatever's on the menu."

The girl went away.

Klassen sighed and shook his head disapprovingly. "She could be your daughter! Well, almost... "

Klassen cautioned the younger cop, "Someday you're going to get older. Women won't treat you the same! Pardon a hackneyed old expression, but you can't keep burning the candle at both ends... forever! Grow up!"

Spencer dismissed the comment, and looked around the café, "You know, this was Ramona Szewczuk' favourite hang-out. She had a bunch of old geezers get together here every Wednesday afternoon, and they'd just sit and talk for hours. She was their computer guru."

"Great pastime for seniors to just sit and talk."

Spencer added, "In about 20 or 30 years, I could be here doing that too... hey, I am doing that!" He chuckled.

If you had to play good cop and bad cop, Spencer was the bad cop. A hard nut to crack. He prided himself in his atheism, which, he felt, gave him an objective perspective on this case and on life in general. Klassen was formerly Roman Catholic. He considered himself a believer but not in the Catholic Church. If anything, he was now a practicing Mennonite because his wife was one. He figured either a Catholic ticket or a Mennonite ticket was a good pass into Heaven. He was on the side of his mother when she said [and this was in her 90s], "You know, I don't believe in religion but I believe in God!"

Both men looked around the *Café* and felt strange sitting there sipping coffee, maybe in this exact spot where Baryon used to sit. They wished she could be here chatting with her old geezers! Spencer, of course, at the age of 32, would be an "honourary geezer."

Klassen recalled that the Church was instrumental in supporting his own family when they first came to Canada back in the early 1950s. "A place to stay until dad found a job on construction, food vouchers to help out and people to talk to so we could learn English." He commented that his church was presently sponsoring a Muslim family from Lebanon, supporting them in a similar fashion, setting them up in an apartment and donating furniture. The husband, Sadit, asked the church to pay for his tuition in a welder's course at Niagara College, which he got from donations.

Klassen saw Christian churches as pulling up the slack where government welfare programs ran short. "Churches do a lot of good," he said, "especially the Mennonite Central Committee, MCC." Klassen didn't know how many churches in Canada were supporting Muslim refugees from overseas.

He wondered if we were cutting our own throats though. He'd heard one report that 18,000 Muslims had immigrated into Canada from Iraq since 2003. There were mosques now all across Canada. There was even a TV show on CBC, "The Little Mosque on the Prairie," where the Catholic priest was often the butt of jokes.

"Maybe the priest deserved it?" said Spencer.

Klassen agreed that the Catholic Church had a lot to make up for. Scandals over pedophilia, abuses in Indian residential schools, and a lot of bad history over hundreds of years. The Crusades in the Middle Ages, Joan of Arc, the Inquisition, Galileo and so on, and so forth. Klassen had studied his wife's denomination, the Mennonites, and found out how they had been persecuted by the Catholic Church during the Reformation in the 1500s, and later on, after the Russian Revolution in Ukraine.

"I remember sitting at the library in St. Catharines. There was an etching of a Dutch guy named Dirk Willems. He ran from his pursuer in the middle of winter, trying to escape persecution in the late 1500s. His pursuer broke through the ice and nearly drowned. Willems turned around and saved the guy. What was Willems crime? He didn't believe in infant baptism. Anabaptists believed in making a conscious choice as adults which, according to the Catholic Church, was heresy."

Klassen went on with the story. "After saving the guy, Willems was arrested, found guilty of heresy and burned at the stake." Klassen couldn't remember the exact date. It was, in fact, May 16, in the spring of 1569.

Klassen enjoyed Spencer's company and this chat about ethics. He phoned his wife to tell her where he was. "I won't be home for supper, having supper here at *Williams Fresh Café* with Detective Spencer. Yes, yes, the verdict came through. The Ibrahims were found guilty and will be going to jail for 25 years. Anyway, I need to wind down after a long day at the trial, and talk things through with Detective Spencer. I won't be home until 9 p.m. or so. Love you."

Spencer assumed that Klassen got a "love you" back from his wife. He smiled. He had always been alone, a confirmed bachelor, and liked it that way. Klassen noticed Spencer's bemused smile.

"You've never been married?"

"No. I'm my own man and I come and go as I please."

"I'm my own man too but I like being married. It's made a man out of me in a lot of ways."

"Like?"

"Like my respect for women. Their grit and determination. I must admit, some of my wife's organizational skills have also rubbed off on me."

Spencer laughed, "I guess I'm still a slob at home."

"My wife and I share the load at home. I learned how to cook, do the laundry and more importantly put things away." Klassen admitted, adding, "It's too bad we can't have kids."

"Think of adopting?"

"Yeah, but we're not sure. We've heard so many stories about taking in other people's problems, like fetal alcohol syndrome babies. We just don't know... and now, I think we're too old anyway."

CHAPTER 38

"Malt does more than Milton can, to justify
God's ways to man."

[A.E. HOUSEMAN 1859-1936]

.....

COFFEE STRETCHES INTO SUPPER
SPENCER FLIRTS WITH WAITRESS!
JUNE 2014

THE MENU CAME. SOME ITEMS SEEMED TOO EXOTIC FOR both Klassen and Spencer. Bacon and Black Bean Nachos? Breaded and Baked Dill Pickles? Both of them went for the Classic Toasted Western. The price was right, and it sounded more familiar than "beans or pickles."

"And to drink?" asked the waitress.

Spencer looked up, already anticipating the answer, "What have you got in beer?"

"Nothing," she affirmed. "If you want something cold, we have Organic Yogurt Smoothies!" Spencer's eyes glazed over. "Bring me another coffee," he said in acquiescence. When the waitress went away, Spencer said that he sorely missed his beer with supper!

Klassen chuckled. "This is a Coffee Pub," he said, "Not a Beer Pub!"

The waitress came back with a full carafe of coffee, and filled their cups. She gave Spencer a piece of paper with her phone number on it. Then she smiled, and went away to get their orders.

"I don't know how you do it?" said Klassen.

"Well, first of all I'm not such a bad looking guy. And second of all, she knows I didn't mean anything by that black remark. She could see it in my eyes."

"Hmm, clear blue, like the open skies." said Klassen.

"They say the eyes are the mirror to the soul," quipped Spencer, "love of life and fun, that's me, no racism in my soul, and an open mind!"

Spencer added, "I think Life is an adventure. I want to keep it fresh, and not find out at the end that I've been asleep all along and never lived. I think that drugs can do that to people, so can fear of living and so can religion."

Now that he had a head of steam up, Spencer added, "Religion can really screw people up and waste lives. Look at the Ibrahims. I like to keep far away from it."

Klassen objected, "Come on. You gotta admit sometimes in the dark when you're alone and things aren't going right, you have something nudging inside of you, where you look to something beyond you for a little help or comfort."

"I admit it but so far I'm doing a good job closing the door to that part of me. I think there is a right and wrong, but no Heaven or Hell. Religions are just man-made stuff about what people think God is or wants."

"Actually I agree with you in a big way, Mennonite that I am."

"The unattractive part of most religions is their interpretations," said Spencer. "I see so many splits and factions, all thinking they have the only right answer, the only pathway to God. There are Catholics and Protestants. Then there are Sunnis and Shiites. Look at the divisions within Christianity and Islam; and on top of that, what about Hinduism and Buddhism and Heaven knows whatever other 'isms' in the world! Who's right and who's wrong... and who cares?" said Spencer with disgust.

Spencer concluded, "It's just not worth fighting for and killing each other over. I think John Lennon was right in singing, "Imagine there's no Heaven." Spencer added, "Except, I think he was wrong in one thing, his hope at the end of the song, that the world will live as one. It never will!"

Spencer was actually preaching to Klassen, who listened respectfully, and nodded his head in occasional agreement. Their meals arrived. The waitress smiled at the two of them, but gave Spencer a special wink, when she walked away. Klassen rolled his eyes. Spencer smiled like a contented Cheshire cat.

He went back to being serious. "Muhammad is supposed to be the last Prophet from God and the Qur'an is supposed to be the final word." Spencer added wryly, "Where does that put Joseph Smith? The Mormons were founded about 1,200 years after Muhammad. Which one is 'the' last prophet and 'the' final word? New religions keep springing up like weeds in the grass."

They made sweeping statements about religion, and their personal convictions, between bites in their food, and their sips of coffee. They acted like they had all the answers.

Spencer said, "I'd make an irreverent Christian, if ever I became one

Klassen commented, "I'm one already." He recounted his last Life Group meeting. He wanted to give two older ladies some insight. "Christ was not a Christian!" he pronounced.

"Whatever do you mean," said the ladies aghast at the idea, because after all, they put their whole Faith in Christ!

"Well," said Klassen. "He was a Jew and a Rabbi. The Christian movement rose up after Jesus was crucified and buried. Christianity took root from Peter and Paul's teachings. The followers of Jesus were known as little Christs or Christians." This was news to these ladies. They couldn't believe it. "Jesus, not a Christian?"

Klassen recalled another incident where he had a little fun at the expense of straight-laced Christians. "Heaven's experiencing budget cuts, you know!" he announced. "The pearly gates had to be torn down, no more roads paved with gold, and no more fancy harps for newcomers. The angels handed out kazoos instead. Gabriel was finally able to balance the books. It was Heaven's way of saving the Almighty dollar!"

Eyebrows lifted. Not everybody in the group found that funny. The youth pastor grinned a little, taking the joke in stride.

Klassen and Spencer finished their meals and ordered more coffee, enjoying their easy conversation. Sunlight still lingered on in the evening outside.

Klassen admitted, "Wally was sure helpful in getting this conviction."

"If he hadn't stumbled on that necklace, and if he hadn't taken the same classes as Alexander and Aamir! How bizarre is that?"

"There's a word for that where coincidences just come together," said Spencer, "A fancy word, serendipity."

Klassen observed, "And if you don't want to be fancy, you could always say, the Hand of God was in there somewhere!"

Spencer commented, "I'm just glad Wally escaped that basement thanks to the sister."

"She had nothing to do with the actual crime... but the parents... well, they have their moral compass screwed in the wrong direction."

"It's too bad our tax money is giving them free room and board for the next 25 years."

"Oh well, that's the system."

Spencer ordered a refill. He liked coffee, about as much as beer. "Too bad Aamir got away. I'd sure like to meet up with him some day, and have my gun go off accidentally in his face."

"Now, that would be tax money well saved," interjected Klassen.

The evening was drawing to a close. Customers were leaving. Both men paid their bill, put a good tip on the table and walked out the door. They shook hands. Spencer said, "Well, we agreed on a lot of things. It was a great evening. Goodnight Detective. I hope Aamir gets what's coming to him."

They nodded at each other and went to their cars, leaving thoughts of religion, Hazirah, Baryon, Aamir and the Ibrahims all behind. Klassen saw the *Café* sign in his rear view mirror. He drove out the parking lot tired. It was a very long supper. He looked forward to getting home to his wife. He couldn't help but wonder, what was Aamir doing right at that very moment?

CHAPTER 39

Of restless nights in one-night cheap hotels

And sawdust restaurants with oyster-shells:

Streets that follow like a tedious argument

Of insidious intent

[*Love Song of J. Alfred Prufrock* - T.S. ELIOT, 1920]

AAMIR IN ISTANBUL
JUNE 2013

ONE YEAR WITH ISIS
JUNE 2014

IT WAS 2 A.M. IN ISTANBUL. AAMIR WAS ELATED WHEN THE plane landed. He booked a cheap hotel from the airport. Soon he was peacefully asleep and dreaming.

His dream was a sweet replay of his escape from Canada. How elated he was when his plane flew over the Atlantic, finally landing in Pakistan. He took another flight, hop scotching to Lebanon, and now he was safe and sound in Istanbul, Turkey. No questions asked, nothing to stop him. He looked like a young businessman. He spoke English and Arabic perfectly. He greased a few palms with big "tips." He awoke at 10:00 a.m. for a late breakfast, first stopping by at the front desk for a bus schedule. While he ate, he planned his trip to Tarsus. It meant a 12 hour bus ride, and then another 6 hours to Akcakale, close to the Syrian border.

The tourist guide gave a speech about Saul of Tarsus, known as Saint Paul the Apostle to Christians. He had been persecuting Christians until he had a miraculous vision on the road to Damascus. The tourist guide, pointed out, to those who didn't know, "This was Saint Paul's conversion."

"Great story," Aamir chuckled to himself. "Paul did a lousy job of planting Christianity here in this region. We're all Muslim!" He entertained his own vision, to convert the whole world to Islam!

When Aamir stepped off the bus in Tarsus, he said to the guide, "As salaam aleykum," [may peace be upon you] and got the greeting back, "***Wa alaykumu as-salaam***." He found another cheap hotel for the night. The next day, he bought another bus ticket, headed for Akcakale.

He was only one among many young men who heard the call to "Jihad." They had been coming since the summer of 2013, entering Syria and slipping across the border from Lebanon, Jordan and Iraq. They still got into Turkey through the summer of 2014, taking advantage of corrupt border guards and slack rules. They used forged passports to evade the secret police of those countries.

Aamir couldn't count the palms he greased. That was the culture in those countries and the barter system. His beard was starting to show. He had made an arrangement with a contact to barter for a Syrian passport, with a new picture, new beard and new name: Hafiz Bashir. He would be the protector of Islam and bring the good news of the Prophet to a new world.

Numerous would-be jihadists, who entered Syria, were dispersed to various sub-groups like the Ahrar ash-Sham and the Nusra Front. The rebel camps were "polyglottal" in nature, speaking Chechen, Tajik, Turkish, French, Saudi Arabian and Urdu from parts of Pakistan and India. It was reported that slack border security into Turkey and Syria was the main reason for this growing number of foreign fighters. There seemed to be an underground railway system, as it were, to transport fighters. The Libyan leader, Abu-Yahya, openly admitted that there was an easy travel route for Tunisian and Libyan fighters, willing to be smuggled into Syria with the help of militant groups.

To the police and to his sister back in Canada, Aamir Ibrahim seemed to have disappeared off the face of the earth. He was now Hafiz Bashir, a new ISIS recruit, so hopeful to get his training in the militant boot camp during the summer of 2013. He intended to train as hard as everyone else and make his body strong, as a soldier for Allah.

It is said that the largest number of foreign fighters came from Libya [several hundreds], then 500 Jordanians, the Saudis numbered more than 300, as did Egyptian Islamists and Iraqis. The total number of foreign Sunnis who entered on behalf of the rebel cause by 2014 was estimated to be close to 10,000 fighters. It is thought that foreign Shia fighters numbered around 10,000 as well. Over 600 foreign fighters were killed in the first half of 2013 alone.

The Syrian boot-camp in which Aamir-Hafiz ended up spoke mostly Saudi Arabian and French. He could get by on French. The leader was Abu Ahmad al-Awani a member of the ISIS military council, ironically also a former member of Saddam's army. Abu Ahmad al-Awani changed his name from Waleed Jassem al-Awani.

Seemed like everybody had a name change. Maybe it was like being born-again? Hafiz's immediate boot commander was Abdul Ali al-Sayed who took an interest in the young man's videography and computer savvy. The jihadist movement could use his skills in the social media. Even Western computer gurus admired how ISIS churned out slick propaganda videos. ISIS also had an English language outreach magazine online, and put out tweets hash tagged to trendy events to achieve world-wide exposure.

Hafiz found himself useful with his video and computer skills, plus he prided himself as a warrior for Allah. He was given army fatigues to wear, an AK-47 rifle and two heavy bullet belts which crossed over his chest. But his instruction was not to engage in the real fighting, let the soldiers do that. Sayed needed Hafiz's computer skills more than his ability to fire bullets.

Hafiz produced a video intended for release the following year, on September 14, 2014 by the *Daily Mirror*. It was a public relations masterpiece. One minute and four seconds long. Short, memorable and punchy with vocal grunt music, like something out of Carl Orff's *Carmina Burana*.

Jihadists in fatigues, rappelling on cliffs, zip lining, marching, pulling tires, doing push ups, engaged in martial arts. Veritable Bruce Lees! Endurance that would make the "National Football League" cringe! The macho stuff was all there, appealing to young men who wanted to have bodies like Sylvester Stallone. It was meant to be a testosterone rush. Created by "The Islamic Front," showing its superiority in military training.

They all wore face coverings. Except for the bearded American camera man at the end of the brief film, following the tough troops from behind. A kidnapped victim? A camera man forced to record the true grit of jihadists? Maybe there was another kidnapped buddy filming this? Do this or die? The name of Allah was not mentioned in the clip? They were selling machismo and warriorship.

When he wasn't videographing or writing the propaganda for a website, Hafiz did push-ups like everybody else, pulled heavy tires and ran for miles in the heat. He became fit, and was proud to be a warrior for Allah, a true jihadist who would change Syria and Iraq and eventually the world!

CHAPTER 40

The Global Village: A phrase coined by Marshall McLuhan to describe the world that has been "shrunk" by modern advances in communications. McLuhan likened the vast network of communications systems to one extended central nervous system, ultimately linking everyone in the world.

[THE GUTENBERG GALAXY: THE MAKING OF TYPOGRAPHIC MAN (1962)]

.....

WALLY'S GLOBAL AWARENESS
ISIS BECOMES ISIL

WALLY DID NOT SHUT WORLD NEWS OUT AFTER HIS ESCAPE from Aamir's basement. If anything, he deliberately became more globally aware. He didn't watch local stations anymore, but turned instead to DW News, "Deutsche Welle," the international news on the BBC. Too bad that Aamir had gotten past Canadian customs. Maybe Canada's shyness about profiling certain ethnic groups made it easier for Aamir to slip by to safety.

Canada liked to think of itself as a hospitable and civilized country. Canada, a pleasant Mosaic where everybody gets along! Well, the idea of a Mosaic was nice, in Wally's mind. Maybe someday the world would be that way! But for now, the Canadian Mosaic was a broken dream in Wally's mind. Aboriginal people had a long list of grievances against "Indian residential schools." Cities also did not blend peoples together very well, but fostered instead, little Italy neighbourhoods, little China towns, etcetera, etcetera. There was ongoing talk of separation in Quebec. How did all this foster Canadian unity, let alone a Canadian identity?

Wally was convinced that Canadians were both naive and lucky. He had a wife who had a good teaching job, and he himself, retired now, didn't have to worry about financial insecurity. Instead, he enjoyed a flexible schedule as a photographer. He had the time to explore the internet, and become more globally conscious. Lot of changes going on in the world, not just in Canada. Canada was regarded as soft by many nations. Was Wally's own easy life merely a reflection of that and a cushy illusion?

Maybe T.S. Elliot was right. April was the cruelest month. It was April 2013 in which ISIS announced the expansion of its operations from Iraq into Syria. The group added the words "al-Sham" to its name, ISI [the Islamic State of Iraq].

"al-Sham" was translated as "the Levant" or "Greater Syria." The name change signified the group's intention to expand beyond present-day Syria. That's where the group's acronym became ISIL. ISIL rampaged through eastern and northern Syria, and by 2014 eventually into western and northern Iraq. Young men were reported killed in conquered villages because they would not convert to Islam. Young women were sold as rewards to the fighters and raped.

ISIS or ISIL was reported to be run by an Iraqi jihadist, Abu Bakr al-Baghdadi. The group was reported to have 6,000 fighters in Iraq and possibly another 5,000 in Syria. It was estimated that 3,000 foreigners joined these jihadists, a thousand from Chechnya, 500 or so from France, Britain and other parts of Europe. There were even recruits from Canada and the United States, eager to join the cause of the Islamic State.

The Guardian, reported a year later, by October 2014, that young recruits filtered into ISIL at the rate of about 1,000 per month, entering Iraq or Syria, one way or another, often with false passports. New jihadists apparently had exceeded 15,000 via 80 different countries. Experts said that many young men simply saw no future in their own countries. Maybe they had been on welfare, coming out with college degrees and no job prospects, or maybe they were just plain disillusioned with corrupt democracies. In Islam, they found "purpose."

Wally saw them as young bullies wanting to exert big muscles. They were macho boys with dangerous toys! How did they become so fanatic? What made these radicalized young men tick? Wally found one family's story in the *National Post* article from 2012.

The Plotnikovs were a Russian-Canadian family wanting to make a new start in a new country. Vitaly Plotnikov moved his family to Toronto, and got a job stocking shelves at a Highland Super Market on Dufferin Street. The family took out their Canadian citizenship in 2008. Their son, William was 15 when the family moved to Canada. He showed an interest in boxing and the martial arts. Mr. Plotnikov said in a *National Post* interview that he was amazed at how fast his son's radicalization had gone. "He had gone from convert to

CHAPTER 41

Just take those old records off the shelf

I'll sit and listen to 'em by myself

Today's music ain't got the same soul

I like that old time rock 'n' roll

[BOB SEGER HIT 1978]

.....

BRINGING BACK THE PAST

MOODY BLUES 1967

CAT STEVENS 1970

"Late Lament"
Breathe deep the gathering gloom,
Watch lights fade from every room.
Bedsitter people look back and lament,

Another day's useless energy spent.
Impassioned lovers wrestle as one,
Lonely man cries for love and has none.
New mother picks up and suckles her son,
Senior citizens wish they were young.
Cold hearted orb that rules the night,
Removes the colours from our sight.
Red is grey and yellow white.
But we decide which is right.
And which is an illusion?

[MOODY BLUES 1967]

Wally was grateful he was seeing Karl de Jong during the autumn of 2014. His nightmares about Hazirah's dead body were becoming more manageable, but the world news was becoming more disturbing. He needed someone to talk to. He didn't know how to look at the world. Indeed which is right and which is an illusion?

One of his idols during his M.A. year had been Cat Stevens. Wally bought the *Tea for the Tillerman* album in 1972. Cat Stevens was coming to McMaster that year, or was it earlier in 1971? Wally missed him, due to a conflict in his schedule. Maybe he was driving back home to visit his parents in Kitchener? He couldn't remember. It would have been an enjoyable concert. Cat Stevens sported curly black hair back then, and a thick beard, and looked like a rock star. His songs were full of introspective lyrics. They were poetic, a sign of a soft, searching artist. Cat Stevens' songs resonated with Wally, who himself was wondering, at that time in his 20s, what was life all about? Where was everybody and everything going?

.....

Cat Stevens 1970
Oh, baby, baby, it's a wild world
It's hard to get by just upon a smile
Oh, baby, baby, it's a wild world
I'll always remember you like a child, girl

On The Road To Find Out 1970
So on, and on I go, the seconds tick the time out
So much left to know, and I'm on the road to find out

.....

Cat Stevens was born Steven Demetre Georgiou, July 21 1948. When he became a recording star, he was known by his stage name, Cat Stevens. He converted to Islam in December 1977, and the following year, adopted the name Yusuf Islam.

"All those name changes," thought Wally. "Signs of him searching, looking for an identity." Wally had gone through something similar. When he became a reporter for *Grande Prairie This Week*, he was tempted to take a "nom de plume," Pierre LeLoup, a pun on the music by Serge Prokofiev. Wally also found it interesting that Cat Stevens contracted tuberculosis when he was overworked on tour with Jimi Hendrix. Wally himself had spent 2 years in a sanatorium in Austria when he was little, recovering from tuberculosis. He felt like he was in good company with Cat/Yusuf Islam... and Chopin!

As a Muslim, Yusuf Islam retired from the music scene for almost 30 years. Just now, in the autumn of 2014, he was finally back with a new album, *Tell 'Em I'm Gone* and a new tour.

Wally could hardly recognize the old rocker from recent photos. Cat/Yusuf looked greyer and more Islamic, a far cry from the Gothic black look in his rocker days. He still had a vibrant voice. "I don't drink. I don't smoke. And I don't do much exercise, but at the same time, I live a very healthy life, and it's definitely helped."

Yusuf had grown up on Drury Lane in England. No playgrounds! That gave rise to his philanthropic acts, especially for kids, "building a school with a big, big playground."

Since he converted to Islam, his life had not been without controversy. On September 11, 2001, when the Twin Towers were attacked, he was quoted as saying, "While it is still not clear who carried out the attack, it must be stated that no right-thinking follower of Islam could possibly condone such an action. The Qur'an equates the murder of one innocent person with the murder of the whole of humanity." Yusuf has repeatedly condemned terrorism and Islamic extremism. [Wikipedia]

Cat Stevens had chosen such a different path than Wally, "on his road to find out." Wally became a Christian. He had gone to the Canadian Mennonite Bible College in Winnipeg shortly after recovering from a nervous breakdown. Wally wondered, if all aware people were actually on the same spriritual road to find Truth or to find God, whether Muslim, Christian or whatever, as long as they were sincere in their search for a moral compass on how to lead their lives.

Wally hated the concept of a Holy War, a Holy War, which was intended eventually to rage outside the Middle-East and possibly become global... in the Modern Age. An article in *The Economist*, June 14, 2014 gave a clear perspective on ISIL: "An extreme Islamist group that seeks to create a caliphate and spread jihad across the world has made dramatic advances on both sides of the Syrian-Iraqi border."

The article went on to suggest that "The Arab Spring" had become "The Jihadi Spring." There was actually a Twitter hashtag, "#jihadispring." America threw all kinds of money at Afghanistan and Iraq, and then certain factions in Syria. The idea of throwing money and equipment their way was to bolster up favoured Middle-Eastern armies and blessing them with ideas of democracy. Somehow that all got derailed, all those benign intentions inside an Arab world. Joseph Stiglitz, former chief economist of the World Bank, and Linda Bilmes of Harvard University, published a book in 2008, entitled, *The Three Trillion Dollar War*. The final question was: "And what's it gotten us?" The final answer was: "A big mess."

Saddam Hussein's "weapons of mass destruction" in Iraq were proven non-existent, after all, to the amusement of cynical critics in the West. Assad in Syria did use chemical weapons for which he was censured by the international community. They were apparently checked, and carefully destroyed in keeping with "the rules of war."

But there were so many assault rifles, rockets and armored vehicles destroying the villages and towns of Iraq and Syria, that one wondered, wasn't the final outcome the same as if weapons of mass destruction were used?

The Economist on June 14, 2014 said, "The Islamic State of Iraq and Greater Syria, ISIS, is a group that outdoes even al-Qaeda in brutality and fanaticism."

There were 120,000 deaths counted between the start of the Arab Spring in 2011 and the start of September 2013. The newly named, "Jihad Spring," was only a promise of more upheaval in the Muslim world, not the rebirth of democratic societies.

Approximately 700,000 Syrian refugees fled to Turkey. Jordan became overburdened with the flood of Syrians. Approximately 150,000 people sought shelter in the Qatari refugee camp. Canada promised to absorb 35,000 of them, after processing. What a mess, both in real-life and on paper!

CHAPTER 42

"Modern Jihad: Tracing the Dollars Behind the Terror Networks" propels the reader into the netherworld of illegal organizations. From the Contras to Al Qaeda, Loretta Napoleoni maps out the arteries of an international economic system that feeds armed groups the world over with an endless supply of cash."

[COMMENT ON LORETTA NAPOLEONI'S BOOK, *Modern Jihad*, PLUTO PRESS, 2003]

• • • • •

THE IRAQI PORT, MOSUL, AND TAL AFAR AIRPORT

JUNE 14, 2014

ABDUL ALI AL-SAYED SENT WORD OUT THAT THE MEN would move out in the morning from their camp in northern Syria. Their objective? Within a few days, Mosul, an

Iraqi port, a "stronghold" with lots of weaponry for the taking. Sayed knew Allah was on their side.

Mosul is a city in northern Iraq half a day's ride, maybe 400 km northwest of Baghdad. Average temperature 95 degrees Fahrenheit in the summer, 55 in the winter. It's a port standing on the west bank of the Tigris River. It is also the capital of Nineveh Province. The name had Biblical overtones, recalling Nineveh from the Bible, an ungodly place that Jonah wished to avoid. The Book of Nahum in the Old Testament had nothing good to say about Nineveh, as a city of corruption. Maybe nothing had changed in all these millennia?

Jihad was on the move. Who could stop the hand of Allah? In mid-June 2014, radical Sunni militants took control of the northern city of Tal Afar and its airport, as ISIS entered its second week of offense with its eyes on Mosul. Hundreds of Iraqi soldiers had been killed in the defense of Tal Afar, while ISIS militants seized more Iraqi weapons and vehicles to equip their men. The Americans had been so generous in equipping the Iraqis with such mobile and effective weapons of destruction.

ISIS fell upon Tal Afar from the west. They were already well armed with assault rifles, trucks and even the FIM-92 Stingers, shoulder-fired infrared homing surface-to-air missiles. Hafiz squatted in the back of one of the trucks which peeled onto the tarmac of the airport. A helicopter was firing up its rotors, almost ready to take off, with several Iraqi officers who decided it was better to save their own skins, than to stand shoulder to shoulder with their men. An ISIS militant jumped off the truck, was handed a Stinger launcher, aimed and fired on the helicopter. He blasted it out of the sky just as it became air-borne. It exploded crashing to the tarmac in a fireball of smoke and twisted metal. The rebels on the truck waved their black banners and cheered, "Allah is great."

ISIS met only pockets of resistance. Iraqi soldiers were fleeing and those who manned their posts met with swift death from bullet or grenade. Hafiz was elated with the success.

A sniper from the airport tower fired two shots. One jihadist grabbed his chest and went down; another met instant death as his brains splattered over his comrades. Hafiz wiped blood from his face. He thanked Allah, it wasn't his blood. Things were not going quite as smoothly as he had hoped.

Militants scattered seeking shelter. Three of them broke through the entry to the tower, and climbed the stairs looking for the source of the shots. Hafiz heard more reports of gunfire and then sudden silence. Two militants returned with a wounded Iraqi soldier in their grasp. He had been shot in the shoulder and leg. He looked defiant.

"This one has courage," said Nadhir, "we will use him as a warning to any others who stand in our way." They loaded the Iraqi onto the truck and drove to the nearest hangar. There they stripped him naked, punched and kicked him senseless; and then tied him to a chair, binding his legs and his hands.

Nadhir did the honours. "Those two men you killed were my friends. Now I seek revenge, in the name of Allah." The Iraqi's eyes widened in fear. "What will he do?" Nadhir drew a knife and made sure someone held the Iraqi's head still. The victim's hands were useless, bound behind his back on the chair. They tortured him all night, revived him, and then tortured him again. They tortured him all night, revived him, and then tortured him again.

At dawn, a ray of sunlight filtered through the window in the hangar. The Iraqi was still alive. His eyes were horrified as the rebel commander entered the hangar and said, "We must move out now. Put a grenade under him, so he can kiss his ass goodbye. No evidence of torture must be found."

As Hafiz and his comrades pulled out in the truck, there was a loud explosion in the hangar. They shrugged their shoulders inconsequentially, and headed onward to Mosul.

Hafiz knew that Allah blessed their cause. Things had to be done to create a Caliphate for pure Islam. He knew war was war, and that a Holy War had to be cruel, to purge the world of infidels.

.....

Wally wished he had magical powers, if plain prayer did not work! He'd wave a magic wand or just wiggle his nose, first, to stop all wars. Then maybe to teach terrorists a lesson. How about a touch of Ebola for all the jihadists? No, that's Old Testament stuff, like the plagues in Egypt. Too cruel. Ironic about the question whose side God was on? God struck down the Egyptians in a sort of Holy War on behalf of his chosen people, the Israelites. Today in 2014, the jihadists think of themselves as God's chosen people who wage a just and Holy War, proclaiming, God is Great, while they kill infidels in the name of Allah. Meanwhile, the Pope prays for world peace from his cushy Papal seat in Rome, and the Western world watches News updates on TV, from the safety of their living rooms.

Well, whose side is God on anyway? Maybe Wally didn't pray hard enough or wish hard enough? Maybe if Wally closed his eyes and concentrated, he could make all guns turn into cameras: either Canon or Nikon, doesn't matter. Just something that clicked and not banged! There's so much beauty to take pictures of in this world.

I see trees of green, red roses, too,
I see them bloom, for me and you
And I think to myself
What a wonderful world.

[LOUIS ARMSTRONG 1967]

How close were we to the flames of Armageddon? What would Iran do with a nuclear bomb? What would a new Islamic State do? What if ISIS overran Assad and found more chemical weapons in Syria? Chemical weapons or nuclear warfare? Would that be the way to destroy the infidels once and for all?

Wally said to himself, "I don't understand this whole mess. What a crazy world." He liked Louis Armstrong's vision of the world.

CHAPTER 43

"Planes and command positions — all of them have fallen in addition to weapons caches. Also prisons were stormed and criminals have been set free. What happened is a catastrophe by any measure."

[WWW.JIHADWATCH.ORG – JUNE 10, 2014 BY ROBERT SPENCER]

. . . . .

ISIS MOVES ON MOSUL
ISIS ARMS ITSELF!
JULY 8 UPDATE, 2014

WALLY INTENDED TO READ THE QUR'AN AT A LATER DATE. But since the internet was so immediate, he googled a curious question: "How do jihadists get their weapons?"

Canadians were so ignorant about what was going on in the Muslim world. Apparently the Americans themselves had left a lot of weapons behind when they went home from

Iraq in 2011 after nine years of war. They had trained and supplied the Iraqi army hoping Iraq would become a stabilized nation now that Saddam Hussein was gone, and that there were no real weapons of mass destruction.

When the Syrian Civil War broke out, the Americans again generously supplied equipment to rebel forces like the Free Syrian Army which fought to topple the Assad regime. Money and weapons also came from Saudi Arabia and Qatar to supply the rebel brigades. The factions and subfactions made Wally's head swim. He couldn't remember all the funny Arabian names, who was Sunni and who was Shiite, and who was affiliated with Saudi Arabia or Qatar or whomever. It was a mess. He thought of the Balkan Powder Keg which he'd studied in high-school history and the causes which led to World War I.

Wally found an article written by Jeremy Bender, in *The Business Insider* issue, July 8, 2014: **As ISIS Routs The Iraqi Army, Here's A Look At What The Jihadists Have In Their Arsenal.** It was a clearly written account... and actually scary! ISIS seized military equipment from fleeing Iraqi soldiers when ISIS overran the city of Mosul. That weaponry made these ragtag fighters into a conventional army to be reckoned with.

He found his answer,"How jihadists got their guns and bullets?" He had been astonished when he glanced at those jihadist photos in the media. Young Muslims rode in Humvees or half-ton trucks and sported grenade launchers and waved black flags and assault rifles. Hefty belts laden with bullets festooned their chests. They wore face coverings and beards. They all looked young, eager and healthy, all willing to go to war and to die! Wally didn't trust soldiers fighting a Holy War with hidden faces.

"You lost approximately three divisions worth of equipment and probably at least three depots in that area,"

Anthony Cordesman, a security analyst at the Washington-based Center for Strategic and International Studies, told *The Wall Street Journal.*

The irony was that much of the weaponry seized in Mosul was actually supplied by the U.S. army to the Iraqi army as a going away present. There were also field weapons produced in Russia, Croatia, China, the Balkans and Iran. What a motley bunch of deadly gifts falling into the hands of ISIS! Jeremy Bender's article gave a list of the impressive artillery which ISIS had seized in Mosul.

. . . . .

AK-47: their standard assault rifle, low cost, durability, availability and ease of use. The AK-47 originally developed by the Soviets. Spread to other armies and "irregular forces" around the world. Light weight, effective and "remarkably easy to obtain."

M79 Osa Rocket Launcher: fires a 90 mm shell, effective against tanks and fortified positions.

Smuggled from Croatia by Saudi Arabia to supply Syrian rebels. ISIS found the M79 rocket launcher an effective weapon against armored vehicles driven by Iraqi Security Forces.

RBG-6 Grenade Launcher: Saudi Arabia allegedly smuggled these from Croatia into Syria. They eventually "found their way" into ISIS's hands.

RPG-7 Rocket Propelled Grenade: The Iraqi Security Forces, the Kurdish Peshmerga, and ISIS all use them. RPG-7s are highly portable, unguided shoulder-launched antitank weapons. Durable and relatively low cost. Simple to use. The grenade range, up to 920 meters.

M198 Howitzer: range 14 miles. Can launch high explosives, rocket-assisted projectiles, and white phosphorus. ISIS likely captured these howitzers from the Iraqi Army after they fled their bases.

ZU-23-2 Anti-aircraft Gun: range 2 miles, designed to strike low-flying targets, as well as armored vehicles. Has been used in the Syrian Civil War, and it is also in the arsenal of the Iraqi Army.

FIM-92 Stinger: shoulder-fired infrared homing surface-to-air missile. Designed by the U.S. and used since 1981. These MANPADs can take down helicopters and aircraft. It is believed ISIS looted FIM-92s from Iraqi military bases.

HJ-8 Anti-Tank Missile: effective against armor, bunkers, and fortifications. The Free Syrian Army (rebel group) used these against the Syrian Arab Army since June 2013. Now ISIS has managed to incorporate these weapons into their arsenal.

DShK 1938 Machine Gun: used as an anti-aircraft weapon and heavy infantry support weapon. Can fire 600 rounds per minute. Can be mounted on cars for easy use and maneuverability. "ISIS likely stole these machine guns from either the Syrian or Iraqi armies."

.....

Humvees: American built. "Acquired" when Mosul was stormed by ISIS.

T-55 Tank Series: Soviet tank produced from the end of World War II through the 1980s. It is estimated that ISIS has around 30 of these tanks,

T-72 Tank: second-generation Soviet battle tank. Entered production in 1971. ISIS has an estimated five to ten T-72 tanks.

.....

Except for the Humvees, which were previously owned American property, ISIS doesn't want tanks and armored personnel carriers like the M113 and heavy armored trucks like the MRAP! It cannot use these multi-million dollar pieces of equipment because they are too cumbersome and costly to operate.

What they want is mobile weaponry, small and easy to use. ISIS seized plenty of that! Experts suggested that ISIS was probably digging big holes to bury the bigger equipment for later use, once the Islamic State actually became a State in that part of the world. Experts feared facing another "North Korea" in the Middle East.

Wally was amazed at the list and the things those weapons could do. He thought of bodies blowing up, limbs lost and lives destroyed. He thought of Canada's Universal Healthcare system and how doctors were trying to replace heart valves, organs and limbs in order to prolong lives. What a difference in two worlds! Young bodies shot to pieces in Syria and Iraq, organs that could have been harvested, somehow saved by the wave of a magic wand, frozen and flown to Canada and other parts of the globe to save lives. Was Wally wrong in thinking such thoughts? Why were Doctors without Borders there in that region, possibly wasting their time? Better to plug the dam with a thumb than do nothing at all. What a tide of man's inhumanity to man... and man's inhumanity to women! All the king's horses and all the king's men...

It is estimated that the military equipment which ISIS captured so far, in the summer of 2014, could equip an army of 200,000 soldiers. ISIS has a vigorous campaign for recruiting young men from Africa, the Gulf States, the Balkans, as well as Europe and even English speaking nations. The rebels are adept at using the internet in propaganda. And they rub salt into American wounds, with the well-known fact that ISIS soldiers were even trained by U.S. personnel at a secret base in Jordan back in 2012! One spokesperson said, "It's a convoluted and embarrassing mess out there in the Gulf Region. Nobody expected our intervention or our hopes for democracy in that region to turn sour like this! Must have seemed like a good idea at the time!"

Meanwhile, the Black Market was doing a brisk business in small arms dealing within Croatia and Turkey.

It seemed like the $25 billion worth of training and equipment provided by the U.S. before it withdrew from Iraq at the end of 2011 was just a big waste, a huge throw-away of money and training swallowed up inside a black hole, called Iraq.

When the smaller Sunni militia swept in on the port of Mosul, 30,000 Iraqi troops abandoned everything, throwing down guns and equipment, even getting rid of their military uniforms, right down to their shoes, exchanging everything for civilian clothes. So they ran, seeking refuge in the Iraqi Kurdistan capital of Erbil 50 miles east.

It was reported that senior Iraqi officers had "simply disappeared before the rank and file even knew the city was under attack." The rank and file tried to blend in with fleeing civilians to get away from ISIS after their commanders abandoned them. The Kurds were amused at the Iraqi disorder and their flight for self-preservation. They were also afraid for themselves because they did not know when the big city of Kobane would be next.

CHAPTER 44

In his book *The Interpretation of Dreams, Sigmund Freud* suggested that the content of dreams is related to wish fulfillment. Freud believed that the manifest content of a dream, or the actual imagery and events of the dream, served to disguise the latent content of the unconscious wishes of the dreamer.

[HTTP://PSYCHOLOGY.ABOUT.COM/OD/STATESOFCONSCIOUSNESS/P/DREAM-INTERPRET.HTM]

• • • • •

MONDAY, 2:00 P.M.
@THERAPY PEARLS AND POTTERY
JULY 14, 2014

"YOU'RE THE THERAPIST," WALLY STARTED, "I WANT TO TALK about my dreams today!"

"How are you sleeping though?"

"Manageable. I don't see the bloody images anymore, but I do get weird dreams ever since I started this notion of writing a novel."

"Okay, get your coffee, gather your thoughts, let's sit down and let's get started. Tell me all about it."

They sat around the coffee table. The ceiling was steepled. The west window was a large triangular one with crystal prisms dangling off the frame. The afternoon sun shone through those prisms splashing rainbows all over the room. Wally liked the dancing colours. He stared at the splashes of rainbow, and summoned up the memory of his dreams. He closed his eyes as he talked.

"It's got to be symbolic," he said. "I've been dreaming about pearls and pottery."

"Interesting," said de Jong in his counselorly fashion. "Go on."

Wally explained his first dream. He'd been gathering pearls. They were still in their clam-shells washed onto a sandy beach by rolling waves. An immense sea stretched back from the beach and Wally was the only beachcomber in view. Wally picked up another clam-shell, worked hard to pry it open and plucked out a pearl. He did that to the next one and the next one, until he had a pail full of pearls. He brought the pail home where he drilled a tiny hole in each pearl. He then threaded these pearls together into a lovely lustrous necklace which was intended to grace his wife's neck.

Then a hand came out of nowhere, snatched the necklace away, breaking it and throwing the pearls back into the sea.

De Jong didn't stop Wally. He took notes. He merely said, "Go on."

Wally talked about his second dream: the potterer. Most often, one dream followed the other in the same night.

"I'd have this clump of clay on my potter's wheel, which is spinning 'round and 'round. My hands are shaping it, all dirty and wet, working the clay up and up into a pot. Gobs of clay would stick to my fingers. The job always got difficult when I had the outside shaped and then I'd have to hollow out the interior."

"Sometimes the structure would sag and collapse and I'd have to start over. I found the chore frustrating, to shape it, get it just right, and then plop, it would just collapse. I know that the pot had to dry naturally, once you get it to the stage where it was shaped."

"I never make it to the last stage though, so I could fire and glaze the pot. I knew it had the potential to be a beautiful work of art. However, in my dream, the clay always fell in my hands and I always had to start over."

"So, let's hear it from you, Wally," asked de Jong. "What do you think this all means?"

"Okay. My English professor would say, it's an allegory. The pearls represent the chapters in my book. They can be beautifully written and I might be able to tie them together into a beautiful book. I'm afraid though, that some publisher will criticize and change my work to the point of destroying it... or the publisher may just reject it outright and say it's rubbish."

"I hear you saying you're afraid to submit your work to somebody for scrutiny," said de Jong.

"You got that right. I'm no Lee Child or Mark Twain."

"Hey you're a baby writer. Your first submission. Look at Robert Frost. Worked on a farm in his 20 and 30s. Family obligations. Didn't publish a collection of his poems until he was 39 years old. Okay, you're older than that... but let's say your other career, 'vacuuming and cleaning the house,' has slowed your progress towards literary fame."

Both Wally and de Jong laughed over that one, "slowed your progress towards literary fame!" "Time for a doughnut break!" they both said in tandem. "And another cup of coffee!" They both got back to the coffee table and eyed the prisms in the window dancing in the sun.

"What else do you see in your dreams, let's take the pottery thing?"

"Well," said Wally. "You have to get your hands dirty if you want to shape something beautiful." He said he saw his photography that way, willing to climb down the gorge at Ball's Falls to get that picture from a low angle looking upwards at the rushing water, catching the blue sky above. He saw that beauty required sacrifice and effort. "It sure was a long and slippery climb down there," he said to de Jong. "Now with this novel, I'm researching war in the Middle East and trying to describe scenes of a bloody battle."

Wally saw his dreams as "getting his hands dirty." He was also afraid that his effort would fail, if a publisher rejected his book.

De Jong raised his eyebrows and quoted Robert Browning: "Ah, but a man's reach should exceed his grasp, Or what's a heaven for?" [1812-1889]

Both men paused, appreciating the poetic insight. Wally finally said, "I've also had this dream about the Crusades, and me charging off to fight the Saracen in the Holy Land."

De Jong harrumphed and said, "How about if we save that one for the next session. Allegories give me a headache. Too much thinking! Men weren't made for it. They were made for finishing their coffees and doughnuts." De Jong nodded at the side counter with a twinkle in his eye. They both chuckled and enjoyed the final rays of sunlight gleaming through the triangular window at the top of the office, which de Jong affectionately called "My Great Room of Meeting."

The routine was to wind down the last five minutes in small talk. "Nice day," said de Jong, eyeing the sun outside the window. "Would have been a great day for pictures."

"Yeah," agreed Wally. "It would have been a great day for pictures!"

CHAPTER 45

She shrugged. "Many people come here; I don't have to read newspapers. The outside world has no interest for me, only the inner worlds. Out there" – she waved a hand – "out there is only negativeness, violence, confusion, hostility – "

[P.13, *The Clairvoyant Countess*, BY DOROTHY GILMAN, 1975]

. . . . .

CHIBOK UPDATE
SPENCER PHONES ABQURAH
FRIDAY, JULY 18, 2014

DETECTIVE SPENCER TURNED OFF THE TV. HE SAT ALONE IN his apartment, just finishing his "TV dinner." It was 6:30 p.m. He was lonely and he was disgusted over the news clip he had just seen. It was the 6 months anniversary of the kidnapping of 276 female students from the Government

Secondary School in the town of *Chibok* in Borno State, Nigeria.

On April 14-15, 2014, the girls from different high-schools in northeastern Nigeria had gathered to take their final examinations. Instead of doing their tests, they were kidnapped.

One hundred armed men showed up at a girls' boarding school. They claimed to be Nigerian government troops sent to protect the students from "marauding terrorists." Staff didn't suspect anything was wrong. The terrified teenagers were ordered out of their beds in the dead of night and herded into Toyota Hilux jeeps.

Four of the girls apparently escaped during the three week trek into the Camaroon jungle. One escapee reported that they were highly prized if they were virgins, that they were raped up to 15 times a day, forced to convert to Islam, and threatened to have their throats cut if they refused.

Nothing had been heard about the kidnapped girls until three weeks later, when on May 5, Boko Haram's Islamist leader, Abubakar Shekau, claimed responsibility for the kidnapping. He bragged about his act on video. He threatened to sell the girls into slavery, and showed them dressed in black all huddled together.

"I will marry out a female at 12. I will do same for a 9-year-old girl, like it was done on my mother Aisha and wife of Prophet."

"Just because I took girls in a Western school, they are worried. I said they should even desert the school, they should go and marry."

Shekau declared Jihad against Christians and Christianity in his video. "It is a war against western education, democracy and constitution." He said that if he was killed better fighters would arise to take his place.

Michelle Obama, the first lady, tweeted support around the hash tag *#BringBackOurGirls*. Various countries, the U.S., U.K., Canada and Israel and others offered assistance to the Nigerian government.

Ebele Azikiwe Jonathan, president of Nigeria and leader of the People's Democratic Party, was criticized for the government's slow and indecisive action in finding the girls. Half a year later, the girls were still in captivity. Chibok soon disappeared from the public's attention as an international issue. The media then centered on the Islamic State of Iraq and Syria, which made better headlines. ISIS and the Ebola outbreak made better news.

When the Chibok kidnapping of the girls happened, somebody tweeted: "I just heard a snippet on the news. What the hell is going on here? Didn't Procol Harum record *A Whiter Shade of Pale* in the 1960s?"

.....

Spencer had Abqurah's number. He phoned her and made it clear that it was purely a social call, now that her parents' trial was over.

"I guess I'm sort of asking you out on a date." He wanted to chat and have a coffee with her. She hesitated, but said, "Yes. It would be nice." They met at the Mohawk Timmy's after her class. They talked about everything and nothing in particular. It was nice! Spencer drove her home and walked her to her apartment door. He felt an impulse to hug her, but instead, said Goodnight.

CHAPTER 46

"Regard the Franj! Behold with that obstinacy they fight for their religion, while we, the Muslims, show no enthusiasm for waging holy war." [Saladin]

[QUOTATION: *The Crusades Through Arab Eyes*, AMIN MAALOUF, AL SAQI BOOKS, 1984]

.....

SATURDAY AND SUNDAY, *JULY 19 AND 20, 2014*

LAURENT, THE CRUSADER

WALLY TOOK OUT A HISTORY BOOK OVER THE WEEKEND from the local library, a history book written by Thomas Asbridge, [not Wally's usual fare since he liked murder mysteries]. The title of the book was, *The First Crusade*, which described the sacking of Jerusalem in the summer of 1099. Out of his obsessive reading during the next two nights, Wally created a fictional character in a dream... and Wally in that dream... became "Laurent," the Crusader!

[Historical facts gleaned from: *The First Crusade* by Thomas Asbridge, Oxford University Press, 2004]

Actually, there were seven *Crusades*, between 1095 and 1291. *The* First *Crusade* was the most successful. The First Crusade was sanctioned by the Roman Catholic Church, under Pope Urban II, to regain access to holy places in Jerusalem. Several hundred thousand Roman Catholic Christians became Crusaders by taking a public vow and receiving plenary indulgences from the church. During the Crusades the term for Muslim was Saracen. The term Franj or Frank by the Muslims meant Westerners, especially the French.

[WIKIPEDIA]

.....

Laurent stood on a hill overlooking Jerusalem, the Holy City, which he had vowed to free. The call went out through all of France and other Christian lands to battle the Saracens. Indulgences were promised by Pope Urban II, forgiveness of past sins. Crusaders would wear the sign of the cross on their chest as a holy sign for a warrior of the Lord. It was a Holy War for Christians against infidels, the Saracens who held the Holy City. Christians would win back all of the Holy Land for Christians, the way it was meant to be!

Laurent eyed Jerusalem in the sweltering heat. June, what a hot month it was! He pictured Jesus eyeing the city as well, over a thousand years ago, deliberately heading back for his crucifixion.

> Now as He drew near, He saw the city and wept over it, saying, "If you had known, even you, especially in this your day, the things that make for your peace! But now they are hidden from your eyes. For days will come upon you when your enemies will build an embankment around you, surround you and close you in on every side."
>
> [LUKE 19:41-43 NKJV]

His fellow Crusaders didn't inspire respect or trust in Laurent. Most of them were rabble. They were uneducated dirt and in it for the fun and the looting. They liked wearing the emblem of the cross on their chests. It made them feel important, and gave them an excuse to do what they wanted. After all, God was on their side, and they would be forgiven.

They could boast and swear about their bravery against those brown skinned infidels, the Saracens. They would skin them alive. They received the blessing from Rome, and they were assured that God would go with them. None of them had ever read the Bible or even knew how to read! It was a good way to escape the labour on the farm, the drudgery of work every day at home. They had a great time drinking and boasting at nights in the army camps. A soldier's life was a good one!

Laurent was an exception. He had been educated. He was the son of a nobleman, a land owner. Also the black sheep of the family! Laurent's older brother, Gerard, stood to gain the lion's share of the inheritance.

Laurent had also sown his wild oats among the village maidens. The Crusades beckoned him for a welcome escape. He heard a man could make his fortune in the Holy Land. Gold and silver for the taking! He had no respect for religion, and did not believe in prayer or the life hereafter. When Urban II called all God fearing men to take the Holy

Land back for Christendom, Laurent only heard opportunity calling... and escape, not a Holy cause! He did not need his father's petty share of the inheritance. He would make his own fortune with the sword!

.....

This is how Wally's dream took shape one night in a deep, deep sleep. He was Laurent standing on a hill above Jerusalem. He bore the cross upon his tunic, as he gazed down upon the Holy City. It was June 1099. He was happy he was the hero fighting on the right side, fighting on the side of God, even though he did not believe in Him.

Crusaders had invaded the Holy Land with several armies. Peter Barholomew urged his troops on under the symbol of the Holy Lance. Arnulf ordered that another standard, a golden cross, bearing the image of Christ be fashioned. He encouraged his followers to gather around it. Different factions, under different symbols changed sides, and many Crusaders defected to Godfrey of Bouillon's camp. He was the protector of the cross with the image of Christ, a more palpable standard than the Holy Lance!

A five-fold cross was also emblazoned upon Godfrey's tunic, the symbol standing for the five wounds of Christ. Smaller crosses were strategically placed in the four quadrants around the bigger cross, representing the four quarters of the world and the four evangelists. A clever design which drew the imagination of the men who went over to Godfrey's camp. Laurent was part of that camp.

.....

"We've taken up our position around Jerusalem," wrote Laurent in his journal, "but we are ill-prepared and not led well in this initial assault on the wall."

"My friend, Raimbold Creton climbed up the scaling ladder which we maneuvered against the wall. I saw a Saracen sword lift high and slice through his left forearm, just as he reached for the top of the battlements. We were forced to retreat. What folly."

"We have two siege towers but we cannot push their wheeled platforms close to the wall. The ditch is in the way! Our leaders challenged the men with a payment of a penny to bring three large stones to the south of the city to cast into the pit. It took three days and nights to fill it."

"We built other siege weapons: a massive battering ram with an iron-clad head, a number of catapults, scaling ladders and portable screens under which our men could hide as they approached the walls."

"Boulogne's cousin kidnapped a Muslim knight, who was scouting out the Christian camp one night. He was a bald-headed man, somewhat corpulent. Perhaps, he came out to relieve himself. We do not know. We asked him to convert to Christianity. When he declined, our knights brought him in front of the Tower of David. The man was beheaded by Baldwin's squire in full view of all, especially the guards on the wall above."

"On another occasion a Fatimid spy was caught taking messages in and out of Jerusalem. He was put in a catapult with the intention of throwing him back into the city. But the wretch was too heavy. He wasn't thrown far enough and broke his neck on sharp stones near the wall."

"It is now the second week of July. Our Crusaders are ready to unleash our rage against the infidels holding the Holy City. We will triumph in the name of God and Jesus Christ our Lord."

"*July 14, 1099 Anno Domini*: The first light of dawn. Horn calls sounded all over our camps. The Saracen thought we were attacking from the south. Instead Godfrey's soldiers had built a siege tower at the northern walls, in front of the city's Quadrangular Tower. But this was a ruse. In the middle of the night, our Crusaders dismantled the tower, moved its parts and re-erected it one kilometer east of St. Stephen's Gate. The Saracens were shocked the next morning to see the siege tower in a new position. Meanwhile, the Crusaders also struck the northern wall with the intent to break through to the main walls."

"*Dawn July 15, 1099:* Assaults were renewed. In the end, the Crusaders prevailed. The wattle screens tied to the siege tower protected those underneath managing to deflect the stone missiles hurled at them from above. Godfrey cut loose one of the screens protecting the tower and fashioned a bridge across the ramparts. The Saracen defense collapsed. Those stationed at the northern wall turned and fled at the sight of the Franks atop their walls."

"I was horrified at our Christian behaviour. Our knights in the name of the Lord sacked Jerusalem on July 15, 1099. How could we behave so badly and think we were right in the name of Jesus? My fellow-Crusader reported this with great joy:

Some of the pagans were mercifully beheaded, others pierced by arrows, plunged from towers, and yet others, tortured and burned to death in searing flames. Piles of heads, hands and feet lay in the houses and streets, and men and knights were running to and fro over corpses.

[ACKNOWLEDGEMENT TO: *The First Crusade*, THOMAS ASBRIDGE, OXFORD UNIVERSITY PRESS, 2004]

"Many Saracens fled to the Temple Mount. The Crusaders went after them and cut them down as far as Solomon's

Temple, 'where was such a massacre that our men were wading up to their ankles in enemy blood'."

"I staggered through the city with sword in hand horrified by the scene. My fellows thought I was fatigued from my own acts of violence but I was not. I deliberately chose not to engage in the slaughter. My fellows did not notice my inactivity. They were distracted. I refused to shed blood, except when my own person was attacked. Every time a Saracen attacked me, he challenged me saying, 'Christian prepare to die. Your fate is sealed at the hands of... Aamir.' I do not know if I was walking in a trance or a dream through all this horror in Jerusalem."

"When Aamir raised his sword, a young maiden stepped in front of the blade saving my wretched life. Remember me, Hazirah, she cried as she fell. I lunged at Aamir with my sword and pierced him through the neck. He fell bleeding from his throat."

" I do not know if that day damned me to the eternal flames; but somehow, I felt right not lifting my sword in the same manner my comrades did against everyone in sight, and somehow I thanked God for this angel of mercy, who shielded me every time Aamir attacked."

"Crusaders were crazed with blood lust that day. They went through the city killing not only Saracen, but gentile and Jew alike. Stabbing women, seizing infants and dashing them against the walls. There was no mercy."

"Our men next cast their eyes on the spoils of war. They grabbed all gold, silver and precious stones that they could carry, entering homes of citizens. It was agreed they could keep the house or palace or whatever they found. They even cut open the bellies of slain Saracens to see if they had swallowed coins. Many poor Crusaders became rich that day."

"I could not reconcile doing God's work and acting like this. It appears that our religious fervour and our barbarism can co-exist within one and the same soul. It is all embraced within our two-sided selves. Rejoicing and weeping from the victory which God gave them, our Crusaders made their way to worship at the Sepulcher of our Saviour Jesus. Covered in the blood of their victims, they kneeled and prayed at the site of Christ's death, and resurrection, and thanked God! How could this be?"

[HISTORICAL EVENTS ATTRIBUTED TO: *The First Crusade*, THOMAS ASBRIDGE, OXFORD UNIVERSITY PRESS, 2004. FICTIONALIZED CHARACTER OF "LAURENT," ATTRIBUTED TO THE AUTHOR OF THIS NOVEL.]

.....

Wally woke from his dream, yelling "The Horror! The Horror!" His wife awakened, startled. She led him to the bathroom, so he could take off his soaked night shirt; and brought him something dry to put on. He apologized, briefly explaining he dreamed that he was in the Crusades attacking Muslims. "You'll have to explain this one to de Jong," she said. "Let's get you back to bed and a bit of a rest."

CHAPTER 47

Unlike Freud, who often suggested that specific symbols represent specific unconscious thoughts, Jung believed that dreams can be highly personal and that interpreting these dreams involved knowing a great deal about the individual dreamer.

[HTTP://PSYCHOLOGY.ABOUT.COM/OD/STATESOFCONSCIOUSNESS/P/DREAM-INTERPRET.HTM]

.....

2:00 P.M. @THERAPY
MONDAY, JULY 21, 2014

"THOU SHALT NOT KILL!"

"THERE'S A LOT THAT'S SIGNIFICANT IN THIS DREAM," SAID de Jong. "But I'll start with the obvious." He explained that a person could not do evil either in a dream or under hypnosis, unless they would actually do that in the conscious world. "Sounds good," thought Wally. "I sure hope you're right." De Jong went on to say that Laurent's choice not to slaughter Saracens with deliberate cruelty, like his fellows, was something his real self would do to uphold the sixth commandment of the Old Testament, "Thou shalt not kill."

De Jong was fascinated by the fact that Wally had mixed Hazirah and Aamir into the dream where Hazirah saved his life repeatedly from the hands of the Saracen, Aamir. "There's a moral choice by Hazirah here which comes out in this dream. The bully will always be a bully. Often the weak have to make sacrifices at the hands of the bully for a higher good."

The counselor continued: "The other thing that strikes me about this dream is that the Crusades are in a sense still going on today. Maybe the Holy Wars between extreme Christians and extreme Muslims will never end. Solomon once said, 'What has been will be again, what has been done will be done again; there is nothing new under the sun'." [Ecclesiastes 1:9 NIV]

He said that Wally's dream about the Crusades pointed out the duplicity in the very nature of mankind. Both evil and good can co-exist in one soul. "You could have given in to the madness which seized the other Crusaders," said de Jong. "But... Wally, you chose not to! It was a choice open to the others too, but they went with their baser urges and their greed. They chose evil and justified it as good."

De Jong thought of people in terms of a coin. "You can call heads, and on the flip side, tails. All people, like all coins [magicians' coins excepted], have two sides to them. Heads is what you let people see of yourself and tails is what you hide from them. You can also look at a coin like good and evil. Let's say heads is good. Of course, a coin can't choose which side it will land on, but a person can! A person has a conscious choice each moment of his or her life to be good or bad.

"Wally, you made a moral choice in the dream," observed de Jong, "to fall on the side of good, not to murder, not to rape and not to steal, unlike your comrades in the Crusade."

As a history buff, de Jong couldn't resist pointing out that the image of the Roman god, Janus, was two-faced. "He's the god of beginnings and transitions," he explained. De Jong relished the point, like a professor in a lecture. "Janus looks to the future and the past at the same time!"

"Wally, I'm proud of you in that dream," he said. "Maybe you were the only Crusader during the entire sacking of Jerusalem whose prayer God actually heard at the foot of the Sepulcher!"

Wally sighed sadly, "The world is still flipping between two sides of a coin... and like Janus, maybe trying to bring the past back into the future? The Crusades and ISIL! For all our technology, I often feel like we are still stuck in the Middle Ages. When will it ever end?"

De Jong nodded his head in quiet agreement, "World War I was supposed to be 'the war to end all wars'... and sadly, here we are today!"

CHAPTER 48

Let me say that the path I did take for a brief period of my life was not of reckless drug use, hurting others, but it was a path of quiet rebellion, of a little experimentation of a darker side of my confusion in a confusing world, lost in the midst of finding my identity.

[JENNIFER CAPRIATI RETIRED AMERICAN TENNIS PLAYER]

.....

YOUNG CANADIANS RADICALIZED

SUNDAY, SEPTEMBER 14, 2014

AMERICA "LOSING OUR WAY"

"THE RADICALIZATION OF MUSLIM YOUTH!" WALLY HEARD that expression a lot in the summer of 2014. Some of those young people weren't even Muslim! They just sought a cause where they could rebel against the greed and disparity they'd seen in "the West."

He read the article about Christianne Boudreau, written by Amarnath Amarasingam Mahdi Qasqas, in the *Toronto Star*, September 14, 2014. Her son, Damian Clairmont, died fighting in Syria last winter. Christianne Boudreau decided to make her son's tragedy her own cause as a mother to stop kids going into crazy wars overseas.

"My knees are shaking so please forgive me. I'm a mother, not a public speaker," she said in an interview at a conference that month. She explained that not just young Muslim men, but mainly men, period, were joining terrorist groups overseas. According to the Canadian government, there are approximately 130 fighters to date that have become jihadists, and the estimate around the country is probably higher than that!

Their names will probably not be made public until they get killed somewhere in Syria, Iraq or Somalia, or wherever they've gone to join up.

These militants still maintain their Twitter and Instagram accounts, which they update with pictures from their travels in various hot spots. They also include political diatribes against moderate Muslims and non-Muslims in the West.

> Damian Clairmont, known as Mustafa among his friends in Calgary, was also known to be a harsh critic of life in the West. Same went for the other young men who departed from Calgary: Salman Ashrafi, Farah Shirdon, and Collin and Gregory Gordon.

They called their former Calgarian friends "hypocrites" or *munafiqun*. That's a charge deeply offensive for many

Muslims, because the Qur'an promises the *munafiqun* an afterlife in the lowest levels of hell.

Family usually can't make sense of it. Christianne Boudreau said that Damian seemed to have found a peace of mind when he told his mom about his decision to go to the Middle East to study Arabic and Islam. She supported her son's decision.

A few weeks later, she got a phone call from her son. She noticed that the country code was Turkish. When he called again, the country code was Syrian. He told his mom not to worry. In the winter he was killed.

So what about Canadians who are already overseas, not killed and want to come back? Some youths joined ISIS with an initial zeal, only to discover that their ideal image of the group fell far short of reality. Should Canada allow them back in?

Like everything in politics and religion, there are discussion groups in Canada which argue the pros and cons of both sides. Should returnees be given a second chance? Can they really be rehabilitated and reintegrated into Canadian society? Maybe that concept of second chances is both the strength and the weakness in our Canadian society. Or is it another point for which extremists laugh at us?

• • • • •

To a large extent, young Muslims were right in their criticism of North American society. It sure helped to have money to get elected in a democracy. Democracy was not free! Greed, sex, racism and poverty were all there. There's an obesity epidemic, gang warfare in big cities, blacks shot by white police, "banksters" who are writing themselves big bonuses, pharmaceuticals making record profits, politicians who keep making promises, while many people are on welfare and scraping by on minimum wage!

The show, "Moyers and Company," hosted a brilliant African-American, Bob Herbert, who wrote a book called, *Losing Our Way*, in which he said that powerful companies and powerful men in office were running America, not for the benefit of American citizens but for their own interests. [As if that's something new!] Money was the bottom line. He pointed at ordinary folk who had two or three jobs at minimum wage, eking out a living. They had part time jobs, so the employer wouldn't have to pay their insurance coverage. Herbert said that it was just insane that the Bush Administration, when it was in power, cut taxes at a time of war, just to get elected. Herbert saw the goal of politicians as getting elected and not as doing anything real for citizens. He said that getting $8 per hour in minimum wages, while corporations and banks were making record profits, was disgraceful and contrary to making the engine of a healthy economy run in the United States. Corporations and banks, themselves, were going to make the economy of the United States go broke because of their greed for immediate profit.

Herbert admired veterans who had sacrificed themselves in what seemed like "wars without end" in Afghanistan and Iraq. He cited the courage of Dan Berchinski who had his two legs blown off by an Improvised Explosive Device [IED] in Afghanistan, and who struggled to walk again with artificial limbs.

CHAPTER 49

First we take Manhattan, then we take Berlin

I'm guided by a signal in the heavens

I'm guided by this birthmark on my skin

[LYRICS LEONARD COHEN 1987,
SINGER JENNIFER WARNES]

.....

FIRST MOSUL [IRAQ]
THEN KOBANE [TURKISH-SYRIAN BORDER]
FIRST WEEK, OCTOBER 2014

ABU BAKR AL-BAGHDADI WAS VIDEOED IN A 15 MINUTE rant. He proclaimed himself to be the Khalifa, which means successor to Muhammad, and the political and military leader of ISIS, now ISIL, with the "L" standing for Levant or Greater Syria, which could mean anything from incorporating Syria and Iraq to incorporating the whole world. That would give a new meaning to John Lennon's song, "I hope someday you'll join us/ And the world will live as one."

Baghdadi laughed at the stupidity of the Americans. Especially President Obama's announcement in September 2014, "to degrade and destroy" ISIS. He laughed at the idea that the President intended to do this, "with no boots on the ground." That was political hot air blown at Americans who didn't want to be involved in another decade of war.

Baghdadi said to his council, "Rest assured airstrikes alone will not vanquish us. *We* are the boots on the ground and *we* will run over Syria and Iraq like a vengeful flood. We will create a Caliphate in the name of Allah and Muhammad, may peace be upon him." He added, "We will become a settled fact of life in the heart of the Middle East."

Media campaigns in dozens of languages were spread over the internet attracting young men to its cause.

"We are marching through city after city," pronounced Baghdadi, "with American weapons! Thanks to the U.S. arming the Iraqi army to the teeth when they pulled out. And that was paid for with American tax dollars!" Baghdadi smiled with great satisfaction under his beard. His jihadists had the cash to buy more arms. When his troops overran Mosul and sent the Iraqi army scurrying away for their lives, not only weaponry was seized but also $500 million from a bank in Mosul.

On July 5, 2014, Michael Snyder wrote this in *WashingtonsBlog*:

To say that the new Iraqi army has been incompetent would be a massive understatement. Not only have they run away like scared kittens from these jihadists, they have also left behind staggering amounts of weaponry for them... We have become a laughingstock to ISIS. They know that we are not going to invade Iraq again. So they are laughing at us as they use our own equipment to take over the country.

The Kurds appealed to the the United States to escalate air strikes. If Kobane falls next, they said, then thousands of Kurds will be in danger of persecution and death. Within the first week of October 2014, it was estimated that 40% of Kobane was controlled by ISIS. Kurdish "Women Protection Units" were training to liberate the western gate of the town.

Kobane is a Syrian-Kurdish border town which is strategically positioned to give a direct link between the Syrian province of Aleppo and its stronghold of Raqqa to the east. Approximately 9,000 jihadists set their sights on Kobane; and were opposed by approximately the same number of Kurds, one third of them women!

It is said that Islamic militants believe that they will not go to paradise if they are killed by a woman. An expert on Middle East Affairs scoffed at the idea. "That may be so. But in most cases, ISIS looks at these women soldiers as a playground for raping and debasing women."

Hafiz laughed at the comment when he heard it on Saudi TV. His troops had ravaged Mosul and were given women as rewards. "For taking the town," said his unit commander, "you might as well take the women too!" Hafiz had no qualms about doing just that. It was a foretaste of Paradise should he be killed as a martyr for the cause.

The world saw another reality in ISIS excesses. The Kurdish women would just be a bigger smorgasbord of sexual abuse for their militants. To the victors go the spoils! It was a dictum of human nature and of armies throughout the Ages, from "The Rape of the Sabine Women," through to the Crusades, through to modern day ISIS conquering Kurdish territory. Same old story!

CHAPTER 50

"Fight those who do not believe in Allah or in the Last Day and who do not consider unlawful what Allah and His Messenger have made unlawful and who do not adopt the religion of truth from those who were given the Scripture - [fight] until they give the *jizyah [tax]* willingly while they are humbled."

[QUR'AN 9:29]

• • • • •

UNITED NATIONS REPORT
THURSDAY, OCTOBER 2, 2014

IN THE FIRST WEEK OF OCTOBER 2014, THE UNITED NATIONS drew up a report on civil rights abuses committed by jihadists. It was based on 500 interviews and produced jointly by the UN Assistance Mission for Iraq (UNAMI) and the Office of the UN High Commissioner for Human Rights.

The report suggested that there were an array of abuses against religious and ethnic communities which "may amount to war crimes or crimes against humanity." It stated that almost 2 million Iraqis had been displaced because of the violence, over 24,000 civilians killed in an 8 month period, and numerous abuses like rape, forced recruitment of children, and desecration of religious and cultural places.

Attacks on Muslims by ISIS [Reported by UN on Oct 2, 2014]:

- On 21 August, a 31-year old man was stoned to death by ISIS after a self-appointed court sentenced him to death for adultery. On 28 August, seven individuals, allegedly Sunni, were executed by ISIS after being condemned to death.
- On 16 July, ISIS was distributing leaflets among Christians [estimated 20,000 of them] in the city ordering them either to convert or to pay "jizyah" (toleration/protection tax), to leave or face death.
- On 22 July, ISIS killed a Sunni Imam in eastern Baquba because he had denounced the organization. Reports allege that on 9 September, another Imam was executed in western Mosul for failing to declare his fealty to ISIS.
- Members of the Shia Turkmen and Shabak communities were also singled out for attacks by ISIS
- On 27 July, ISIS abducted 20 young students and a Sufi Muslim leader in Mosul. The students were studying the Holy Qur'an when the attack was carried out on the al-Rawtha al-Muhamadiya Mosque in the Muthanna District, eastern Mosul. The gunmen also destroyed some tombs of Sufi sheikhs located inside the mosque. The whereabouts of the abducted students is unknown. Families of the abducted stu-

dents have pleaded with the Sunni leadership of ISIS in Mosul to release their family members.

- UNAMI/OHCHR received reports that a number of women who had refused to wear the veil were beaten by ISIS in Mosul. On 21 August, media reported that ISIS beat with sticks women who were not wearing the veil in markets in the city. Allegedly, some women reacted, throwing stones at their attacker.

.....

> "I will cast terror into the hearts of those who disbelieve. Therefore strike off their heads and strike off every fingertip of them"
>
> [QUR'AN 8:12]

James Foley was beheaded in the later part of August 2014, maybe August 19. He was an American freelance journalist and photojournalist of the Syrian Civil War. He had been abducted November 22, 2012 in northwestern Syria. Foley was the first American citizen to be killed by "Jihadi John."

Ali al-Sayyed was beheaded c. August 28, 2014. He was a Sergeant in the Lebanese Army. ISIL captured him during the Battle of Arsal. ISIL member Abu Musaab Hafid al-Baghdadi posted pictures of his beheading on Twitter.

Steven Sotloff was beheaded c. September 2, 2014. He was an Israeli-American journalist reporting for *Time Magazine* and allegedly *The Jerusalem Post*. He was kidnapped in Aleppo, Syria, in 2013. A video was released showing Jihadi John beheading Sotloff.

.....

> But though I have wept and fasted, wept and prayed,

> Though I have seen my head (grown slightly bald) brought in upon a platter,
>
> I am no prophet—and here's no great matter;
>
> I have seen the moment of my greatness flicker,
>
> And I have seen the eternal Footman hold my coat, and snicker,
>
> And in short, I was afraid.
>
> [*Love Song of J. Alfred Prufrock* – T.S. ELIOT, 1920]

Other beheadings were grossly carried out and put on the internet during the summer of 2014. The names of those who died and how they died should not be forgotten, some identified and some never to be identified. The list goes on:

- Abbas Medlej, a Lebanese Army soldier
- an unidentified Kurdish soldier
- up to 75 unidentified Syrian soldiers, their heads and bodies displayed along the streets
- David Haines, British aid worker c. September 13, 2014, kidnapped near the Atmeh refugee camp near the Turkish border. A video of Haines' beheading was entitled, "A Message to the Allies of America" and released September 13, 2014 by ISIL.
- Alan Henning, British humanitarian aid worker, beheaded c. October 3, 2014. A video was released by ISIL on the internet
- Hervé Gourdel, a French citizen and moun-

taineering guide, kidnapped on September 21, 2014, while hiking in Algeria. He was beheaded c. September 24. His video was entitled, "A Message of Blood for the French Government."

- The video is similar to other ***ISIL*** beheading videos. It opens with a news clip of French President ***François Hollande*** and a title screen. It then shows Gourdel handcuffed and kneeling in front of four armed masked men. After Gourdel delivers a statement, one of the militants reads a statement. In it he declares that this kidnapping and execution were in response to the order of ISIL spokesman ***Abu Mohammad al-Adnani*** to attack citizens of countries participating in the US-led coalition against the Islamic State. Like the other IS beheading videos, it does not show the actual beheading, but the final scene does show Gourdel's dead body with his severed head in his lap, and then the fighters holding it up.

  [HTTP://EN.WIKIPEDIA.ORG/WIKI/2014_ISIL_BEHEADING_INCIDENTS]

The Syrian Observatory for Human Rights reported on October 1, 2014 that ISIL had beheaded 10 individuals near Kobane, two males and three female Kurdish fighters, four Syrian Arab rebels and a male Kurdish civilian. It is reported that the beheadings are often carried out in public and the public is told that any dissent will not be tolerated.

The Khaled Sharrouf incident outraged Australians and much of the world. In 2014, Khaled Sharrouf, an Australian citizen, joined ISIL. He posted a photo on the internet of his seven-year-old son holding the decapitated head of a Syrian soldier. The incident was strongly condemned and raised concerns about ***Australian Muslims*** going abroad for terrorist activity, and the possibility that the recruits returning home for further attacks.

David Cameron, the British Prime Minister, put this on Twitter: "The murder of David Haines is an act of pure evil."

The White House also commented via Twitter: "The United States strongly condemns the barbaric murder of UK citizen David Haines by the terrorist group ISIL [ISIS.]"

Outrage was expressed by Europe and the West via newspapers and the internet. There was even support from Muslims against these beheadings. After the Gourdel incident, for instance, hundreds of Muslims gathered in the Grand Mosque of Paris to protest the acts by ISIL. Dalil Boubakeur, the leader of the French Council of the Muslim Faith, led the protest, joined by thousands of other Muslims around France.

.....

But ISIL continued to expand and move from city to city in Syria and Iraq with seeming impunity. Airstrikes did not stop them. ISIL now were the "boots on the ground" that couldn't be stopped and they were on home turf!

ISIL thumbed its nose at the United States which seemed to have become a laughingstock not only for the Islamist militants but for many people around the globe. Things were not forgotten from the days of the useless Viet Nam War and Nixon's Watergate scandal and the huge lie about "weapons of mass destruction" in Iraq and the billions spent in America's foreign war in Afghanistan. And this at a time, when America's proud heritage of "democracy" was a lie, with its years of slavery behind it and with its continued racism in front of it. Historians could not deny America's long tradition of imperialism for control of anything from the banana republics to the oil enriched countries of the world.

The United States ignored its own problems at home, with the turn of the second millenium, instead of healing itself from within: 50% poverty among its citizens, a sizeable welfare state, obesity, a hodge-podge of healthcare, continued racism, 55% of its annual budget insanely earmarked for the military, propping up its sagging economy with the printing of 4 trillion dollars of paper money out of thin air, and borrowing massive sums from China and other countries to keep afloat, so that the national debt stood at almost $17 trillion by 2013. Some experts predicted that the U.S. economy would inevitably come tumbling down like a house of cards, which would see the middle class destroyed, more widespread poverty worse than the Great Depression and hyperinflation rivalling the Weimar Republic shortly after World War I.

ISIS leaders were not stupid. They were aware of America's history and it internal problems. They might just be [ironically] the David who would slay the world's Goliath and make him topple to the ground, ready for his head to be chopped off, ignominiously slain!

And from America's perspective? Before ISIS grew any bigger, there might be no other choice than to retract the policy of "no boots on the ground' over there and to stimulate America's economy with the rapid manufacture of more war equipment: armaments, boats, planes and rockets. There's nothing like another war to pull the economy out of a slump! With Russia involved, the whole thing might just escalate and explode like a Middle East Powder Keg to start World War III. Would that be the beginning of the Apocalypse or Armageddon?

Wally hated to think about things like that. Yes, he was aware of what was happening world-wide. But there was a part of him which censored those fears and shoved them to a hidden corner in his mind. Most people he knew hated war, violence and bloodshed, he being the foremost among them. He liked to mind his own business. He recalled the advice in Voltaire's *Candide* [1759]: "Let us hoe our own garden." It was a private activity which did not cross into somebody else's garden; it also made the best out of one's own plot and whatever it could produce. Wally was convinced that what most people wanted was to have their own little space, which they could call their own, to be left alone, to work, to marry and to have children without the fear of being conquered or being dominated by a dictator. But down deep, he knew that when it came to governments and the power struggles among classes and wealth, that dream of being left alone was only an idealist's illusion.

"Don't worry, be happy!" [Bob Marley 2009 song]

CHAPTER 51

It is difficult to conceive of an interpretation which could arrive at *any other* conclusion than that the practice of beheading is justified, and in fact *commanded*, by the Qur'an itself. The Qur'an explicitly says to "**strike at their necks,**" and authoritative Islamic commentators (not just modern jihadists like Islamic State) interpret this as a justification and sanction for the practice of beheading.

[HTTP://WWW.ONEPETERFIVE.COM/PRACTICE-BEHEADING-JUSTIFIED-ISLAM/]

.....

HAFIZ'S ACT OF VIOLENCE
HAFIZ'S SECRET MISSION
THURSDAY, OCTOBER 2, 2014

HAFIZ WAS CALLED INTO A SECRET MEETING IN THE LITTLE house just outside of Kobane. It was a humble house, nothing special, equipped with no running water or toilets, unnoticed. Perfect as a camouflage for temporary headquarters. The next objective would be to move against the Kurds guarding strongholds within the town.

"As salaam aleykum," said the ISIS unit commander. Hafiz responded, ""'***Wa alaykumu as-salaam***."

Abdul Ali al-Sayed faced Hafiz and offered him a small cup of Turkish coffee. He had acquired a taste for it. "You have done well with our videos, but now we want you to be on the other side of the camera. We will test your resolve to please Allah. If you pass this test, then we have a bigger mission for you."

"And how am I to please Allah?"

"We need you to behead the next victim to show the West we will not be stopped!"

Hafiz's chin lifted with determination at the challenge. "It will be done."

Hafiz was dressed in black the next morning at dawn, a frightening facsimile of Jihad John. His nose and lower face were covered in a black executioner's head covering. He held his sword in hand. The victim was led in under the rising sun, outfitted in an orange jump suit. He was made to kneel. He was drugged to be submissive, as Allah wished. He had been a Kurd defending Kobane.

Another videographer stood by, a Muslim. Hafiz launched into his speech. "This is what we do to infidels. Let it be a warning to the Western world, that we will not be stopped, that we will purge the decadence out of all non-believers. The Islamic State will rule, in the name of Allah and Muhammad, may peace be upon him." With that Hafiz swept his sword back and forward in a smooth arc.

Hafiz was called into a meeting again with Al-Sayed. They greeted each other as before: "As salaam aleykum," said the ISIS commander. Hafiz responded, ""*Wa alaykumu as-salaam*."

Hafiz accepted the Turkish coffee and they talked. "You will be smuggled across the Syrian border, to be flown back to Canada. Your mission is to plant explosives in the subways of Toronto."

"We want to demonstrate our power in your former country, in Montreal, Toronto, Winnipeg and Vancouver." He continued, "We have a few smaller cities in mind too, to show how deep our hands can reach. We will take our war to their soil! Their nightmare of 9/11 is not over!"

Since Hafiz had lived near Toronto, he was the logical choice. "Our contact will wait for you there at Union Station. The password is, "How about them Leafs" The answer from your brother will be, "Time to win the Stanley Cup, eh!" Hafiz couldn't help but think how funny this sounded in the Arab world.

Al-Sayed went on, "Everything is arranged and paid for. You will have a bank account in Kobane, Ankara, Frankfurt and Toronto. You will have a Turkish passport and a new name." Hafiz got briefed on the details. Al-Sayed ended his briefing, "May Allah bless your mission."

CHAPTER 52

And when the night is cloudy, there is still
a light, that shines on me,

shine until tomorrow, let it be.

I wake up to the sound of music, mother
Mary comes to me,

speaking words of wisdom, let it be.

[THE BEATLES - 1970]

.....

THE EYES TELL ALL
VISITING THE PARENTS
FRIDAY, OCTOBER 3, 2014

ABQURAH LAY IN BED IN THE DARK IN HER APARTMENT. SHE had the radio on, Classical 96.3 FM, "Beautiful Music For A Crazy World." She was listening to *Nocturne* hosted by

Marilyn Lightstone. At the moment, Rimsky-Korsakov's *Scheherazade* was playing, "The Young Prince and Princess," an enchanted love story.

Infidelity lay behind the concept of 1,001 nights... and so did "murder," depending on how you look at it. A Persian king's wife was unfaithful, he had her executed [probably beheaded]. He decides that all women are the same, and so he marries a series of virgins, and has them each executed the next day, before they can prove themselves unfaithful.

When he runs out of virgins, the Vizier's own daughter, Scheherazade, volunteers to marry the king. She spins a story every night, leaving it at a cliffhanger, before she finishes it the next night and starts a new story. The king finally relents and loves her at the end of 1,001 nights.

The Young Prince and Princess was a lovely piece of music written by Rimsky-Korsakov in 1888, but the beauty of the music was very opposite to the concept of a king executing his brides day after day. The old Arabic story is shrouded in romance, but it underscores the age-old struggle between good and evil. In the big picture, you might say, Heaven and Hell. An eternal struggle!

Abqurah kept the radio on all night. She awoke at 6 a.m. to get ready for her morning classes at Mohawk College. She had enrolled in courses which she thought could lead her eventually into social work or possibly criminology.

Subjects of interest included, "Domestic and Workplace Violence," "Cults and Terrorism," and "Criminal Psychology." She had personal experience with her own family's tragedy; and she wanted to use her own tragedy in helping Muslim immigrants in Canada. She knew what it was like to be a stranger in a strange land.

Abqurah watched the 6 o'clock news in the evening at supper. CHCH reported the latest beheading, showing a still photo of the victim and the executioner standing above him. The news anchor played the pre-recorded message with the disguised voice. Abqurah recognized the executioner immediately, from his eyes. "Aamir," she whispered horrified. He had dropped off the face of the earth for more than a year, only to resurface like this!

She contacted the police department right away. Not even the quiet music and soothing voice of Marilyn Lightstone put her to sleep that night. She had an appointment with Detective Spencer the next day, after her class and after her Timmy's shift in the afternoon.

"It's him, I know it's him," she said to Spencer in tears. She looked up at him from her hijab. Spencer thought Arabian women were more beautiful with the head covering because it emphasized their faces.

"At least, we know where he is and what he's doing now," said Spencer. "Your past is always going to haunt you. You have to come to grips with that." Spencer suggested a counselor. He knew of a good one. Just the talk would be good.

"I'm so glad you're working and in school," he said, "You're creating your own independence, which a lot of women in your culture don't ever get." He added, "If there's anything else you see or hear about your brother, let us know. If he ever comes back to Canada, we want to nail him."

That last comment unsettled Abqurah. "If he ever comes back to Canada? Oh my God, what if he does?" Abqurah was seriously thinking about becoming a Christian. Her brother would not be pleased!

. . . . .

She visited her parents in jail. This had been arranged with Detective Spencer's assistance. It had been just over 3 months since the trial. The parents resented her being out there and them being in here, "with these criminals."

"Didn't you think what Aamir did to Hazirah was wrong?" asked Abqurah.

"It was Allah's will. The family was dishonoured," said Adl.

"But all she wanted to do was marry Alexander."

"He was a Christian and an infidel."

"I'm thinking of becoming a Christian."

"If only Aamir could hear you now!"

The mother, Yaminah, bowed her head in shame. She was silent. Abqurah tried to explain.

"I know that Christians have had their history, just like our Muslim forefathers. But I feel I am drawn towards this Jesus and his words."

Adl proclaimed, "You are my daughter no longer. You are dead to me." Both parents turned to go.

CHAPTER 53

"The Prophet was given the strength of thirty (men)." Muhammad (hadith 24) apparently claimed that devout Muslims would be given the sexual strength of 100 persons upon their arrival in Heaven."

[72 Virgins - Dr. AVI PERRY, 2009]

.....

LIKE A CHAMELEON
INTRODUCING JORIN ASLAN
SUNDAY, OCTOBER 5, 2014

HAFIZ GOT RID OF HIS MILITARY PARAPHERNALIA, GUNS and clothes within the ISIS lines. He shaved his beard and before long, he looked like an ordinary Turkish citizen, wanting to escape from the rebels like everyone else. He got a false passport in short order.

He was escorted safely into Kurdish territory by a cab driver who had no loyalties to any cause, except his own pocket book. Hafiz put a bullet in the man's head and kicked him into a field in the countryside. He wiped the gun and threw it into a ditch. Hafiz kept his switchblade, a weapon of choice. He drove off in the cab, parked a block away and registered at the "The Oasis Hotel." The price looked right on the marquee.

He glanced at his new Turkish passport with satisfaction. He was now: Jorin Aslan. The first name meant high, upper, as in rank. The last name meant lion. He would be a proud lion, a strength to be feared! Jorin Aslan burned Hafiz's old passport in the sink and flushed the evidence down the drain. He was once again, reborn!

Jorin dreamt a pleasurable dream that night of his eternal reward in Jannah [Paradise]. He felt content and safe. 72 houris [virgins] would be given to him. He dreamt of those virgins with veils over their faces; and as he lifted each veil, the face behind it was... Amy. Amy, Amy... Amy, 72 times over! He whispered, "Impossible!"

Jorin awoke in a heavy sweat in his cheap hotel room. He knew what he had to do. He had another day before his bus would leave for Ankara. He went to a local café not far from the hotel. Two Kurdish women were chatting. They were part of a group of Kurdish women fighters taking turns in trying to liberate the Western Gate of the city. One said she wished she had the courage of Dilar Gencxemis who blew herself up killing several ISIL militants. "We'll show them how women can fight," she said, "They think that women cannot fight them. But we're not afraid."

Jorin introduced himself. "I couldn't help but overhear. Is it true that the jihadists are afraid of being killed by a woman for fear of going to hell?" Jorin explained that he was trying to get back to his elderly mother and father in Istanbul, away from all this craziness. He had been in Kobane on business, to start a cab company, when ISIS cut his plans short. Beler was the talker while her companion, Asti, seemed shy.

Asti was a pretty little thing, 18 years old. Long black hair, sultry eyes, a button of a nose and a cute little mouth. She still looked like a kid, and was nervous with Jorin's presence. Beler was older, 20, and more confident where men were concerned. She had long flowing brown hair, bangs that hovered over her forehead. Her eyes were brown and inviting to Jorin. Her mouth full and sensual.

Beler tossed her head back and boasted, "Yes, jihadists believe they won't go to paradise if they are killed by women. That is why they flee when they see us. I witnessed it personally at the Celaga front. We monitor their radio calls. When they hear a woman's voice on the air, they become hysterical."

She was quite proud of the new strength that young Kurdish girls found in this confrontation with ISIL. Asti said she had to get back home. Beler stayed back intrigued by this handsome Turk with a lion's name.

She excused herself to go to the washroom. Jorin followed her, clubbed her with his fist, and pulled out his knife. The act was done quickly. He convinced himself she was just another infidel. He was doing God a favour.

He wiped his blade and slid stealthily out the back alley, like a cat. Even if he would have left out the front door, no one would have noticed him anyway, or cared inside the crowded café.

His stolen cab was still where he left it. He was amused, "I could start my own cab company!" He drove himself back to the hotel, again parking a block away. He showered, had a drink, and a light meal in the bar, and then he slept very well that night. The bus ride to Ankara had all been pre-arranged through other contacts. He travelled light, just a backpack loaded with his passport, a fake credit card, extra clothes, and a copy of *The Holy Qur'an*.

CHAPTER 54

The Wizard prepares to get Dorothy home in his hot air balloon but Toto chases a cat. Dorothy follows, and it leaves without her. The good witch of the North arrives and tells her that she can still return home by tapping her heels together three times and repeating, "There's no place like home."

[*Wizard of Oz* NEAR END – 1939 MOVIE]

.....

ON THE ROAD AGAIN!
MONDAY, OCTOBER 6, 2014

IN THE AIR AGAIN!
TUESDAY, OCTOBER 7, 2014

ANKARA WAS 11 HOURS AWAY BY BUS. THERE WERE SEVERAL checkpoints and toilet stops on the way, but basically nothing he could not bluff his way through. That evening, Jorin signed into a five star hotel, "The Divan Ankara Cukurhan," and slept soundly in a much better bed. He was scheduled to fly out of the "Esenboja International Airport" the next morning on Tuesday, October 7.

Jorin found his bank, withdrew money in Deutsch Marks and Canadian Dollars. He booked the 7:00 a.m. flight from Ankara to Frankfurt, Germany. It was a three and a half hour flight, though extra time had to be taken into account, with the shuttle bus, baggage time and customs. Frankfurt to Montreal was a grueling 8 hour flight with a meal, but 7 hours would be gained back in the day going west. He had no problem at Customs, using his perfect English with the occasional "eh" thrown in.

Jorin relaxed and took advantage of the promise of a pleasurable flight advertised in the brochure: "Enjoy specially selected *food* and beverages on board *Lufthansa* flights worldwide and experience culinary delights." The stewardess asked if he wanted anything to drink from the bar. He asked for coffee, black. The Qur'an forbad alcohol. Jorin/Hafiz/Aamir had to keep his body pure.

> "O you who believe, intoxicants, and gambling, and altars, and arrows of chance are tools of affliction used by the devil. You shall avoid him so that you may be successful."
>
> [QUR'AN 5:90]

In mid-flight, he wondered how many infidels the plane would kill if it crashed into Ottawa's Parliament Building. Topple the tower! Let the symbol of Confederation crumble! Would the Prime Minister of Canada be killed? Or was he out at some G7 Conference somewhere or at his cottage? Jorin sipped his coffee, letting his mind wander into revengeful realms.

It took 8 hours for the flight to arrive at "Montreal Mirabel Airport." It was 2:00 p.m., Tuesday, October 7th. Jorin found a Thai Restaurant in the food court and ordered Pad Thai and a mixed vegetable rice dish. Then he found a cab which took him to the Via Rail Station. He suffered jet lag and did not look forward to an additional 5 hour trip by train to Toronto's Union Station.

In Montreal, he had arranged for his Toronto contact to meet him at the Union Station. Jorin would wear a red Fez. He looked more like a Shriner trying to sell tickets to a circus than an undercover terrorist. His contact came to him immediately. It had been a long exhausting day for him. It was 7:00 p.m., Tuesday evening.

"How 'bout them Leafs?"

"Time they won the Stanley Cup, eh?"

Jorin felt stupid saying the password while wearing a red Fez. But it worked. He put the red Fez back into his backpack. "I'm Umar," said the contact. "You will be my guest." They left, neither of them real Canadians, nor real Leaf fans.

CHAPTER 55

"I believe in an America where the separation of church and state is absolute... where no church or church school is granted any public funds or political preference, and where no man is denied public office merely because his religion differs from the president who might appoint him, or the people who might elect him."

[HTTP://WWW.UNITEVOTERS.COM/CHURCHANDSTATE.HTM - PRESIDENT JOHN F. KENNEDY, SEPT. 12, 1960]

.....

CAESAR'S COIN AND THE LEAFS
TUESDAY, OCTOBER 7, 2014

THOMAS ERIC DUNCAN
WEDNESDAY, OCTOBER 8, 2014

THE PRAYER MEETINGS HAPPENED EVERY TUESDAY EVENING at the church at 7:00 p.m. The routine? Weather and easy banter for about 10 minutes, a reading of Sunday's scripture and what it means. Then prayer concerns. And finally coffee [or tea] and cookies at 8:00 p.m. with chatting until 8:30 p.m.

Both Jake Klassen and Jonathan Evans looked at prayer meetings as encouragement to carry out their police duties. It was a good way to spend Tuesday evening among friends. When they got home, they always had something interesting to talk about with their wives before bedtime.

Evans was 15 years younger than Klassen, yet, he had deep worry lines on his face. He liked his hair short and parted neatly on the right side. He rarely smiled, and when he did, it was with lips pinched together. You'd think he was Steve McQueen!

He appreciated Klassen's insights, both on the job and at the prayer meetings. It was great that they belonged to the same church, and the same police force together. They made it a policy not to talk religion on the job. However, at the prayer meetings, they prayed for police officers in general terms. Politicians especially were never above prayer at these meetings!

Sunday's topic had been the "render unto Caesar" passage:

> Tell us therefore, What thinkest thou? is is lawful to give tribute to Caesar, or not?
>
> But Jesus perceived their wickedness, and said, Why tempt ye me, ye hypocrites?
>
> Shew me the tribute money. And they brought unto him a penny
>
> And he saith unto them, Whose is the image and the superscription?

> They say unto him, Caesar's. Then saith he unto them, Render therefore unto Caesar
>
> the things which are Caesar's, and unto God the things that are God's.
>
> When they had heard these words, they marveled, and left him, and went their way.
>
> [MATTHEW 22:17-22 KJV]

Klassen reread the passage out loud. He observed, "Well, Jesus doesn't deny the authority of the State! I'd suggest, the coin was a great way to illustrate the separation of Church and State!"

"I never thought of it that way!" commented one of the ladies. "Maybe Religion should butt out of affairs of state, and the state should protect the freedom of all religions, as long as they don't break the law." Klassen acknowledged that when Christendom forced its religion upon people, and burned them at the stake, there were problems of terrible injustices. He could see the Islamic State repeating that same mistake in its conquered territories, creating a theocracy under Allah and combining it with Shari'ah Law. "They are making the same mistake we Christians made in the Middle Ages, combining the Church and State, with no freedoms for other religions."

Klassen commented that Muhammad approached his conquered territories with more enlightenment in the 7th century, than the Islamic State is currently doing in modern times. "The Constitution of Medina," he explained, "guaranteed that non-Muslims would have political and cultural rights, as well as freedom of religion. Now, that was pretty enlightened of Muhammad, back in 622 CE!" He added that Muhammad's original intentions were not followed by leaders who came after him, reinterpreting his message by their less tolerant goals.

Klassen recognized that Muhammad did a magnificent job of unifying all the tribes and races within the Arabian Peninsula into one huge community, called an "ummah," in which all groups had rights.

"He took 22 years to do all that, and could have used more time, had he lived longer," Klassen said. "Jesus preached his simple message of loving God and loving your neighbour, within the span of three years. It was impossible, however, for him to challenge the Roman Empire, during his lifetime, although he confronted the authority of the Pharisees and Sadducees within his own Jewish community."

"I see a different meaning in Caesar's coin," Olive interrupted. "I see a craven image in the coin, like the worship of money and like false gods." Someone else proposed the idea of counterfeit money, and then, how these hypocrites, who approached Jesus, pretended to admire his wisdom, while all the time wanting to ensnare him!

"That's still going on," said Olive. "Look at the ads. All those law suits on TV. Lawyers haven't changed!"

"How about Muslims who pretend to be good citizens when they really aren't?"

"You can't paint them all with the same brush!" somebody objected. "What about the Catholic Church?"

Jonathan Evans, as a former Catholic, spoke up. "I was surprised after I graduated from an all boys Catholic high-school. A priest was convicted of pedophilia, and another priest had hit a student, slapped him across the room, and was never charged."

Evans continued, "All the priests wore black cassocks and white collars, as if they were specially chosen by God." Klassen's eyes widened with interest.

"I'm listening."

Evans said, "Well, it wasn't all bad! The Catholic School Board started a high-school orchestra in that school. I chose the violin."

"You don't strike me as being a musical guy, especially the violin, being a cop and all."

"Anyway, last month I went to our class reunion, its 25th anniversary. I graduated in 1989." Klassen did some quick math in his head. That put Evans at about 45. "Hmm. He's catching up to the old geezer age!" he thought.

Both Klassen and Evans, in fact, could have joined Baryon's Wednesday afternoon coffee klatch of geezers at *Williams Fresh Café*, had they worked for the Hamilton Police Department. Evans went on about how his high-school group had grown so... well, so old. Rounded tummies, wrinkled faces and white hair. They looked like muppets.

"The thing was," laughed Evans, "I was one of them! Well, maybe not the rounded tummy, but I had all the other features." He said that he learned something important from his old Chemistry teacher, from grade 12.

"The guy was a priest and now he was married and had two sons." Evans related how he had a private conversation with this former priest.

Evans had asked him, "Why'd you quit?"

"I saw how bitter other priests got as they grew older. They all felt cheated, like they missed something in life. I didn't want to end up like them."

The former priest confided that he went back to Grad school where he met a nice lady. They fell in love, got married, and that was the end of his priesthood.

Evans regretted he didn't ask the former priest if he got excommunicated from the Catholic Church, or if he attended Mass anymore. The priest said he still believed in God, but a different God, and a different church, than he was taught.

Evans went on to say that the priest started a successful counseling service for ex-priests and for parents who had troubled kids, especially sons. He admired the priest's courage. Evans was convinced that many priests still had good hearts; at least they started out that way.

An older lady, Olive, switched the topic suddenly. "We all know about false priests in the Catholic Church. What about Muslims?" she asked. She was worried about radicalized Canadian youths who put up a false front in society to promote Islam. "But the big question," she asked, "is how you tell extremists from moderate Muslims?"

Klassen put in, "The fruits of the spirit. I would look at their effects. Whether the way they practiced their religion destroyed or built something up." He continued, "Right now, I'd see ISIL as counterfeit Muslims, like a bad coin, because they are killing women and children in the Middle East, like it's the Middle Ages!"

Evans said, "Christians, themselves, had nothing to be proud of in the Middle Ages! They ransacked and plundered the Holy Land, all in the name of Christ. I don't think Jesus would have approved!"

Olive cut in, "Who's 'the good guy' in one century and who's 'the bad guy' in another?"

Pastor Greg finally cut in and steered the conversation back to Sunday's sermon about "render unto Caesar." He explained that the tribute the Jews paid to Rome was actually a tax in those days. He compared that to the tax the Muslims exacted from non-Muslims after the Qur'an was written over 600 years after Christ. The name of the tax was the "*jizyah*," imposed wherever Islam ruled on the Arabian Peninsula.

Pastor Greg finished with a decision, "Well, enough history!"

"I second that," said Evans.

Pastor Greg was the group's peace maker and official time-keeper. He was of average height and somewhat stout, as a sure sign that he liked his food, and maybe one too many desserts! He still had a boyishness about him for his 30 years, and his eyes twinkled behind his spectacled face. He always smiled, like he was friends with the world. He never wore a suit and tie, but preferred to wear jeans and T-shirts, or polo shirts, if he was going formal.

Pastor Greg cleared his throat, as he turned his head and smiled at everybody. They settled down for prayer. On the list was a concern for a father in the church, age 44, who had cancer, a senior who was in the hospital with a broken hip, a teacher stressed out in her job, and generally, the radicalized youths going over to fight for ISIL, both in Canada and around the world.

They took turns praying around the table. Klassen found that somehow he could never pray at these meetings. To him, it sounded like a grocery list and he had problems with that. He bowed with respect and hoped that the prayers would work.

Pastor Greg finished the session. That was the signal, "Coffee time!" The ladies brought in the coffee carafe, mugs and cookies. Could there be anything more Mennonite, a sort of hold-over from the old days, than the ladies clustering together and talking about grandkids on one side? The men talked about sports.

"Hey, how 'bout them Leafs?"

.....

Jorin Aslan did not need a prayer or a coffee. He was happy to be in Toronto, on that very evening at 7:00 p.m., already planning the best way to fulfill his secret mission.

Meanwhile, in another part of the world, his unit commander entertained devious plans of his own. Abdul Ali al-Sayed called in his second in command. What did he think of the idea? Was it feasible?

He wanted to use servants of Allah, Muslim brothers in Liberia and Sierra Leone, who were willing to contract the Ebola virus deliberately to spread the disease? They would die as martyrs for Islam and deserve Paradise! Maybe some of them might even be volunteers there, or "aid workers?"

Could ISIS somehow export Ebola as a weapon of mass destruction against the United States and Canada? Al-Sayed and his lieutenant brainstormed the possibilities.

Al-Sayed liked the idea of targeting Washington; but also, the cities of Montreal, Toronto and Vancouver, because Muslim militants always seemed to squeeze underneath the radar there in Canada. Al-Sayed was encouraged with the thought of spreading Ebola especially into the United States. He was happy to see how a hospital in Dallas had treated Thomas Eric Duncan.

"The first question they ask is if you've got insurance," said Al-Sayed. "Then they look at your color and if you can pay for it." Duncan had no coverage and no money. He was sent away from the hospital, allegedly without proper care.

Finally he was re-admitted after a two day delay; and died later on Wednesday, October 8, after having coughed on, who knows how many people? Texas Health Presbyterian Hospital issued a public statement that Duncan had been cared for by a team of over 50 doctors and given the most appropriate of care! They just didn't have the ZMapp drug available. Some people thought it was a well delivered public relations response.

Sayed laughed, "The system will work for us, if we find the right martyrs to go ahead with this scheme. They don't need to report to any hospital. Allah be praised for Ebola!"

CHAPTER 56

> "Let us remember: One book, one pen, one child, and one teacher can change the world."
>
> [MALALA YOUSAFZAI]

.....

NEWS @11:30 A.M.
THE NOBEL PEACE PRIZE
FRIDAY, OCTOBER 10, 2014

WALLY TURNED THE TV ON AT 11:30 A.M., FRIDAY OCTOBER 10, 2014. Malala Yousafzai, 17, was speaking, thanking the Nobel Peace Prize Committee for being named co-recipient of the prize along with Kailash Satyarthi, 60. Malala is the young Pakistani Muslim girl shot by the Taliban in 2012 for speaking out about the rights for girls to be educated. Kailash Satyarthi, a Hindu, has championed the rights of children since 1980, speaking out against child slavery in India. His approach is similar to Mahatma Ghandi in peaceful protests and demonstrations.

The joint honour came at the end of a violent week between the India and Pakistan border which left 17 people dead, with another 100 seriously injured, as these "estranged neighbours" traded mortar and small arms fire.

Wally just caught the last 10 minutes of Malala's speech, her mouth slanted slightly sideways from the assassination attempt when she was only 15. She wore a brightly green coloured sari with a hint of her black hair showing at the top of her head covering. She spoke from Birmingham, England where she now lives and goes to school, eventually to become a doctor... or a politician.

"She's a talkative little thing," thought Wally. He heard her say that she was thankful for her father "not clipping her wings." She believed girls should have an identity and equal rights to a boy. Tears came to Wally's eyes. "Yep, she'll become a politician... and a good one." Wally hoped in his heart that Malala would live long enough to do some good in her country, and not suffer the same fate as Benazir Bhutto, the former Prime Minister of Pakistan, who was assassinated in December 2007. "Heaven forbid," thought Wally, "that Malala's fate is yet sealed before the kid can do some good in the world." Some crazies could get at her again before she was even grown up.

Malala was in chemistry class when the announcement was made, that she would be sharing the prize with someone else who was working for children's rights.

Malala is the youngest person to receive the Nobel Peace Prize. She wants the Prime Ministers of India and of Pakistan to come to the presentation ceremony in Stockholm, Sweden, in December. She added that it is important to have peace between the two nations, that awarding the Peace Prize to a Pakistani Muslim and an Indian Hindu, "gives a message to people of love between Pakistan and India, and between different religions."

.....

On the same day, Friday October 10, 2014, it was announced by the Supreme Court of Canada that the 17 million dollar lawsuit against Iran was denied. The court said that Zahra Kazemi's death was a "tragedy" but family cannot sue a government like Iran due to Canada's State Immunity Act.

Kazemi was a Canadian journalist imprisoned in June 2003 in Tehran and allegedly raped, brutally beaten in prison where she died 18 days later. Her son, Stephen Hashemi, has been trying to sue Iranian officials for over a decade. Iran has repeatedly refused to return Kazemi's body to Canada.

CHAPTER 57

"If the freedom of speech is taken away, then dumb and silent, we may be led like sheep to the slaughter."

[GEORGE WASHINGTON]

.....

3:00 P.M. @TEA
KYIV EVENING CONCERT
FRIDAY, OCTOBER 10, 2014

TEA TIME CAME AT 3:00 P.M. THE JEWISH COUPLE DOWN the street, Ben and Raisa, had invited Wally over.

"We haven't seen you in ages," said the wife. She had some time on her hands now that

she'd published another novel. She was an author and a Shakespearean scholar.

"Why didn't you move to Collingwood?" asked Wally one day. "Jordan is such a teeny community with farmers and Mennonites. You'd be happier in a more artsy place."

The wife responded, "We wouldn't have met you, Wally."

They liked talking about movies, books, and ideas. Tea time consisted of decaf coffee and mini-doughnuts which in this case, tasted a bit rancid, courtesy of Wally, who had bought them for half-price from the grocery store.

"Actually, I only brought them to get rid of the evidence," quipped Wally. He explained that his wife wanted him to keep away from desserts. She wanted him to lose his dough-boy tummy. "I've lost ten pounds already, but I don't have an iron resolve! My spirit is willing, but the flesh is weak." He patted his tummy, sipping his decaf and munching a doughnut.

As usual, the talk centered around health issues and doctors' visits. Then it veered into the more interesting subjects of movies and books. Wally had seen an old black-and-white flick the other day, "Angels Over Broadway," a 1940 film starring Rita Hayworth, Douglas Fairbanks Jr., Thomas Mitchell, and John Qualen. Qualen's character had nothing to live for after he embezzled three thousand dollars from his boss. He wanted to jump off a bridge and end it all when a policeman passed by. So instead, he wandered aimlessly, and by chance, met a writer and a con man who got him into a high-stakes card game so he could win back the money and pay his boss back.

It seemed like a convoluted plot, but Wally enjoyed the shenanigans and the poetic monologues thrown out by Thomas Mitchell's character, the drunken playwright. It was a well-acted film and had great cinematography. Wally loved those black-and-white films!

Robert Ludlum's Jason Bourne series engrossed Wally's reading pleasure at the moment. He loved murder mysteries with fast-paced suspense and smart dialogue. Espionage and murder, that was the ticket!

When Wally had first met Ben and Raisa, he was reading the "Hardy Boys." He loved the adventures Frank and Joe got into, and how the adolescent duo solved mysteries, often with the inadvertent help of their buddy, Chet Morton. *The Tower Treasure* started the series off, and there were more than sixty books in all, great for a teenager's mentality... and great for Wally's too, since he considered himself, "young at heart." He enjoyed Franklin Dixon's novels immensely and didn't mind getting teased by his friends about reading "adolescent material."

He graduated to more "adult reading" since his new friends moved into the neighbourhood. Ben had read Stieg Larsson's "The Girl with the Dragon Tattoo" and David Guterson's "Snow Falling on Cedars." Ben basically pushed these thick novels upon Wally one day to take home. Wally said he'd try to return them before the turn of the century! It seemed like Wally's tastes in literature made a quantum leap in sophistication every time he had tea at Ben and Raisa's house. Wally soon digested the full trilogy by Stieg Larsson and added David Guterson's sad story about the Japanese immigrant family to the collection of more profound things he had read, [other than the Hardy Boys].

Wally also reveled in Robert Parker and Robert Ludlum novels through his wife's influence for "lighter" literary entertainment. Eric van Lustbader had been contracted to continue the Bourne series after Ludlum's death. Van Lustbader had produced several excellent stories, including "The Bourne Betrayal," Wally's current read.

Bourne was tracking down a kidnapped friend, CIA deputy director Martin Lindros, who had discovered suspicious shipments of uranium in Ethiopia. Wally was glad the book described a made-up story and not reality! Heaven forbid, if an underground organization ever did find a way to ship fissionable material and a nuclear device from Ethiopia to Nigeria into the hands of the crazed Islamists, "Boko Haram." Wally refused to entertain such a notion. He was content to live in Canada which was mostly a land of kindness, where the scary things in the books he was reading were just literary entertainment and imaginary happenings.

Wally's friends were very artistic and accomplished. Ben was a composer of music, and both, Raisa and their middle-aged son, Asher, were authors. Asher was finishing his first novel. Wally often wondered, considering all their common interests, whether he would have had a similar friendly relationship had a Muslim family moved down the street.

During tea time, the husband shifted the conversation away from books. He had written a piece of music in which the ending lyric went, "So be it." The big question was: Where should the emphasis go? On the first word, on the second, or on the third? The emphasis had to dove-tail with the importance of the note in the music.

The conductor, whose orchestra was rehearsing Ben's piece, felt the beat should fall on the word "be," but Ben [the composer, after all] preferred the stress be put on the word "so." Wally couldn't believe the verbal energy which was consumed in the differing viewpoints about where the beat should fall in these three simple words! What a passionate discussion on "So be it!" Wally wondered what emphasis God put in His words when He created the Universe?

Asher and Wally took the initiative, voicing their opinion that *any* of the words could warrant the stress of the beat. It depended upon the context, whether it was sung in anger or in submission. Ben, as composer of the piece, smiled agreeably over their stance.

Wally enjoyed the lengthy repartée and the passion expressed in arguing Ben's case over the conductor's. Wally appreciated the fact that the three little words were hugely and personally important to Ben. It was a question of integrity and ownership. Like Wally rewriting and polishing his own novel over and over again, with little changes, to achieve the correct verbal emphasis and meaning of each sentence.

Finally, Wally said out of the blue, "Malala got the Peace Prize!" They all agreed that she deserved it, though none of them, not even Wally, could remember the name of her co-recipient, except that he was Indian, a Hindu, and much older than she.

"I guess you have to be the youngest recipient ever, and shot in the head, so people will remember your name," Wally said. He had been impressed by her speech that morning on TV.

He figured it was a cowardly and barbaric thing that the Taliban had done to this child. "What makes them think the way they think?"

Ben observed that a psychological study claimed that a person's brain had already made a decision before he or she ever acted. "It's already in their synapses," he said. "The decision is there! Where does that come from?"

Oh-oh, Wally thought. Here we go again with topics out of my depth, light years away from the "Hardy Boys!"

He jumped into the verbal fray anyway. He proposed that actions, even spontaneous ones, came from what he called a "container of values, ready-made," built up from birth through upbringing and experience. It was culture, religion, or society at large which created a person's predispositions.

"I think that's where our morals come from," said Wally.

Ben and Raisa tried to pin decision-making onto something more technical, having to do with the brain's chemical processes and nothing to do with any "spiritual guidance from a moral compass."

"When you do something, the brain has already decided to do it before the brain is even aware it made that decision," said Ben. Wally tried to wrap his brain around that one and came away dizzy. They were getting into a purely intellectual exercise of words... lots of fun and no answers!

Where else could Wally get his fill of philosophy and things that didn't get the dishes done at home! He saw that it was 4:30; and time to make supper for his wife. She always came home late from school, expecting a meal ready after a hard day teaching kids. Wally thanked Ben and Raisa for the "tea time" and told Asher, "We'll have to talk about how to write a novel, sometime."

"Just stop when you get to 80,000 words," said Asher. Wally had no idea what that number would feel like in words. He would just keep on writing until he felt it was done.

.....

Wally and his wife took in a concert that Friday evening by the "Kyiv Symphony Orchestra and Chorus." It was part of a Canada and Ukraine Friendship Tour, held at the Glenridge Bible Church in St. Catharines. The flute player was excellent and the orchestra, as a whole, sounded professional. The choir did a marvelous job, making the rafters ring. Handel, Bach, Tchaikovsky and Rimsky-Korsakov were all represented in the repertoire, as was Ukrainian folk music by composers like Lysenko.

Wally wished there were more of a concert though and fewer words from the podium. He appreciated one point which was mentioned. The orchestra was headed back to a cold winter in Kyiv where the Russians might turn the gas lines off again which fed Ukrainian furnaces.

Wes Janzen, the conductor, remembered directing the group when they all wore coats in the rehearsal hall last winter; and he could not see the faces of his choir, because of the mist coming from their cold breaths when they exhaled. The conductor confessed that people would die that winter if the Russians cut off fuel lines into Ukraine.

Wally slipped $20 into the collection plate. It was only last March 2014 when Russia annexed the Crimean Peninsula and now Eastern Ukraine was threatened with incorporation as well. Wally wondered how the Kyiv Symphony and Chorus would fare through the coming winter, once they returned to their homeland? He wondered how warm Putin himself would be this winter?

> Man is the only Patriot. He sets himself apart in his own country, under his own flag, and sneers at the other nations, and keeps multitudinous uniformed assassins on hand at heavy expense to grab slices of other people's countries, and keep them from grabbing slices of his. And in the intervals between campaigns he washes the blood off his hands and works for "the universal brotherhood of man"- with his mouth.
>
> ["THE LOWEST ANIMAL," MARKTWAIN]

A week after the concert, the President of Russia, Vladimir Putin and the President of Ukraine, Petro Poroshenko, came to an agreement, "within parameters," that gas would not be cut off to Ukraine in the winter. Upon hearing the good news, Wally thought, "My, what a deft move by Putin. It makes him look like a real good guy."

The next day, Saturday, October 11, 2014 Kobane was burning, as U.S. airstrikes created huge clouds of haze and smoke over the city, where ISIS strongholds were supposedly located.

CHAPTER 58

Should I, after tea and cakes and ices,

Have the strength to force the moment to its crisis?

[*Love Song of J. Alfred Prufrock* - T.S. ELIOT 1920]

.....

WILLIAMS FRESH CAFÉ
SUNDAY, OCTOBER 12, 2014

SPENCER AND KLASSEN HAD ESTABLISHED A FRIENDSHIP during and after the trial of the Ibrahims. They occasionally met for a coffee at *Williams Fresh Cafe* just opposite McMaster University. Spencer ordered his coffee, black. A different waitress served them. Klassen ordered his coffee with cream and his usual slice of pie [whatever was on the menu].

"What happened to that pretty young thing who gave you her phone number?" asked Klassen.

"Oh nice girl. But she left to go to university out west... She wanted an experience with an older man."

"I suppose you were that experience? And willing to accommodate?"

"Yeah. But I'm getting too old for this kind of thing. I'm 32, for Chrissakes, and I don't do the bar scene any more. I'm tired of shooting out lines just to pick up young girls. I can't quite explain it, but something is happening inside of me that wants something, well, more permanent."

Klassen took that comment with a grain of salt... but maybe there was some truth in it. Klassen noticed that Spencer wasn't eyeing the waitresses like he used to. Maybe he was sick.

"So what's changed?"

"You remember Abqurah? Well, I've asked her out a couple of times. She said, Yes."

"Come on!" objected Klassen. "She's half your age!"

"Not quite. I'm 32 and she's 21. I like young women, but it's somehow different with her."

"Spencer, it's not just the age difference. There's culture and religion. And besides, you were professionally involved with her previously, as a cop!"

"All that swept aside... I really like her! I feel comfortable with her and we can really talk. Besides her parents are in jail, and she's trying to make something of herself."

Klassen thought a moment. "Okay, I see how you are attracted to her. You may even love her. But she's still a Muslim and Heavens, you're an Atheist."

"I never said I was... well, completely. You were right, I'm searching for something bigger than myself for inner peace. This damn world doesn't offer it to me."

Klassen chewed a piece of pie and sipped his coffee. Coffee helped him think, chewing did too. He finally said, "Well, good luck on this one. We each choose our own road in the end. I hope you're on a good one with this kid. Just don't hurt her." Spencer's eyes watered a bit. He remained quiet. "Not for the world," he thought. "Not for the world!"

CHAPTER 59

"There's some evil in the best of us and some good in the worst of us."

[DR. MARTIN LUTHER KING JR.]

. . . . .

JORIN AND UMAR

TUESDAY, OCTOBER 7, 2014

UMAR WAHIDI BROUGHT JORIN HOME. HE WAS 26 YEARS OLD and lived in a downtown, third floor apartment, by himself. He was of medium height, about half a foot shorter than Jorin, but stockier. His black hair was neatly trimmed, and so were his black beard and mustache. He had dark circles around his eyes though and a hooked nose. His eyes blinked a lot which made him look suspicious. If it were not for his blue dress shirt, a polka dot tie and black blazer, one could easily think he was a Muslim terrorist.

Umar spent a lot of time on Facebook and Twitter. Somehow through social media, secret messages always got through to him from overseas.

They discussed blowing the top off the CN Tower but high explosives were impossible to sneak in with 4 Sentinel II machines or explosives trace-detection portals at the entrance. The machines could detect anything from plastic explosives to drugs, sniffing air particles that come off people, like a mechanical sniffer hound which smelled you from head to toe. They decided that a martyr flying a plane into the Tower would make more sense, just like 9/11 in New York. Jorin and Umar relished the symbolism of blowing the top off the CN Tower. "Ah, that would be a sight to see," said Umar. The plan involved too many complicated details though. Neither of them had a pilot's license, so flying a plane into the tower was out of the question. Hijacking a plane seemed too risky. However, the thought of knocking the top off the CN Tower gave them immense imaginary pleasure.

Jorin finally decided, "Subway sabotage is what we must do! Just carry a backpack of explosives onto one of the trains at rush hour, or just hide the backpack behind a seat somewhere at the Union Station. Timed, of course, to go off after we leave the scene."

They could phone the police station afterwards, using an electronically altered voice. "Which group should claim responsibility?" asked Jorin. "How about, 'C-JAH', Canada Jihad At Home!" Both of them broke out in laughter. They enjoyed finding an acronym with a ring to it! Jorin sobered up. He had second thoughts about the acronym. "Hmmm. Sounds like a radio station!" They both laughed again.

Jorin and Umar discussed the 2006 plot which was foiled by an undercover agent. The group known as the Toronto 18 was arrested, and charged with terrorism, and intent to kill or maim. They wanted to detonate bombs on three consecutive days to stretch out the fear factor in Canadian society. Targets included CSIS headquarters in Toronto and a military base off the QEW.

"There were too many people involved," said Jorin. "The fewer, the better." That's why he liked his own plan for sabotaging the subway, involving only Umar and himself.

"Agreed. A backpack timed with explosives," said Umar.

"We will leave it, *forgotten*, under a seat."

"Friday just after work hours would be a choice time. We will not only kill the most numbers but spoil the weekend for all of Toronto."

"Picking a Friday could be doing them a favor! They'll at least have something to talk about in the bars and the coffee shops around the city. Nobody will be bored... unless they watch the Leaf game!" Jorin and Umar rolled over in laughter.

.....

TTC Report published in 2006:

"In light of the global experience with terrorist bombings on trains and, most recently, the arrest of numerous GTA residents on terrorism charges on June 2, 2006, further consideration must be given to improve public safety through changes in design of the new subway trains. This action is consistent with TTC Safety Policy."

Studies, reports and recommendations came out since the Toronto 18 plots made the headlines in 2006, all to ensure the safety and security of passengers using the services of the Toronto Transit Commission.

Most people who read updates online about the TTC felt that the reports sounded like public relations gobbledygook, talking about extra cameras, more phones and more "special constables" on patrol. The special constables never worked out. They weren't real policemen anyway; and they weren't really trained.

It always came down to one question, who would pay for all this? The city got caught in all kinds of Public Relations banter... and no real improvements were made!

Jorin and Umar, in the meantime, contacted their sources, and got the plastic explosives they needed and the timer. It took a couple of days to make it all happen. They carried their "things" up the stairs in grocery bags, just two bachelors bringing home provisions for the fridge. The old building didn't have an elevator, so climbing the stairs was no big deal for healthy young men.

Mrs. Nussbaum, a 70 year old lady, lived on the second floor, just below what she called, "her two bachelors." She'd hear them murmur, in a strange dialect, at night through the ceiling. Even English words were just unintelligible human noise to her. Actually, it lulled her to sleep.

Mrs. Nussbaum carried her own grocery bags up the stairs every Saturday afternoon, which were filled with actual groceries. For her it was no easy task, so she put her bags down on the steps, half-way up to her apartment. She'd take a spell to breath, and then pick up the bags again for the rest of her trip. Sometimes she pictured Mount Everest.

Jorin and Umar were empty handed that Saturday afternoon, and met the old lady at the landing, laden with her grocery bags. Jorin nodded at her and walked on by. Umar stayed behind, and offered, "Here, let me get those bags for you!" Mrs. Nussbaum smiled and loaded Umar's arms up with her two heavy bags. Jorin, embarrassed turned back, and took one of the bags. They walked Mrs. Nussbaum to her apartment, and deposited the bags on her kitchen counter.

Jorin turned to go, already with his foot in the hallway. Mrs. Nussbaum took Umar's arm and offered him a $10 bill. "Five dollars for each of you," she said. "That was so kind." Umar refused the money with a smile. "It's something I would have done for my mother... for free!" he said.

When they were inside their own third floor apartment, Jorin berated Umar for helping the old lady. "She is a Jew! In the name of Allah, why did you offer to help her?"

"Jew or not. She is old." said Umar. "It was no big deal." He turned away from Jorin. End of the discussion.

They turned to their own grocery bags, unloaded and sorted their "things." They put their bomb together in their little apartment, just the two of them. Once done, they celebrated by a treat out, coffee and cakes at Starbucks on Saturday night. They sipped their lattés and gloated, while Canadians were busy in the bars and clubs, getting drunk and trying to pick up women, or maybe watching the Leafs lose another game.

CHAPTER 60

I'm guided by the beauty of our weapons
First we take Manhattan,
then we take Berlin

[LYRICS LEONARD COHEN 1987,
SINGER JENNIFER WARNES]

. . . . .

UNION STATION @4:30 P.M.
WEDNESDAY, OCTOBER 15, 2014

SUNDAY PASSED AND THEN MONDAY. JORIN GOT ANTSY. HE did not have the patience to wait out another couple of days to Friday. By mid-week, he said, "Let's head out!" It was a Wednesday afternoon, already October 15th. He figured that the mid-week commute was good enough to make their point. He shouldered the backpack. Umar followed behind. They got to Union Station at about 4 p.m. Things looked crowded, and by 5 p.m. there would be the usual rush to get home.

"Where shall we leave the bag?" asked Umar in the Dari dialect. "It is set to explode at a 5 p.m."

A dark complexioned woman nearby caught the question. She had given up wearing her hijab two years ago, not wanting to stand out from among other Canadians. Sabeen was a Syrian refugee and understood the foreign conversation perfectly. She kept her eye on the two young men plotting to kill and maim commuters at 5 o'clock. "What shall I do?" she asked herself. She had grown to love Canada, a somewhat naive and benign country, her adopted country. Again she asked herself, "What shall I do?"

"Stop thief!" she yelled. Pointing at the two young men, "They stole my backpack!" Jorin and Umar saw the policeman shoulder his way through the crowd. They were not going to stick around and be caught with explosives red-handed. They dropped the bag and ran, soon lost in the street.

Sabeen explained to the police officer what she had overheard, and that the bag contained explosives which were timed for 5 o'clock precisely. It was 4:50 p.m. There was no time for a bomb squad. The police officer saw the men's washroom nearby. He cleared everybody out, and left the bag in a stall, thinking that might smother some of the explosion. He warned people to keep clear of the washroom and get out of the station. He wouldn't want to be sitting on the can right then!

The sound was nothing he'd ever heard before. The explosion blew the door off its hinges and reverberated throughout the Union Station. Backup was called and Sabeen was taken away in a cruiser to be questioned.

.....

"Now then," said Sergeant Riley. "We're they your co-conspirators?" Sabeen was not impressed. She demanded a lawyer. "Try to help and look what happens, get profiled because of the colour of my skin!"

Jorin and Umar came back into the apartment breathless. They would have to wait to see if anybody was killed or hurt in the explosion before they claimed credit. An initial report came over the TV that same evening at 6 p.m.

"Explosion at Union Station. No one was injured. Police say that it was probably a prank concocted by a local gang. Damage was restricted to one washroom. 'What's this country coming to?' asked one witness."

Sergeant Riley went back to check out the scene. He interviewed the young police officer who had enough presence of mind to throw the suspicious bag behind a stall in the washroom.

"So, Officer Dawson, what can you tell me about this incident?"

"The gal overheard two suspicious looking men, probably Afghans, plan to leave a bag inside the station or maybe the subway to blow things up at 5 p.m. She understood their dialect... and that was just plain luck for us."

"Yeah, it was. Do you think she had anything to do with it?"

"No. Otherwise, she wouldn't have been the whistle blower."

"What a bloody mess," said Dawson as they assessed the damage in the washroom.

"Would have been more than a bloody mess, if somebody was sitting on the toilet at the time!" quipped Riley. At least, he thought *he* was funny.

Riley told Dawson, "You'll have to come down to the station so we can get a full report on this incident." He explained, "The TTC lawyers want to get the station back to running smoothly as soon as possible. They don't want to upset TTC commuters by a mere blow-up of a washroom!"

CHAPTER 61

There will be time, there will be time

To prepare a face to meet the
faces that you meet;

There will be time to murder and create,

[*Love Song of J. Alfred Prufrock* - T.S. ELIOT, 1920]

. . . . .

THURSDAY, OCTOBER 16, 2014
AMY ST. CLAIR, VIOLINIST

AAMIR FELT ANGRY THAT THEIR PERFECT PLAN WAS SPOILED by stupid chance. He and Umar argued whether it was in Allah's will or not. Jorin told Umar that they had to take a break and mentally regroup. He said he had things to do in Waterloo. He would be back within a week.

Aamir rented a car. He drove towards Kitchener, got off on Hwy 6 at Morriston. He parked at a Tim Horton's to buy a coffee; and while he was at it, a Boston Cream doughnut. He figured he was half way to Waterloo.

A regular sat with a bunch of his buddies, "Lots of crazy stuff happening in the Middle East... and in Africa." Aamir sipped his coffee quietly. "Over 4,000 people died of that Ebola crisis. You'd think modern medicine could cure that." "Not so easy," said his pal. They were busy chewing their doughnuts. "They don't have modern medicine in Africa. Nobody washes their hands there."

Aamir thought, "Or here, for that matter! Look at the washroom!"

"Hey, are you from the Middle East?" asked an old man, addressing Aamir. "What do you think about all this ISIS stuff?"

"I think they should kill Assad and take over the Middle East," retorted Aamir.

The old gent didn't expect this answer. He objected, "Hey, that doesn't sound very Canadian!"

"What is Canadian?" questioned Aamir. "Canada was taken away from your aboriginal Indians."

"Yeah, but we made something of this country."

"What did you make? A country of cream puffs, lightweight cowards who had to have a Tim Horton's on the Front in Afghanistan when they went to war."

"Oh yeah, then what are you doing in here?"

Aamir felt like grabbing the old fart by the collar. He prayed, "Allah give me strength." He got up, stepped out the door, and threw the uneaten doughnut into the trash can. He got into his car, taking the coffee with him. He figured coffee would calm him down.

Before he knew it, he passed the Schneider's Billboard off the 401 Highway. Time was 10:45 a.m. Temperature, 20 Celsius, a good temperature for a sunny autumn day!

He got to the Waterloo Motor Inn by noon. He signed the registry, "Ibrahim Lincoln." The desk clerk didn't even look at it; probably wouldn't even get the pun if he glanced at the page. Free Wi-Fi. That was good! He had his iPad. He ate in the restaurant. Ordered a French Stuffed Chicken Supreme, stuffed with goat cheese, served with sweet potato mash, covered with "pommery mustard cream." He sipped another coffee, black.

Satisfied, he retired to his suite. He thumbed through the white pages and found "A. St. Clair" on 35 ½ Hazel Street in Waterloo. Telephone 519-0000.

Aamir had his bag of tricks with him. He put on a fake mustache, and headed for Wilfred Laurier University, taking the bus instead of his car. He tracked down Amy St. Clair, M.A., Teaching Assistant in the Music Department.

The registrar informed him that there was a free concert given by her the next day in the Theatre Auditorium. The program: Amy St. Clair on Violin, playing a selection from Felix Mendelssohn's Concerto Opus 64, Allegro Molto Appassionato. Accompanied by Marcus Scholtz on piano.

"A Jewish piece," thought Aamir. "How choice. They've always had a monopoly on the violin."

He would sit at the top of the Theatre, back row, and see his old girlfriend play. Actually when he heard the performance, he was surprised at how far she had progressed… and how he hated her for it. He could not picture her subservient to any man, as it should be! He knew what he must do. He snuck out of the Theatre before the performance finished, and headed to the bus stop, back to his hotel room. How would he do this?

Meanwhile, Amy finished her performance with a light number, Percy Grainger's arrangement of "English Country Garden." The audience was tickled pink.

Aamir phoned her that night, just to hear her voice... even the brief, Hello, Hello? He hung up. Amy was disturbed by the silent call but pushed it out of her mind.

CHAPTER 62

Almost all our heroes have all of the following five traits: education, compassion, willingness to share dreams, inspiration, sacrifice. By following these five steps, you will prepare yourself to take action and to do the best you can when the time is right.

[HTTP://MORALHEROES.ORG/
HOW-TO-BECOME-A-HERO]

.....

THE STALKER
THE RESCUER
FRIDAY, OCTOBER 17, 2014

AAMIR STALKED HER THE NEXT DAY, AND FOUND OUT which car she drove. That night, he waited for her in the parking lot. She put in late hours at the school, often until 11:00 p.m. Maybe he would talk to her, knock her about a little. He was ready, with his fake mustache but real switchblade. He wouldn't need the Sig Sauer P229, he'd obtained on the streets in Toronto, 9mm, 13 round capacity. Compact and great for concealment. Aamir relished the thought of using the knife instead.

He approached her, blade out.

"Aamir?"

"Yes, there is nobody who will hear or see you in the parking lot this late at night. Aren't you the dedicated one to put in such late hours?" "Start the car!" he commanded.

"You're a murderer, you killed your sister."

"It was Allah's will. An honour killing."

"What honour? She was a woman."

"Women need to stay home and be wives."

"Not with men like you. You're insane." She gulped, "Are you going to kill me?"

"Yes," said Aamir.

"Please, please don't do it."

"Impossible!" he hissed back.

He edged closer to the car, the door open. He took out her violin and smashed it to the ground. The first gesture of revenge. He was going to force Amy to drive to the far corner of the lot where he would make his second gesture of revenge. He was going to force himself on her for old time's sake, one last time.

Just then a Campus Cop pulled up in his vehicle. He got out and confronted Aamir. He was just as tall as Aamir, a good 6' 2." His black hair was tied in a tight ponytail at the back. They let campus cops do that? His eyebrows angled sharply over piercing eyes. His mouth was straight and serious. He meant business. The cop didn't go for his gun.

"Looks like you've got a knife there buddy. You're under arrest."

That was a really lame thing to say, thought Aamir.

"Are you a hero? Come and take it from me," he challenged.

"Okay," said the cop, "I'm a hero." But he didn't make the first move.

Aamir struck out at him. The cop made a deft move, and knocked the knife from Aamir's hand. Aamir grabbed Amy and threw her into the cop. He jumped into the car, and screeched out of the parking lot, not looking back. The cop didn't pursue. He made sure Amy was okay.

"You shouldn't have let him get away. He's a murderer, killed his sister."

"Wouldn't have been a safe police chase. I'm calling it in. What did you say his name was?"

"Aamir Ibrahim."

"That honour killing from last year? Really publicized?"

"That's the one."

"We'd better call the Hamilton Police Department too, and let them know this guy is back."

"I'm surprised you faced him unarmed!"

"I've got a black belt in Tae Kwon Do. I don't go looking for trouble, unless trouble comes looking for me." Amy could see Steven Seagal saying that very thing.

She stared down at her open violin case. The neck of the violin was broken, a clean break at the neck. Amy couldn't help but think that her own neck could have been like that, cut by Aamir's vengeful stroke of a knife.

Her attention reverted to her smashed instrument. "Oh, my poor, poor violin," she moaned.

"Lady," said the cop, "it's only a violin. Your life's gotta be more important than that. Consider yourself lucky." Amy wasn't so sure. Steven Seagal didn't quite understand, "My violin is like my lover, it is my way of singing to the world." She wondered if her instrument could be repaired... and how much it would cost. Thank God, she had a job!

They put her broken violin carefully back in the case and then placed it in the back of the Campus Police cruiser. The cop said, "Let's get you to the police station and report this. My name's Jerome Lavigne by the way. That's French."

On the way, Amy found out that Jerome took this night job to help pay for his tuition. He was enrolled in the Kinesiology Program at the University of Waterloo during the day time, working as a Campus cop at Wilfred Laurier at nights. He liked combining his interest in sports, and science, and hoped to make a career out of rehabilitating injured professional athletes someday. He planned to finish his degree this semester.

.....

Meanwhile, Aamir signed out of the Waterloo Motor Inn before midnight Friday night. "Was everything satisfactory?" asked the desk clerk.

"I have an appointment in another city this morning," Aamir said, paying for two nights with cash.

He headed for Hamilton in the wee hours of Saturday morning. His next stop was his sister and maybe another honour killing! Especially because of the deal she had made against her parents with the Crown Attorney's Office. He looked for a hotel on the escarpment, close to Mohawk College. He knew his younger sister always wanted to enroll in social work and be a "do-gooder." Her favourite motto at home used to be, "Am I trying to *do good* or make myself look *good*?" How he hated that saying!

CHAPTER 63

If I could reach the stars, pull
one down for you

Shine it on my heart, so you
could see the truth

That this love I have inside, is
everything it seems

But for now I find, it's only in my dreams

[ERIC CLAPTON 1996]

.....

THE HUNK AND THE KNOCK-OUT

SATURDAY, OCTOBER 18, 2014

AMY ST. CLAIR KNEW WHAT SHE WANTED. SHE ASKED Jerome Lavigne out for a coffee at Starbucks. He said it was too rich for his pocket-book, so they arranged to meet at Tim Horton's instead, off King Street. They were going Dutch treat.

There wasn't anything electric between them, but they found themselves comfortable with each other. Amy was intrigued by this strong man's skill in the martial arts, and in his ambition to become a sports therapist. He wasn't just a hunk, though he was a hunk. He, on the other hand, thought Amy was a knock-out with an unusual musical talent. She was already a "semi-professor" on the Laurier campus. He wondered what she was doing with him?

They ordered their coffees, each a double double. No doughnuts. "Something in common," Amy thought. She wondered amusingly, "A good foundation to build a relationship on?"

"You saved my life." she said. "I feel like I can't just say, thanks, and let you go. At first, I thought it was Steven Seagal who saved me."

Jerome put on his best Jack Webb impersonation: "Just doing my duty, Maam." He was hooked on old crime shows. The reference went above Amy's head, but she thought it was funny. "Something likeable about this one," she thought. He confessed he didn't watch Steven Seagal movies, or Sylvester Stallone, or Arnold whathisname.

Amy got the conversation back on a serious track. "I've kept myself from going out for a long time. Aamir was a difficult boyfriend. I fell for his good looks when we first met, but I didn't know what he was really like. He became too possessive and too crazy. I got scared and wanted out of the relationship. When we broke up, I breathed fresh air. That's when I came to this university. It's been just me and my violin ever since."

Somehow, the tune of "Me and My Shadow" popped into Jerome's head. He almost whistled it. Amy told him she was performing another noon concert that Wednesday.

Would he come? He glanced at his cell phone scheduler and beamed, "Yep, schedule's free. I would love to come!"

Amy found there was more to Jerome than meets the eye. Once you got him talking, he opened up like a flower, and chatted enthusiastically about music, books and world affairs. He asked Amy if she had ever heard Jazz Violin played by the likes of Stephane Grapelli?

"No?" asked Jerome. "I've got a great selection of CDs at my place!" Sounded like a pick up line. "Come and see my etchings sometime?" Amy felt safe though. She'd have to come up and listen to his CDs... sometime!

They stared at each other and smiled. Sipped their coffees. They switched to books, sounding each other out. Amy had her favourite book, *Atlas Shrugged*, by Ayn Rand, in her purse. She pulled it out, and flipped it to a dog-eared page. She wondered about Jerome's opinion of strong women. He said he liked them. He'd read *The Female Eunuch,* by Germaine Greer, and he agreed with her, that men had dominated everything too much, too long. He agreed that it took a woman twice the work to get the same respect on the job.

Amy finally got her finger on the quote in *Atlas Shrugged*. She explained the context in the book: too much government, too many bailouts! The economy was broke. They needed somebody to jump start the nation's economy before it slid into another Great Depression.

.....

Galt: "You want me to be Economic Dictator?"

Mr. Thompson: "*Yes!*"

"And you'll obey any order I give?"

"*Implicitly!*"

"Then start by abolishing all income taxes."

"Oh no!" screamed Mr. Thompson, leaping to his feet. *"We couldn't do that . . . How would we pay government employees?"*

"Fire your government employees."

"Oh, no!"

. . . . .

Jerome agreed, "Yep, that's the way I see it. Too many big shots controlling too many things, and nobody willing to give up their power."

They both sidled up to the counter and paid for a refill, double double again. A common bond! Jerome said he was reading Tavis Smiley's new book, Death of A King, the real story of Martin Luther King Junior, his last year of life. Jerome said he got interested in the book, after watching a TV interview of Tavis Smiley by the Well Read show host, Terry Tazioli.

"Smiley wasn't happy," said Jerome, "that after almost 50 years, since King's death, those triple threats he fought against were still there."

"What triple threats," asked Amy.

"Racism, poverty and militarism!" pointed out Jerome.

He explained that King was against the Viet Nam War because of the billions of dollars America had spent overseas in a losing war, when the country had all its own problems at home. King saw the triple threat of racism, poverty and militarism in America as the very threats which could destroy America's democracy today!

"Half the United States is in poverty," pointed out Smiley. Jerome, watching the show, just shook his head when he heard the statistic.

"Hmm." thought Amy. "A guy who knows social issues... and cares! The guy has possibilities." Amy liked that they had hit if off right away. They respected each other's tastes in music, though not the same music, books, though not the same books, and world

affairs, well those were the same issues the world over. "It's a good start for a relationship," thought Amy. "Besides, he's not bad looking."

She thanked him again for saving her from Aamir. "Lucky you were there!"

"Maybe it wasn't luck, maybe it was meant to be!"

Amy wondered how Aamir ever got the way he was? They both agreed that all religions, any religion could be twisted into extremes, into things they were never meant to be. "Islam is so weighted in favour of the men," she said, "it's feet are stuck in the Middle Ages."

"That's an attraction for all these macho guys going overseas to fight for ISIS," commented Jerome. He smiled sheepishly, "I must admit having four wives might be an attraction for me too... hmm, maybe half a dozen?"

She frowned.

He brightened, "Sorry. Just a whim. I wouldn't really do it."

She challenged, "You'd better not! If I were the first wife, I'd lay down the law about that!"

They both laughed. They agreed that if women won rights in the Islamic world, about equality, education, jobs, owning property, bank accounts, and not wearing burkhas... well, just the plain right to personhood, the change would have to come from women themselves. He said that women needed to rebel against wearing burkhas... and not support such a terrible tradition.

"It won't do," said Jerome, "if a female Muslim approached the Driving Bureau in a burkha, and insisted on her religious freedom to have her picture taken in the burkha for her driver's license."

"I don't know if the burkha has ever been an issue; but I think, the hijab is allowed as long as the face is visible," offered Amy.

Jerome related a funny incident he'd run across on the internet. An Austrian guy, Niko Alm, applied for a driver's license wearing a spaghetti strainer on his head. He insisted it was a religious headgear. He was an atheist, who said that the sieve was a requirement of his religion, pastafarianism.

This got Amy chuckling. "You can't be serious?"

"Oh, he was! He claimed he belonged to a light-hearted faith, the pastafarians, who worship at the Church of the Flying Spaghetti Monster. He insisted on his rights!"

"Did he get them?"

"Eventually yes. The Austrian authorities insisted that he get a doctor's certificate first, that he was psychologically fit to drive. It took three years of red-tape; but at the end, he was issued his license with his photo wearing his official sieve as a religious headgear."

"Making ridiculous points with ridiculous religious rights," Amy said. "It can undercut common sense. Are Muslims going to respect the rights of our own traditions, if they ever take over?" she questioned.

It sounded like something which couldn't be answered with just another cup of coffee, so Jerome left it alone. They smiled at each other. Were they bonding? They were so unlike and yet the same!

She liked the fact that he wasn't a macho guy, though he had a nice build. What was more important was his personality. She felt that he was not someone who had to be right all the time... and when she talked, he listened to her!

"Yep, the guy has possibilities!" she thought. When they left Timmy's, she intended to walk back into the university campus. He would catch the shuttle bus at University Avenue for a Kinesiology seminar at the U.of.W.

"Don't forget about my noon concert on Wednesday!" she called back to him.

"I'll be there," he assured her. "This could be the beginning of a beautiful friendship!" [Casablanca film, 1942]

CHAPTER 64

I don't want clever conversation
I never want to work that hard
I just want someone that I can talk to
I want you just the way you are

[BILLY JOEL SONG - 1977]

.....

SPENCER AND ABQURAH
THE NEXT LEVEL
SATURDAY, OCTOBER 18, 2014

SPENCER CONSIDERED HIMSELF A LUCKY MAN. MAYBE blessed was more like it. It wasn't exactly a spring and winter match, more like spring and mid-summer! Spencer ignored the 11 year age difference, the culture and the religion. Everything, except love! He just had her on his mind all the time. He felt love, affection, passion and respect, all rolled in one.

Spencer picked her up after an evening class, and drove her home to her apartment. They talked about plans, his career and her schooling.

"You know, schooling for a girl is frowned upon in my culture. Let alone having a white boyfriend." There was something in the back of her mind which somehow wanted to finish by saying, infidel. She tried to deprogram herself, to shake off the past, and wrap herself in a new religion, like a new coat.

Detective Klassen had kept in touch with her, knowing how sad her family situation was. He wanted to help her, so he told Abqurah about his church's Mennonite pastor who could explain Christianity to her, if she really wanted to know. Klassen gave her a little preliminary background about the Mennonite culture and religion. Mennonites also had a history of being persecuted, so they understood what intolerance meant. They broke away from the Catholic Church in the 16th century because they believed in adult baptism, not infant baptism. That's why they were called Anabaptists. They were hunted down for their beliefs and killed by other so-called Christians.

Klassen said, "I guess Muslims have similar problems, like between the Sunnis and the Shiites. My pastor is a good guy though, and knows a lot about Christians... and Muslims too."

Spencer listened attentively to Abqurah, as she recounted how Klassen prompted her to explore Christianity. Spencer found it funny; maybe ironic was the better word for it, for their being in her apartment talking about life, love and religion. Spencer told her that he'd like to stay with her that night.

"I have to have a ring on my finger first," she said, with a glint of determination in her eye.

Spencer smiled and kissed her goodnight.

They went shopping the next Saturday, at the Limeridge Mall. She picked a less expensive ring at *Ben Moss Jewelry*, a tiny ring, rose gold, with swirls, and a teeny diamond in it, about $250 worth. It was Zirconium, which didn't mean anything to Spencer, except that it was within his budget, and he liked the little ring. Looked nice on her finger.

"It's not the price!" she said. "But it is what I want! It's elegant… and I love it… and I love you," she said.

He paid cash. He beamed at her, and gave her a hug right in the store. "We'll size it to a 7," said the clerk, "by this afternoon, say 2 o'clock?"

They were there in plenty of time to pick up the ring. Spencer wanted Abqurah to wear it, before they met Detective Klassen for coffee at *Williams Fresh Café*, later that Saturday afternoon. Spencer was pleased as punch to show Abqurah off to Klassen. He wanted Klassen to see her hand with the new ring on it. She'd made an honest man out of him. "Now that's a strange concept," thought Spencer, "marriage, Christianity and me!"

. . . . .

The irony did not escape Klassen as the two sat down just after 3:00 p.m. They ordered their coffees and Klassen was pleased that they all ordered a slice of pie. Klassen didn't want the other two to watch him demolish a slice by himself.

Their talk meandered comfortably from this to that. Spencer and Abqurah talked about jobs and school and wedding plans. Klassen basically listened. He also had news about Wally, the photographer, who had discovered Hazirah's body. Wally, himself, was in therapy to deal with his nightmares; and to face the fact, that murder can happen within a very civilized society.

Klassen told Spencer and Abqurah that he and Wally occasionally met at Timmy's in Jordan for coffee. Klassen added good-naturedly, "Maybe I'm having too much coffee... and too many doughnuts and pies!" He slipped a forkful of pie into his mouth with a merry twinkle in his eye.

Spencer's cell phone rang. "No rest for the wicked," he commented. He flipped the phone open and then with a quick decision said, "Excuse me. Police business!" He left the table to talk outside in the parking lot. He came back in a few minutes, all serious and all "Detective" now.

"I've got bad news," he said, "Aamir's been spotted in Waterloo, and he might be heading back this way." Abqurah looked stunned. She had hoped this part of her life was over. "How could this be? I thought he was somewhere in Syria or Iraq with ISIS. He actually got back into this country?"

"Yes, with a different passport and under a new name. Who knows what it is?"

Spencer explained that Aamir had waylaid his old girlfriend, Amy St. Clair, in the parking lot, at Wilfred Laurier University, late Friday night. He had drawn a knife. He was accosted by a young security guard who disarmed him. Aamir pushed Amy into the officer, and escaped with her own car which had been left running.

Spencer said, "That guy's got more lucky horseshoes up his rear end than most people." He looked at Klassen and Abqurah and sighed, "Well, that's the update." He added quietly, "And now he's probably on his way here!" Abqurah sat there dazed.

.....

Aamir had all of Saturday to plan. He rented a motel room and thumbed through the white pages. "Ah, here it is. A. Ibrahim, Mohawk Court Apts, 30½ Mohawk Rd W. (905)

546-2222." He caught up on his sleep, and had a late breakfast across the street from the motel, at a Wendy's. He found an ATM and took out several hundred dollars from his account. ISIS took care of its people! He went back to the motel to snooze a bit more. Later that afternoon, he went to *Canadian Tire* and bought a bicycle, cash. He loaded it into the back of his trunk, and tied the lid securely down with bungee cords.

That night, he contacted a buddy from the old days, and paid cash for a Sig Sauer handgun which he hid in the trunk. Almost 80% of American law enforcement agencies have chosen the Sig Sauer P229 for reliability and safety.

He slid the gun along side the trunk's "doughnut tire." "How apt," he thought, realizing the irony. "Doughnuts and cops!"

He collected a few rocks from a ditch, and put them in the trunk. The switchblade in his pocket was added assurance. He smiled, "Switchblade if I get into the apartment. Rocks if I don't. Sig Sauer just in case."

Aamir slept well Saturday night, after watching an old Abbott and Costello movie on "getTV." It was supposed to be a 1949 classic, "Africa Screams." "How stupid!" he thought. "No wonder Westerners have soft brains!" He fell asleep after midnight, planning to launch his attack, late Sunday night, with everything well prepared.

CHAPTER 65

My heroes are those who risk their lives every day to protect our world and make it a better place - police, firefighters and members of our armed forces.

[SIDNEY SHELDON – WRITER OF BOOKS AND TV SHOWS]

• • • • •

POLICE PROTECTION
SATURDAY, OCTOBER 18, 2014

THE DEATH THREAT
SUNDAY, OCTOBER 19, 2014

SPENCER SLIPPED HIS .38 INTO THE HOLSTER UNDER HIS jacket, and headed back to Abqurah's apartment on Saturday evening. He'd phoned her that he was coming. He said through the door, "It's me. It's Ed." She opened the door.

They went out for supper at a Thai Restaurant. Spencer had one beer. She had a Pepsi. She didn't seem to mind him drinking one beer.

Spencer had drawn night shift, so he called in a favour, and made sure he and his partner sat in a patrol car all Saturday night outside of Abqurah's apartment. He paid for the coffee and doughnuts to keep them going. He was off duty the next two days, so he could give Abqurah his full watch-dog attention.

He took her out for Sunday breakfast, stayed for lunch, and then in the afternoon, they took in a Sunday matinée, "Frozen," and shared a large bag of popcorn. They had a long walk back to the apartment, as the sun slowly set in the autumn sky. Before they knew it, it was supper time, 6:00 p.m. They ordered a pizza, Hawaiian double cheese. Spencer didn't care. If a bullet didn't get Aamir, maybe a double dose of gas might blast him into Paradise.

"I'm staying the night. I'm your official guard dog," he said seriously. "Don't argue. I'll sleep on the couch."

She fingered her engagement ring. "I'm courting you," he teased with a twinkle in his eyes. "So don't worry... .no funny business."

"Do you think Aamir will come after me?" asked Abqurah.

"*You bet your sweet patootie," he commented.* "Aamir's on a mission and it's not from Allah! He wants plain and simple revenge, which he calls honour."

Abqurah and Spencer talked. "In my culture," she said, "names mean something."

"Well, actually my name means something too," admitted Spencer. "My mother liked the poet, Edmund Spenser. My actual name is Edmund but I prefer Ed. Cops on the force call me, Spencer. My name's with a 'c' and the poet's name is with an 's'... except I don't write poetry."

"Maybe you should," said Abqurah. "It would be romantic." Spencer harrumphed. "Just don't make that a requisite for courting you," he said. "How about your name?"

"It means genius," she said simply.

"Whoa! Now I'm in trouble. I can see you're going to outsmart your husband at every turn."

"Isn't that the way it's supposed to be?"

Spencer figured he was already outsmarted. He had nothing to say. They watched the Sunday evening movie on TV until about 10:00 p.m. Spencer couldn't remember what it was about. Maybe a chick flick? Usually, those things didn't stick in his mind.

He paid attention though when a loud thud rebounded off the wall outside. The next rock smashed through the window. Spencer turned the TV off, and then the lights. They heard Aamir yell, "Allah is watching you, Abqurah. He will have his revenge." Then silence.

Spencer called the police station. "Hi, it's Detective Spencer. We've received a death threat by some nut outside. Can you send a patrol car down here to arrest him?" They sent a patrol car right away. Spencer wouldn't have to shoot Aamir if they caught him, but Spencer's own preference was to put a bullet in the guy's head.

The patrol car sped along with its lights flashing and its siren blaring. It passed some guy on a bicycle, without lights, heading in the opposite direction. "No lights," said the driver. "Let him go. Head for our call first!" said his partner. They were at the apartments within minutes.

One officer checked the neighbourhood, nothing there. Another rang the apartment unit. They came upstairs. "Nada, nothing, zip. We couldn't find the guy. I see there's a broken window and a rock. We'll make out our report." "Humph," thought Spencer," hit and run. Just like Aamir!" He also wondered how wise it was of the police to drive in with flashing lights and the siren? That would have been an obvious tip-off for Aamir to get the hell out of there.

Spencer convinced the police to guard the building with their patrol car all Sunday night. They joked about it being a Timmy's "gig" again, with more coffee and more doughnuts. Spencer chuckled. He would hold the fort inside the apartment with his sidearm, and he was glad he had a patrol car on the outside. Abqurah felt doubly safe. She explained that Aamir had always been recluse as a child, and then he caught some kind of religious bug when he was a teen.

"He was never affectionate as a brother," she said, "He could have done so much with his life, other than pumping gas at dad's station. When it came to computers, he was a whiz. He could have gone into engineering or become a programmer, made an easy life for himself... but the Qur'an and my parents mixed him up."

"Well, I've wasted a lot of years myself when I was young," admitted Spencer. "But since I've passed my 30th birthday, I've grown up some, and I've been looking for more permanent things in my life." He explained that he hung out in bars during his 20s, which now, in hind-sight, was one big waste of time. He was lucky he had trained as a cop and enjoyed the job. The closer he got to 30, the more he kept away from the bar scene. He concentrated now on his career; he had made detective in short order.

Wastin' away, wastin' away
Too much of nothin' every day
Wastin' away, wastin' away
Too much of nothin' every day

[*Baker Street Album* - GERRY RAFFERTY 1978]

The TV was off. Abqurah and Spencer fell asleep leaning against each other on the couch. They dozed on and off throughout the night. They talked on and off and dozed again. What were their dreams? How would they spend their lives together? They talked about family. How would they not make the same mistakes as their parents? "If I could," said Spencer, "I'd wrap up Forever and give it to you!"

If I could save time in a bottle
The first thing that I'd like to do
Is to save every day
'Til eternity passes away
Just to spend them with you
If I could make days last forever
If words could make wishes come true
I'd save every day like a treasure and then,
Again, I would spend them with you

[JIM CROCE SONG 1973]

A ray of sunlight woke them up early Monday morning. Abqurah got ready for her day of school. They made toast and coffee. Spencer turned the TV on again.

A snippet of news on CHCH reported that Nicola Jones had died on Sunday, October 19, 2014. She was the Morning Live weather reporter for the station.

Chris Beattie, Jones' ex-husband, confirmed today that Jones, 41, passed away at noon Mexico time on Sunday – but not before their young son spoke to his mother via telephone.

She suffered from an aggressive form of cancer since last April. She flew to Mexico for surgery and died in a hospital there. Nicola loved to have fun on the air.

Abqurah said, "She was so young! And here people are deliberately killing each other in the Middle East."

Spencer uttered, "Yeah, like here with your nutty brother!"

Spencer never liked the term, "ex-husband." He wondered out loud, what went wrong there in that marriage between Nicola Jones and her ex? Why'd they divorce? They had a little kid together. "I hope that never happens to us!" said Spencer. She snuggled closer to him on the couch and they kissed.

The old saying is, "It never rains, but it pours!" They heard the TV newscaster say that Raphael Ravenscroft, the musician behind one of the most recognizable saxophone solos, on Gerry Rafferty's hit, *Baker Street*, died of a suspected heart attack on Sunday at the age of 60. Ravenscroft went on to work for icons like Pink Floyd, Abba and Marvin Gaye. The news report concluded with this amusing quotation from *The Guardian*, read by the TV news anchor:

> Ravenscroft is reported to have been paid £27 for the Baker Street session in the form of a cheque that bounced. The hit reached No 3 in the U.K. charts and No 2 in the U.S., and Rafferty was said to have earned £80,000 a year from royalties.

"Boy," thought Spencer, "we've got a flood of good news this morning! Ravenscroft dying on the same day as Nicola Jones, and our death threats from Aamir! What more can we ask for?"

Spencer wasn't shy about using his influence with the police department. He made sure Abqurah had an escort for the day. An APB was sent out with Aamir's last known name and description. They sent word out to airports, but they weren't sure what good that would do. What name did he go by now? What passport was he using? Where was he going?

CHAPTER 66

> "Let those fight in the way of Allah who sell the life of this world for the other. Whoso fighteth in the way of Allah, be he slain or be he victorious, on him We shall bestow a vast reward."
>
> [QUR'AN 4:74]

.....

BILLY BISHOP AIRPORT
MONDAY, OCTOBER 20, 2014

UMAR STILL HAD AN ADRENALIN RUSH FROM THEIR NEAR escape at Union Station. "Maybe there are too many of us in this country," he thought. "What are the chances that somebody would understand our private talk in the Dari dialect? Isn't anything sacred anymore?" Umar thought it was funny that people were talking on their cell phones all the time in public, on the street, in stores, the washrooms! "I guess there's no privacy anymore!" he muttered to himself.

He was getting anxious to do something while Jorin was gone. But what? The wait was driving him crazy. He knew it was a feeling which often got him into trouble. But he dismissed the idea; and thought instead, what it would be like to see the CN Tower burning.

A satisfying image crossed his mind with the CN Tower tumbling in flames. He looked through the Yellow Pages and found what he wanted: "Flying Instructions. Call Mike, licensed pilot, 416-3333. Reasonable Rates."

Umar made an appointment with Mike at the Billy Bishop Airport on the island for 10 o'clock Monday morning. It was just a matter of taking the ferry across.

Billy Bishop Airport is commonly known as the *Toronto Island Airport*. It's a small airport located on the Toronto Islands within city limits. It's named after Air Marshal Billy Bishop, a Canadian *World War I* flying ace who won a Victoria Cross for his ability to shoot down enemy aircraft. In less than six months of actual *flying* time, Bishop had downed 67 enemy planes.

Mike greeted Umar cordially. "You look like you're from the Middle East. I'm sorry for profiling you, but I'll need to see your driver's license, some kind of ID that you're a Canadian citizen and I need to get character references, once we sign the contract for lessons. I take cash or credit card."

Mike Feeney was a seasoned pilot, 45 years old. He liked to think of himself as a cowboy of the air, so he wore fancy western shirts on the job and a stetson. When he flew out on a job, he always left the Stetson behind in the office. He supplemented his parcel delivery service for small to middling companies by opening a flying school for people thinking they'd like to be able to fly. They could hang a framed copy of their pilot's license on a wall somewhere, just to impress family or business clients. A topic of discussion.

Mike took a look at Umar's driver's license and memorized the name. It looked okay. He asked him a few innocuous questions like why he wanted to fly. "To impress the girlfriend," said Umar, not wanting to make up a complex story. While Umar filled out the necessary form, Mike plied him with chit-chat. Had he been in Canada his whole life? Yes, born here. Parents were from Afghanistan. What did he think of Mayor Rob Ford? His private life should remain private. He was doing a good job for the tax payer though. How about them Leafs? Umar smiled. Time they won the Stanley Cup!

Mike needed the business, so he asked if Umar wanted to see the *2014 Cessna 172S Skyhawk SP*. He led Umar out to a private hangar.

"Isn't she a beauty?"

"Yes, she is," agreed Umar, pulling a Glock from the small of his back. He pointed it at Mike and said, "I'll take a free lesson right now." Umar draped his jacket over the gun.

Mike was instructed to get clearance for take-off. Umar pictured the CN Tower in flames. Mike didn't fasten his seat-belt. He didn't tell Umar to do so, ignoring the first rule of flying safety.

The morning had cleared. Streaks of sunshine broke through a blue sky. As Mike and Umar took off, it looked like a perfect day for a test flight.

"What do you intend to do?"

"How about if we head to the CN Tower, and have a real close look at it?"

Mike's plane was headed away from the Tower, actually headed further out on Lake Ontario because that was the direction of his take-off from the tarmac.

"Do you know who Billy Bishop was?" asked Mike.

"No," said Umar.

"I didn't think so," said Mike.

He banked the plane steeply on its side, before Umar could react. What was the guy going to do? Shoot him? Mike didn't care if he got shot right there and then. At least, he had the choice of when and how he'd die, if the plane went down.

Mike opened his door and rolled out, as the Cessna took its steep dive sideways. Umar was too stunned. "This stupid infidel didn't follow instructions!"

The plane spiraled out of control into the lake, crashing upside down in a big splash. Mike was lucky as he plummeted, landing feet first in the lake. He broke both his ankles. Great! How long can you tread water? A motorboat nearby headed his way, threw him a lifejacket and pulled him in. The owner had already called 911.

"Damndest thing I ever saw!" said the skipper. "What happened?"

Mike explained that his Cessna was hijacked. "That guy was crazy. He wanted me to fly into the CN Tower." Mike shook his head with the next thought which came to mind. "My insurance rates are going to go through the roof!"

Mike was interviewed from his hospital bed, lots of metal and screws in his ankles. Demerol helped him feel better, almost euphoric in a painful sort of way.

First the police interviewed him and then he slept. Then the newspapers, *The Toronto Reporter* and *Toronto Today*, and then he slept. Part of the newspaper article read:

> **Monday, October 20, 2014: Shortly before Noon, Hijacking of small aircraft at Billy Bishop:** Hijacker was killed in a crash into Lake Ontario. Only injury reported was the pilot who bailed out in a trick turn, and broke

his ankles when he hit the water. "There are some nutty people out there in the world," said Mike Feeney, the pilot. "The guy wanted to knock out the CN Tower. Must have been a terrorist, though you'd never know it. He even showed me his driver's license. Umar Wahidi. He was a Canadian citizen, for Heavens sake!"

CHAPTER 67

> "O you who have believed, seek help through patience and prayer. Indeed, Allah is with the patient."
>
> [QUR'AN 2:153]

.....

NOON NEWS
ANOTHER ABOUT FACE!
MONDAY, OCTOBER 20, 2014

JORIN WAS CONVINCED THAT HE COULD GET A GOOD NIGHT'S rest in the cheap hotel where he was registered as "Alan Sayed." He had a leisurely breakfast there at 10:00 a.m. on Monday morning, and sipped his coffee with satisfaction that he, at least, had unnerved his sister, leaving her wondering if he would be back or not. He would not be back; he had other, bigger plans in mind, than the tempting honour killing of his younger sister.

By 11:00 a.m., he got on the ramp to the 403 and then the QEW, heading back to Toronto. His bicycle was secure with bungee cords in the back of the trunk. The morning sun had given way to overcast skies by noon Monday. Dreary day! Jorin turned on the radio.

He heard, "Hijacking of small aircraft at Billy Bishop. Hijacker killed... Umar Wahidi, a naturalized Canadian citizen, hijacked the Cessna. The pilot said, Wahidi wanted him to fly the plane into the CN Tower."

"Shit!" Aamir blurted out, hitting the steering wheel hard. "He couldn't wait. I told him I'd be back within the week. Stupid waste!" That was bad news. He couldn't go back to the apartment. He had to spend another miserable night in another hotel or motel, somewhere in Toronto. "Well," he thought, "I must come from a long line of nomads!" His anger subsided to amusement.

Jorin found a Value Village where he bought two changes of clothes. Syria was still warm in October but November could get cool. His backpack would come in handy.

He found an ATM and withdrew enough money for travel. Thoughtful funds from the Islamic State. Handy electronic cash!

He still had his iPad, so he could scour the internet for news about the Holy War in Kobane. He found a Tim Horton's with free Wi-Fi. "Timmy's, the poor man's Starbucks!" He sipped his French Vanilla and ate a Boston Cream doughnut, while he accessed the internet.

He googled Sofia, Bulgaria. Not far from Turkey. *Sofia-Vrazhdebna Airport*, two terminals which he could see on GoogleMaps. Every week, at least 56 domestic flights and 896 international flights depart from Vrazhdebna Airport in Sofia. He found cheap flights!

He drove straight to Pearson that Monday afternoon and bought a one way ticket, cash, to Sofia, Bulgaria. $658. He told the airline agent that he hated credit cards. Get too many Canadians into debt.

The flight was going to leave at 2:00 a.m. Tuesday morning. Arrival time in Sofia, Bulgaria, 9:00 a.m. Bulgarian time. Add 7 hours. That's going to be some jet-lag!

It was only 3:00 in the afternoon Monday in Toronto. Lots of time to plan. "I love it when a plan comes together." That line seemed familiar to him somehow? Jorin arranged his schedule in his head. What would he do next?

He drove back downtown, and abandoned the rental car with the bicycle still in it, in an underground parking garage, in the middle of Toronto. Just left it there! It would take the police some time and sleuthing to find out who rented the vehicle or owned the bike?

Jorin took the Downtown Express to the Pearson International. Registered at the Holiday Inn nearby, a three star for $125 a night, with a shuttle service early Tuesday morning. "Great. I should have been a travel agent," chuckled Jorin. He had more than enough travel money to hop-scotch into Bulgaria, then Turkey and back into Syria.

He bought himself a good supper at the grill with Jihad money, and then settled in for a 4 hour snooze in his his posh room. He slept soundly; wake-up call for the shuttle to Pearson at midnight. He found himself sitting in the *Canada Air* lobby in plenty of time for his 2:00 a.m. flight, Tuesday morning. "We are marching to Bulgaria," he hummed in his head.

CHAPTER 68

"Anyway, it is important to know that the Muslim fundamentalists never really started any war with the US. The US had always started the trouble! Take Osama Bin Laden, for instance, if you read up on his history and the reasons why he declared the war on the US, then you would see that he did it because of the U.S. excessive aggression on the Iraqi people."

[HTTP://WWW.ANSWERING-CHRISTIANITY.COM/FORGIVENESS_AND_REVENGE_IN_ISLAM.HTM]

.....

CHAMELEON AND NOMAD

TUESDAY, OCTOBER 21, 2014

JORIN HAD NO PROBLEM PASSING THROUGH CANADIAN Customs. Turks are the good guys. He was travelling to Bulgaria to open a car rental business, and then going back home to Turkey to visit family. Before he knew it, he was in the air. He settled comfortably back into his seat and caught up on his sleep. "Just another day in Paradise," he thought.

Jorin/Aamir didn't feel bad that he did not succeed in killing his younger sister. He got some satisfaction just out of the harassment. The thing he truly felt bad about was not being able to kill his former girlfriend, Amy. Oh well, Allah may yet have his revenge.

Umar's attempt to fly a plane into the CN Tower would have been a grand spectacle, had it succeeded. have succeeded! Too bad... but a Cessna? Would it have been big enough to do the job? Jorin was confident that the day would come when other jihadists, even Canadian born, would carry on this Holy War. He wondered if the police had found his car yet in the old parking garage. The bicycle in the trunk would baffle them.

He looked out the window as his jet flew into the East, toward Sofia. It was about 8:00 a.m., Tuesday morning. Grey clouds scalloped the sky like dirty waves far below, as far as the eye could see. It must be raining down there. He held hopes that the weather would be less bleak further east. But here at 30,000 feet the sun shone bright, and to Aamir, it was symbolic of the sun that would shine over the whole planet, once Islam purged the world of infidels. He itched to join his fellow jihadists in ISIL.

The sun irritated his sleepy eyes. He closed the shutter and fell asleep again. He liked to think, "In Allah's arms."

The plane taxied on the tarmac of Sofia International. Before long, he found himself sitting in yet another airport lobby at Terminal 2. He retrieved his backpack from the conveyor belt. Customs had been no problem. He found a little café in the lobby and paid in American dollars. International currency, recognized by Christians and Muslims alike. The Almighty Dollar!

Jorin perched his iPad on the café table. Googled Canadian News: "Monday, October 20, 2014, Police gunned down Couture-Rouleau, 25, in Saint-Jean-Sur-Richelieu, Quebec, just 30 minutes outside of Montreal. The man mowed down two soldiers in the parking lot of an auto-insurance outlet. Sources said the incident happened just after 11:30 a.m."

"Police suspect that the man had become a radicalized Muslim. One of the soldiers died later in hospital, another was injured. In an interview the next day, on Tuesday, Public Safety Minister Steven Blaney said that he denounced this '*terrible act of violence against our country, against our military, against our values*'."

"Hah, good news at last," scoffed Jorin silently. "A Holy War within the very doors of Canada... 'against our country, our military, our values.' Bah!" "Bah!" he said out loud.

He sipped his coffee and spotted another item of interest. Handy having free Wi-Fi at the airport. Almost every one had a laptop, an iPad, or a cell phone. He should have shares in Apple! He scrolled down. "Ah, here it is!" He touched, Tuesday, October 21, Kobane News:

"Kurdish fighters in the battle for the Syrian town of *Kobane* weathered a fresh onslaught by fighters from the Islamic State of Iraq and the Levant."

He couldn't wait to get back into the thick of things, to fight for an Islamic State which was true to Allah and the Prophet, Muhammad, may peace be upon him.

He found another ATM. He withdrew more Islamic State money. Some American dollars, some Bulgarian Levs, some Turkish Liras, and finally some Syrian Pounds. He figured that the similar names of currency in Italy and the U.K. must have been hold-overs from colonial times. Who knows the history of imperialism? He didn't care. The money would get him lunch and a plane ticket to Ankara, Turkey, that very afternoon. He didn't have to stay in Bulgaria over night, basically an Orthodox Christian country.

Bulgaria's traditional religion according to the constitution was about 80% Orthodox Christian. Islam was 10%. "That could be remedied," Jorin thought.

He googled information on his iPad through Tripadvisor: "Your one-stop shop for finding the best *flights from Sofia* to *Ankara*. Simply tell us where and when you want to travel and we'll do all the legwork for you. 816 flights from Sofia to Ankara every week."

Jorin bought a one way ticket from *Turkish Airlines* for 163 Euros. He had a light lunch and spent time on his iPad until the plane came in at 2:00 p.m. It would take 4 hours to Ankara, via Istanbul. He would be in Turkey at 6:00 p.m., supper time Tuesday. He googled for a place to stay over night in Ankara. Always plan ahead.

Jorin booked online. *Hotel Capital*, a three star, $47 per night. He didn't want ISIL to track his expenditures and think him extravagant.

His flight set down at *Esenboğa International Airport* on schedule. Jorin was bone tired. He looked forward to a leisurely supper at the hotel, maybe not the most luxurious hotel he had seen online, but the buffet looked good. He passed customs with his passport, just another Turkish citizen trying to make good in the car rental business, a member of the thriving middle class.

He ate at the hotel. Before he went up to his room, he stopped at the front desk, and asked for a 9 o'clock wake up call for the next day, Wednesday morning. Closing the door to his three star room, Jorin's eyes took in the wallpaper with displeasure. Large lotus flowers in stark black and white faced him. He whispered to himself, "Either that wallpaper has got to go, or I do." He figured it wouldn't make much difference once he turned off the light and fell asleep. He said, “Goodnight,” to the wallpaper. ”After all, tomorrow is another day!”

CHAPTER 69

LATE TUESDAY, THE POLICE WERE SURE THAT AAMIR HAD escaped [once again] and probably did what he did before, somehow got out of Canada. Who knows where he was? "I'd still like to put a bullet through his head," said Spencer to Klassen over coffee, "I don't care if he is her brother or not. Some brother!"

.....

PSYCHOPATHIC HISTORY
TUESDAY, OCTOBER 21, 2014

Abqurah's brother had always been difficult, even when they were kids. She knew there was something wrong with him. It was only years later, when she could put a name to his weird problem. Aamir was the "family psychopath," just the way he treated animals, and the way he took delight in insulting his sisters. When he was 12, he pestered his father to buy him a pellet gun; and he'd wander into the woods, taking delight in shooting birds. He got quite good at it. Cats occasionally disappeared around the neighbourhood.

Miss Smith, his grade 6 teacher, tried to do a "heritage show 'n tell" in class. She asked the kids to dress in a costume or bring something from their parents' or grandparents' country of origin. This was a way to explain the Canadian Mosaic to the children. How Canada is made up of different nationalities in this wonderful land of ours, and how we all get along together! Miss Smith got the idea that year, in Social Studies, because she had a few Chinese kids, Afghan children, East Indians and several kids of European origin, all in one class.

Aamir wore a "Pashtun" outfit that looked like a pair of pajamas. Heiner wore his "Lederhosen" and a green hat with a feather in it. Chen wore a bright red jacket with yellow dragons embroidered into it. Ada wore her green "sari" to school.

Miss Smith had a "fashion show," and had the kids explain where their ancestors came from, what the costume was called, and why they came to Canada. The kids gave standard answers, Canada was nice, and it had good jobs.

The problem came at recess. Heiner said the wrong thing to Aamir. "Those look like pajamas!" That was enough. Aamir gave him a bloody nose. Heiner's Lederhosen was sprinkled with red. The teacher on duty broke up the fight, not before Aamir took a verbal swipe at Heiner again, calling him a "Nazi."

Both boys sat in the principal's office that day at opposite ends of the room. The secretary kept an eye on them. Mr. Laflamme talked to the boys and sent them back to class. He would have to fill out a report, which was just another daily chore he hated doing, and then, he'd have to phone the parents after school. Was this why he was getting paid the big bucks? Mr. Laflamme took another Tylenol.

Aamir showed his short temper at home too. He would say nasty things to his sisters. Hazirah and Abqurah were teased about becoming Westernized, that they had presumptuous ideas about being equal to boys. Both of them had their eyes set on college; he didn't. Aamir was a whiz at computers. He liked doing things by himself, and so he wasn't keen on a plan for his future, certainly not for making a living. He needed nothing and nobody.

As he got older, he had been given several chances to save money for either college or university. The first was as a drywaller through a house builder friend of his father's at their mosque. Drywalling made him sweat and gave him rough hands. The following summer, another friend said there was an opening at Silverline Concrete. It meant shoveling cement and carrying buckets of it into tight corners on a job site.

Aamir lasted one day and went back to pumping gas at his father's station. He liked to sit there behind the counter and collect the money... and read books, especially The Holy Qur'an.

Hazirah disliked her brother. Abqurah despised him. He was a jerk and he was lazy. He really became obsessed with the Qur'an and with the Hadith, which was the interpretation of the Qur'an. Abqurah followed her family's customs, but wearing the hijab, and then praying 5 times a day felt like a mindless chore to her.

When Hazirah didn't come home last year, her parents said she ran away. Abqurah didn't believe them. She had suspicions that something else was up, but she couldn't put her finger on it. Hazirah wouldn't just dump Alexander, nor would she leave home without letting Abqurah know what was going on. The parents seemed to get used to Hazirah not being around. Aamir seemed not to care.

CHAPTER 70

"Beyond work and love, I would add two other ingredients that give meaning to life. First, to fulfill whatever talents we are born with... Second, we should try to leave the world a better place than when we entered it."

[MICHIO KAKU – THEORETICAL PHYSICIST]

"You will never be happy if you continue to search for what happiness consists of. You will never live if you are looking for the meaning of life."

[ALBERT CAMUS – FRENCH PHILOSOPHER]

[HTTP://WWW.GOODREADS.COM/QUOTES/TAG/MEANING-OF-LIFE]

. . . . .

DETECTIVE EDMUND SPENCER PERSONAL THOUGHTS
TUESDAY, OCTOBER 21, 2014

DETECTIVE SPENCER FOUND IT HARD TO ACCEPT THAT A brother, a blood relative, could kill his own sister and call the killing "honourable." There was honour in killing an enemy in war, if the strength and the weapons at least gave each of them an equal chance! But an honour killing based on a religion? Richard Dawkins claimed that believing in God was a kind of mass hysteria, a delusion. That's why churches got together as a support group in this insane dream that some Consciousness somewhere in the eternal universe actually saw you and cared for you. Spencer tried to hang on to the solid anchor of his Atheism more tightly when he ran across this case where Aamir killed his sister, in the name of Allah. Where's the honour in that... and where's God?

But deep down, Spencer was not a hardened Atheist. He felt a weakness inside him, that he wanted support from something bigger than himself, because indeed, it was a crazy world out there! He found a need to hold onto something spiritual, comforting, something that buoyed him up in the darkness and loneliness of the night.

He frequented beer parlours less and less in the past two years. He felt he had no more vacuous lines to hand to women. He used to use anything from, "Hey, good lookin' whatcha got cookin'" to "I'm just a lonely boy, lonely and blue." He couldn't believe what stupid lines sometimes worked! But as he passed the age of 30, he had had enough of games. Too many years wasted! He wanted something... well, permanent.

His lifestyle did not satisfy him. He lost interest in bars, women and religion. Well, maybe not women so much. Just the games involved. With religion, he became adamant as ever that God was a completely insane idea. Oh, Spencer came across Muslims who were nice people, hard working, and seemed pretty level headed; and he respected the privacy of their own beliefs, but he preferred not to get into a discussion with them... or with Christians.

Abqurah had shown Spencer an old family album. There were not many pictures taken throughout the years; and the ones, which were included in the album, were mainly of Adl, the father, and Aamir, the son. The picture taking, it seemed was relegated to the female side of the family, so one or all of the females were left out of the photos.

There was something in Aamir's eyes, evident even in old photographs of him, which made a person uncomfortable, like something was missing! The only description which came to Spencer's mind was, "there's no soul in those eyes."

One picture showed three of the Ibrahims, mom, dad and Aamir. Nobody was smiling. Both girls were missing. Aamir was a smaller replica of his father. Both of them eyeing the camera with a hardness in their eyes. The mother, Yaminah, had a stern face but cast her eyes down in the picture, looking very submissive. Weren't you supposed to smile in a picture and say, "Cheese?"

What an unhappy family, one inevitably spiraling into a path of self-destruction, shaken up by culture shock in a strange land. They might have had a better chance of survival in the Middle Ages in the Middle East. Strangers in a strange land, who tried to make their microcosm survive in the cultural Mosaic known as Canada.

It wasn't just because of Hazirah's murder or Abqurah's hatred of her brother that Spencer obviously despised Aamir. If Spencer wouldn't have known any of that; and met Aamir, as a stranger on the street, he was sure he'd dislike the guy. Spencer's sixth sense would tell him, there was something wrong with him... bells would go off, like a warning, don't trust him!

Spencer had a brother and sister of his own. Both younger. Josh and Megan. Josh was 28 now and Megan was 25, the baby of the family. Spencer used to toss the football around with Josh when they were younger. In the winter time, they'd take two orange pylons, their hockey sticks, and a red ball to the local school. Spencer would con his brother into being goalie and pepper the red ball passed his shin guards. Occasionally the kid got to shoot "the puck" too.

Josh became a bank manager. He had three kids of his own. And Spencer was proud of the fact that his kid brother deliberately made family time for his kids and played with them.

Spencer was in police training and still living at home when his sister entered high-school. He'd help her with her homework when she asked, especially with Math. When she brought a boy home in grade 11, Spencer teased her about "the guy." Was he the one? Was he good enough? How would he support her? Megan gave him "the look."

Megan's goal was to work in Public Relations. She was good at talking, and good at research, and writing reports. Maybe Human Resources? Maybe law school? Too young to know for sure. She eventually settled for law school. She liked the lifestyle it afforded her. Fashionable clothes, a nice apartment and eating out in restaurants.

"So, you practice law for the perks?" asked Spencer. "Partly," she confessed. "What I love is arguing a case; I love the research, and then coming up with a great defense. I like winning in court." Spencer had lost enough arguments with his sister to appreciate her persuasive ways and her logical mind. She flowered into an independent woman at law school.

His own family was so different from the Ibrahims. Spencer was glad that his parents were not zealous about their religion, like the Ibrahims apparently were. They could not recite the Bible, chapter and verse, but they led quiet lives of respect for others, and raised their kids with a sense of fair play. "It doesn't all come from the Bible, you know," said his dad, "you gotta know what's right inside of you."

When Spencer got to be a cop, he ran across some pretty bad people. The experience was an eye-opener. He saw how the world worked. He found he had less and less use for the Bible or for God. He followed the law; but became, one tough cop. Because of the nature of his chosen profession, Spencer became a confirmed Atheist and a confirmed Bachelor. Aamir should have confirmed those convictions in Spencer even more. However, getting to know Abqurah, all those hard convictions became unravelled in him.

CHAPTER 71

Behold, children are a gift of the LORD, The fruit of the womb is a reward. Like arrows in the hand of a warrior, so are the children of one's youth. How blessed is the man whose quiver is full of them; they will not be ashamed when they speak with their enemies in the gate.

[PSALM 127:3-5 NASV]

.....

DETECTIVE JAKE KLASSEN
MORAL AND LEGAL IMPERATIVES
TUESDAY, OCTOBER 21, 2014

DETECTIVE KLASSEN NEVER MET AAMIR. JUST HEARD stories about him from Abqurah. First through her testimony in court, during the trial of her parents, and later, when he got to know her, through Spencer, stories about her brother over coffee times at *Williams Fresh Café*.

The guy was a psychopath. A religious zealot who had extreme ideas about his religion to kill people who did not follow the true Faith of Islam. First his older sister, Hazirah, who fell away from the path, and now, coming back to Canada, to pick off people who put his parents behind bars. Aamir was, in truth, an animal full of revenge, not a tool of Allah in a Holy War!

Klassen was glad he had met Abqurah. She presented another dimension to the family and to Islam. Abqurah actually seemed sane in the midst of her crazy upbringing.

When Spencer first told Klassen about dating Abqurah, 11 years younger, Klassen thought Spencer was, "robbing the cradle." His opinion tempered when he had met Abqurah at *Williams*. She had sensible things to say. Her eyes showed she was gentle and intelligent. Maybe there's hope here, thought Klassen. He gave both of them the benefit of the doubt.

How could she come from the same family that produced Aamir? From what he saw in court, Klassen judged that the aberration came from Adl, the father. The father domineered the family, with constant harping about the Holy Qur'an. Allah demands this or that! Adl insisted that the "salat" prayers had to be observed, without fail, 5 times a day facing Mecca.

Abqurah was a thinker and questioned her father's strict routines. Aamir, on the other hand, found a cushion of comfort in strict rituals.

Klassen began to see how a mind like Aamir's was set on rules; and would become radicalized, and even participate in a Holy War, with a crazy zeal to defend the honour and righteousness of Allah, and his Prophet, Muhammad, may peace be upon him.

Klassen was grateful for the son and daughter he had. Jake and Katie. Jake was 40 now, a solid citizen, a general contractor who made a good living building nice homes in the Niagara Region. He had been married to Irene for 18 years and they had two kids of their own.

Katie was 35, a hair dresser who ran a brisk business through her shop in Niagara-on-the-Lake. She was still single and a career woman, an entrepreneur who liked her lifestyle the way it was. Klassen had made comments about her settling down with a man years ago. But he came to terms with the fact that his daughter just liked her life fine, the way it was! He loved her and Facebooked regularly, though this was not his favourite way to communicate.

Klassen prayed at meals when the kids were growing up, and he'd pick out a short verse from the Bible, "to think about." But he wanted them to bring God into their lives when they got older, as a conscious choice of their own. They would go to church together as a family when the kids were kids and as they grew up... well, then it was up to them. There was nothing he could do about it. Klassen figured, it was, "in the Father's Hands." He felt sorry for the Ibrahims who were so controlling of their kids. Klassen saw the dad as, "a Qur'an thumping extremist," and now, Aamir, the son, had become that, a chip off the old block!

As a cop, Klassen wouldn't go so far as putting a bullet in Aamir's head, like Spencer wanted to do. Klassen instead wanted to bring the man to justice, by the book, under Canadian law for the murder of Hazirah. Klassen had a moral and legal imperative to follow. Spencer had a sense of justice. Aamir had nothing!

CHAPTER 72

"Morality has nothing to do with talent. If you have talent enjoy it; and if you don't have morality, work on it."

[WALDEMAR GUENTER - POET]

.....

WALLY GUENTER
WHAT MAKES HIM TICK?
TUESDAY, OCTOBER 21, 2014

WALLY WAS AS YET AN UNDISCOVERED TALENT, ONE WHOSE star might never rise, because of the nature of the business in professional photography. The phone didn't ring off the hook for wedding gigs; however, Wally was content enough to take the little business he got. When he wasn't working on wedding pictures, he was busy with scenery pictures. Wally enjoyed his "retirement," was passionate about his photography and happy with his married life.

He loved his wife dearly. She sometimes teased him that she came a close second to his first love, the camera. Wally had tried teaching some years ago but found that disciplining students was not his strong suit. He had a nervous breakdown and so quit the teaching profession. The camera, he knew, didn't talk back, and he enjoyed pleasing couples with their wedding photos much more. When he didn't have a wedding to shoot, he'd take his camera and look for scenery pictures all over the Niagara Peninsula.

His wife, a teacher, gave Wally the freedom to do that. She never threw it in his face to go out and get a "real job" that pays. She knew that her husband couldn't cope with the pressures of being a teacher again, or a real-estate agent, or a car salesman. They did just fine the way they were.

Fourteen years ago, Wally had acquired a Public Relations Diploma at Sheridan College, going back as an adult transfer student. He was offered a job in the Public Relations office at the Sunnybrook Hospital in Toronto, but that meant uprooting and moving to the big city. Wally's wife liked the cozy environment around Jordan. The busy, noisy life of the big city held no attraction for her.

Wally learned how to use a computer at Sheridan College. He found the experience painful because he was the oldest one in the class. But he learned to love what the computer could do, especially when he discovered Photoshop for enhancing his pictures.

Wally's wife? Well, she hated computers, despite the fact that her teaching profession demanded a certain proficiency in it. She didn't like social networking, Facebooking, Tweeting, or the inordinate time people wasted on these networks, gossiping and sharing things they shouldn't share. "As far as I'm concerned," she said, "I prefer my name not be mentioned on the internet at all!"

Wally declined the offer of a job at the Sunnybrook Hospital. He decided to supply teach locally, take photography and web design courses at Mohawk College, and try to drum up a wedding photography business within the Niagara Region.

Well, the business side of wedding photography never happened. But Wally and his wife came to terms with that; and eventually, Wally took on the role of "house husband." He had suppers ready when she got home from school at 6 p.m., and he saw to it that the house was reasonably clean. He joked with his wife that "dusting" was not in his job description. Though, since she brought in the pay cheques, he felt obligated to do his part in the marriage, as much as humanly possible…"for a man." Generally, he did pretty well!

. . . . .

Wally was horrified when he found Hazirah's bloody body. He had taken out "a mental health day," to enjoy the Bruce Trail with his camera, when he made the gruesome discovery. How could somebody do that to another human being? Instead of something to bolster up his mental health, he found something to disturb it.

Wally was eventually grateful that Detective Klassen had given him his card and suggested that Wally go see a counselor. After Leonard died of cancer, Wally had more and more recurrent nightmares. He needed to find some way to get some sleep. De Jong was a great help.

Wally had married into a Mennonite family and attended church with his wife. From what he saw, Mennonites had always pitched in a helping hand when somebody moved or when somebody was sick. They seemed like a pretty grounded folk.

He couldn't fathom how a religion could demand the death of a relative for not staying within the same religion. He couldn't see how Aamir could kill his sister for having a white boyfriend or for wanting to become a Christian. He was aware that Christianity had its dark periods in history but this was the 21st century!

The keyword among religions seemed to be "peace." Peace was obviously absent in this era of jet planes, computers and going into outer space, considering the tension in the Middle East and so many other parts of the world. The Middle East, especially, was erupting like a restless volcano, spewing forth death and destruction at unexpected times. He wondered if Armageddon would erupt from there?

Wally was afraid when Klassen told him about Aamir throwing a rock through the window at Abqurah's apartment. Somehow, Aamir got back into Canada with a false passport, and was tracking down people who put his parents in prison. He even threatened his old girlfriend, a music professor at Wilfred University. Was Aamir going down the list? Would he eventually get to Wally?

This is where Wally could have gone to pieces. He had suffered a nervous breakdown before, so his psyche and his body were permanently damaged, and sensitive to any kind of stress. He was surprised, however, at how well he did after the traumatic discovery of Hazirah's body three years ago. And now, with Aamir back in Canada... more stress! But he was holding up quite well.

Wally had found stability with his computer, his photography, and making suppers for his wife. And Heaven forbid, if anything should happen to his loved ones, his wife? In a strange way, he was grateful that they didn't have kids, in case Aamir came after his family.

Klassen said he'd send a patrol car around to Wally's house for a couple of nights, just to be on the safe side. "To be on the safe side," thought Wally, "is there a guarantee?"

CHAPTER 73

"Ah, modern love — it all seems so trite when compared to the traditions of yore. Before Beyoncé was telling us to put a ring on it and greeting cards were expressing our feelings for us, young lovers were vying for each other's attention with strange and fascinating courtship rituals."

[HTTP://FLAVORWIRE.COM/369990/STRANGE-AND-FASCINATING-COURTSHIP-TRADITIONS-AROUND-THE-WORLD-2]

.....

COUNSELLING AND COFFEE
TUESDAY, OCTOBER 21, 2014

SINCE THE TRIAL WHICH PUT AAMIR'S PARENTS IN JAIL, Detective Spencer and Abqurah established a warm bond which transformed into love between the couple. They liked meeting for coffee and chatting about the future.

Both of them had met with Pastor Greg that Tuesday at 10:00 a.m. on Spencer's day off. Abqurah had booked off work and had no classes to attend. They were scheduled to meet with Pastor Greg again later that same day at 3:00 p.m. at the church.

Pastor Greg was a young man of about 30, recently married himself. He said it was important for a married couple to go on a date, once in a while. "Make it a habit," he suggested. "Appreciate each other. Forgive the faults and encourage the strengths." Who could argue with that?

"So what do you think of Pastor Greg?" asked Abqurah after a sip of coffee at Timmy's shortly after the morning meeting.

"He's pretty young," said Spencer.

"So are you," encouraged Abqurah. "You're only two years older than he is."

"Well, I guess I can take some advice from a young whipper-snapper," joked Spencer. He had lightened up immensely, both as a cop and a man since he had gotten to know Abqurah. It was hard to play bad cop now in the interrogation room.

Spencer had always been the bad cop, and now he felt like he was mush, a softie giving his criminals the benefit of the doubt when he arrested them. No more knocking their heads "accidentally" on the door frame when he put them in the cruiser. Didn't matter. Spencer liked his new self. Gerry Rafferty's lyrics came to mind from his song, *I Was A Boy Scout:*

And I was going into something that was feelin' good
It was something I could understand
I was going into something, it was feeling free
I was singing like a reborn man.

It was ironic. The song was about leaving religion and finding freedom in rock 'n roll. Spencer was transformed but not like Gerry Rafferty. Spencer felt that Christianity and Abqurah gave him his new freedom. He felt free and grounded at the same time. He was changing, going through a metamorphosis of the soul, and he was happy about it. "I'm singing like a reborn man," he thought, as he looked into Abqurah's brown eyes. They both sipped their coffees and smiled at each other.

It was because of his feelings for Abqurah that Spencer took an interest in her culture. He actually read the Qur'an from cover to cover but somehow, it did not quite sit well with him. He also read biographies about the prophet, Muhammad [may peace be upon him]. Spencer shared his thoughts with Abqurah about the Qur'an, and about things in Muhammad's life which made him uneasy. Abqurah likewise had questioned things in the Qur'an and in the Prophet's life, especially about his sexual prowess with his multiple wives and about the fact that this man of peace was a military leader. So how could he produce a book of peace and follow the way of Allah?

She remembered the lesson Jesus taught in the Garden of Gethsemane, during the time of his arrest, where Peter struck the ear off a servant with his sword. Jesus said, "*Put your sword* back into its place; for all those who take *up* the sword shall perish by the sword." [Matt. 26:52] This was so different than Muhammad [may peace by upon him], who led men into bloody battle and had hundreds of the Banu Qurayza Jews beheaded.

Both Abqurah and Spencer preferred to embrace the Jesus of the New Testament who said, "Let the little children come to me," [Matt. 19:14] than the Messenger of Allah, who said, "When you meet those who disbelieve, strike their necks [until] you have inflicted slaughter upon them." [Qur'an 47:4]

Spencer had a lot of new things to learn, and Abqurah had a lot to unlearn before she grew in a new direction.

.....

Pastor Greg had treated them sensitively in the first session. "This could be a hard case," he thought. Abqurah was a Muslim. Ed Spencer was a recent Atheist. Both of them were in a place of delicate balance.

The first session was encouraging. Abqurah and Spencer were willing to admit to an ulterior motive for being there, for becoming Christian. They wanted something better than they currently had in their lives. Right now, there was emptiness and a longing. They wouldn't even call it a need for religion; maybe spirituality was more what they were looking for?

Pastor Greg understood Abqurah's emptiness. That her brother's extreme interpretation of the Qur'an had led him to destroy the family. To kill his sister and to land his parents in jail. Abqurah herself was basically unsullied by Aamir's craziness, though she kept quiet about her suspicions when her sister had disappeared. She tried to believe that Hazirah had simply run away from home. Now her culture and religion seemed dead to her.

Pastor Greg was gratified that Hazirah and Spencer were in his office. "If you want to become Christians, you must have an authentic search for the Jesus of the New Testament, otherwise you won't have a life changing experience." They admitted that their starting point was not Jesus, but a search for something better than what they've had in their lives. They wanted to get rid of this emptiness.

"Go to the New Testament," said Pastor Greg, "if you haven't been there and read it." He suggested Abqurah read the Gospel of Matthew. "And for the recent Atheist," remarked Pastor Greg. "I want you to go through the Gospel of John."

"Oh, before I forget," said Pastor Greg. "I want you both to read 'John 5' together, *The Sermon on the Mount*. Abqurah you can read that portion to Ed. That might introduce you best to what kind of person Jesus was, and what kind of heart he had for humanity."

> Blessed are the poor in spirit,
> for theirs is the kingdom of heaven.
> 4 Blessed are those who mourn,
> for they will be comforted.
> 5 Blessed are the meek,
> for they will inherit the earth

Pastor Greg said bringing up "baby Christians" was not an easy job. He thought "tough love" was necessary at times. He had the experience before when someone didn't take the sessions seriously. He said flatly to those people, "Come back when you're serious, and when you're ready."

"Transformation," he pointed out, "just doesn't work like magic. It doesn't come from a ritual, or a prayer, or a blessing, or me sprinkling Holy Water on people. They can walk away from empty rituals and have nothing. It's got to be authentic, and only that way, can people make the change themselves inside."

"Ed," said Pastor Greg. "You would do well to read Alistair McGrath's answer to Dawkins. The book is, *The Dawkins Delusion*." Pastor Greg's eyes twinkled with irony.

.....

Abqurah was a more difficult case, thought Pastor Greg. Her sister was murdered. "I'm suggesting you get a good counselor," he said. "It doesn't have to be a Christian one... but since you're interested in Jesus, I can recommend the name of a counselor who is both a therapist and a Christian... and somebody who's read the Qur'an." Pastor Greg wrote down a name for her and a phone number. "You can ask if your fiancé can sit in on the sessions."

Pastor Greg said he had friends who were Muslim, who wanted to be married as Christians but wear the traditional wedding garb of their culture. "You have to come to terms with your traditions and your culture and who you are," he said. "Sometimes it's tricky, especially if you're changing religions in mid-stream."

He admitted that people often tried to make God suit their needs, no matter what religion they came from. For himself, he said, God the Father and Jesus His son, were something which spoke to his heart. "The God in the Bible is the God who works on the ground," he said. He felt that Islam had "a more distant God."

.....

Abqurah and Spencer finished their coffees at Timmy's. They were glad they had seen Pastor Greg. They felt they could trust him with their thoughts, like he trusted his thoughts to them. There was nothing forbidden or secretive in their discussion with this young Mennonite pastor. "A good guy," said Spencer.

On the way out of Tim Horton's, Spencer couldn't help satisfying his curiosity. He asked the elderly lady who had served them, "So how's Tim Horton's treating you?"

"How do you mean?"

"Do they pay you minimum wages, at least? Benefits?"

"They pay us minimum wages, yes, and we can always buy into the benefits. They treat us just fine!" she said.

Spencer had noticed that the age range working there included mostly college students or older women, retired, looking for extra income.

The lady pointed out, "Tim Horton's also supports a Children's Camp."

Spencer thought, "Probably a tax dodge... At least a worthy one."

He nodded at the ladies behind the counter. Held the door open for Abqurah; and headed back to the car, hand in hand, all smiles.

CHAPTER 74

"Today's wives might be more independent, and good for them; but today's husbands are more serious, mature and committed than ever, and we should be applauded for it."

[JAKE WALLIS SIMONS, OCT 8, 2014:

http://www.telegraph.co.uk/men/relationships/11148366/Todays-man-takes-marriage-much-more-seriously.html]

.....

PASTOR GREG
COACH AND ENCOURAGER
TUESDAY, OCTOBER 21, 2014

PASTOR GREG WAS HAPPY THAT ABQURAH PROMISED TO GO to a professional therapist. Having her older sister murdered, by her own brother, was a double whamee! Actually, it was a triple whamee, since her parents were in jail.

"I'm glad you have an authentic desire to encounter the Jesus of the Bible," said Pastor Greg. He stopped himself, not wanting to sound like a TV evangelist. He switched topics to marriage counseling.

"Four out of 10 marriages end in divorce," he said. "Let's not make you two part of that statistic!"

He was encouraged to see the love in their eyes. He had already talked about an 11 year age difference, their different culture and religion and their jobs. Ed, as a police detective, had a dangerous job, and Abqurah, as a would-be social worker, would face her own stresses at her job. "You've got to find a balance in everything," said Pastor Greg, "and find time or rather, make time, for each other. Don't be married to your jobs!"

"Sounded like good advice," thought Spencer. "Doing it is another thing!"

Pastor Greg could see them as real Christians by the end of December. By the end of January, he would sign them up for the 6 week session in marriage counseling. They needed some foundation as Christians first.

"So," said Spencer, "What do we talk about in marriage counseling?"

Pastor Greg gave them the run-down:

Conflict Management – how you guys argue. There have to be rules and there have to be time outs and cooling off periods. The best is not to argue!

- Money – Often a bone of contention between two married people. Who is the bread winner? Who earns the most? Do we share equally? Have separate bank accounts? How abut a budget?

- Faith – Another big issue. Who is set in their beliefs? Who is less strict? Who is willing to set a Christian example outside of church? Who lives their Faith? Is the couple united in their Faith?

- Family Dynamics – How do you treat each other's side of the family? Do you get along with the in-laws? Do you support each other if there is "butting in"?
- Backgrounds – How much is traditional, how much modern? Do you want to include both your cultures?
- Wedding Day – What kind of wedding day do you want individually? As a couple? Are you agreed on costs? Photographer, church, hall? Who's invited? What about the ceremony?

Pastor Greg finished by saying, "At the end of the day, marriage is about the couple. It's not the ceremony or the wedding dress, not about the size of the ring or number in the wedding party. It's about you two." He added, "It's about the love you have for each other and it's about a commitment as long as you both shall live." Pastor Greg could see they stood a pretty good chance of staying together despite the odds.

CHAPTER 75

Definition: House Husband is a man who stays at home and cleans the house, takes care of the children and so forth, while his partner goes out to work.

Big Bang Theory, Season 5: "The Shiny Trinket Maneuver" – Howard was upset to learn that Bernadette dislikes and feels uncomfortable around children. However, she has agreed that when they marry, she will work, while he stays at home to raise the children.

[HTTP://BIGBANGTHEORY.WIKIA.COM/WIKI/HOWARD_AND_BERNADETTE]

.....

WALLY'S BUSY AFTERNOON
TUESDAY, OCTOBER 21, 2014

WALLY WAS A "LIBERATED" MAN. SOMETIMES TRADITIONAL images of where he should be in his career would tug at the back of his mind. Men still had a notion of being the breadwinner and of having accomplished this or that at certain points in their lives. Well, he and his wife had come to an agreement that he would handle the house, and she would bring in the pay cheques. She had a way with kids in her teaching job which made them respectful students. So Wally contented himself, with his computer, his camera and his house chores. He was "a reborn man" and "a house-husband." Who would have accepted that... 50 years ago?

He placed his sandwich on the TV tray with a glass of milk. He thought about what to have for supper. Cut up the potatoes, boil them first, then fry them with onions and bacon, lots of butter, salt and pepper.

He finished his lunch with "The Strange Love of Martha Ivers," a 1946 movie, starring Van Heflin, Kirk Douglas and Barbara Stanwyck. Wally loved black and white movies, the "film noir" tradition. He loved not only the stories in the movies but also the history during the era in which they were made. He loved getting moral lessons out of those old movies – something that would make him a better man where he could say to St. Peter, "Hey you've got a man with deep character here walking through the pearly gates here! I got my best qualities out of black and white movies!"

"Hmm," he thought, "how do you get a deep character, watching old movies?" There was a side of him which considered movie buffs shallow, escaping from real life on "the silver screen." Well, it was his hobby and it didn't hurt anybody.

The movie depressed him anyway, so when he swallowed his last bite, he turned the TV off. "Okay, house-husband, let's clean the bathroom!"

He got a pail of warm water, a wash cloth, some paper towels and Windex. The worst part of the chore was removing all the stuff on the counter by the sink and later putting it back. He started with the Windex and the mirror. Wally held the image of Tim Horton's in front of his mind. It had been the carrot today, the reward which prompted him to finish this chore.

Klassen had the day off, so they agreed to meet at Timmy's for coffee at 3:00 p.m. Wally finished cleaning by 2:30, while "The Strange Love of Martha Ivers" played itself out somewhere in TV land. He knew how the plot ended anyway: with the rich husband and wife shooting themselves, and Van Heflin driving out of town with his girlfriend to find a new life together, somewhere off the silver screen. If the Beatles hadn't seen the movie, Wally figured they already knew life's lesson from it: "Money can't buy you love, yeah!"

Wally put everything back on the counter around the sink. He'd do the vacuuming tomorrow. Tomorrow had worries of its own. No need to worry today.

. . . . .

Like Spencer and Klassen, Wally and Klassen had established a special friendship. They often met at Tim Horton's, and just chatted about their jobs, sports and the progress Wally was making with his counselor, Karl de Jong.

Klassen actually preferred this venue over *Williams Fresh Café*. He was getting sick of pies. So whenever he met Wally, he ordered a Boston Cream doughnut and a coffee, "double double." He felt more like a cop when he hung out at Timmy's. Nice change.

Wally held the door open at Timmy's with his shillelagh. It had become part of his personality by now; and he loved gesturing with it, pointing at objects with it, shaking it with emphasis when he was making a point. Quite an effective little tool.

They ordered, they sat, and they stared at their coffees. "So how's it going?" asked Klassen.

"I'm grateful I don't have to wear that dreadful space boot anymore over my broken ankle. A couple of months of hobbling around on that thing were quite enough," responded Wally. "I like the cane though."

"Anything new on the Karl de Jong front?"

"He's helped me with techniques to lessen my nightmares. I don't get bloody images in my head anymore like I used to. I think trying to write a novel is a creative diversion for me, and strangely enough, I am having fewer scary nightmares."

"How's the book going?"

"I'm on chapter 75, and trying to figure out how to squeeze another 75 pages out of this thing. It's hard controlling this beast, which wants to run away in all directions at the same time."

They sipped their coffees. People next to them looked. Who were these kooks talking about books and beasts? What about regular topics like the killing in Quebec or Ebola? Hey, how 'bout them Leafs?

"So," asked Wally, "how's police work? Do you ever relax at all?"

"Ironically enough, I'm reading detective stories, by Dorothy Gilman," confessed Klassen. "She's the lady who wrote the Mrs. Pollifax series about a widow who becomes a spy for the CIA. Mrs. Pollifax is the only elderly lady spy who has a double talent for karate and gardening. The author died in 2012, at the age of 88 from Alzheimer's."

Klassen paused reflectively and continued, "She knew a lot about human nature, and oddly enough, plants. She loved gardening and herbs which she put in her novels. Alzheimer's is such an insidious disease to wipe out all that knowledge and intelligence; and reduce them, to senility. What a shame!"

Wally commented, "Cancer's not a nice disease either." He paused and asked, "Which one of her books are you hooked on now?"

"*Thale's Folly*. It's about a young guy, Andrew Thale, who is asked to check out an old property left to the family. When he goes to Massachusetts, he finds four eccentric squatters have taken over the vacant house."

"Not my cup of tea," said Wally. "I like Star Trek. It's a great way to get off this planet." They both laughed.

Wally liked old time rock 'n roll. The last time they had been at Timmy's, Wally suggested that Klassen google Gerry Rafferty and get a taste of the songs in the album, *City to City* [1978].

"Catchy tunes," admitted Klassen. "I like *Baker Street*. Wow, what a saxophone solo."

"Yeah, the lyrics aren't bad either," quipped Wally.

Klassen couldn't quite remember all the lines, but he thought of his friend, Detective Spencer, that hard nosed cop who had recently switched his life around. "He's gonna give up the booze and the one-night stands and then he'll settle down in some quiet little town and forget about everything."

"Maybe that'll be good for him," thought Klassen. He smiled at Wally. "Detective Spencer has taken a shine to the victim's sister. Did you know?"

That was news to Wally. He never thought a cop would get personally involved with the people in a case. "Isn't that against the law or policy or something?" asked Wally.

"Not really. The trial is over. The parents are behind bars, and Abqurah is on probation, but the kid is at Mohawk College, trying to make something of herself. She's even thinking about becoming a Christian. Spencer and Abqurah are also thinking about getting married."

"Wow. That's some 180 degree turn. Wouldn't sit well with her brother. Look at what he did to Hazirah!"

.....

There was a lull in the conversation. Two ladies made their way to the next table with their coffees. Wally overheard them say they were glad for this break before they continued on to Buffalo. They set their coffees down and one of them looked at the huge photo on the wall behind Klassen.

"I've never known what Tim Horton looked like," she said, "and now I know. He looked like a big lummox with a brush cut straight out of 1950. Must have been before the hippies got into hockey!"

Klassen and Wally laughed. Klassen was a walking "Canadian Guide to Hockey Trivia," so he chimed in, "Yeah, he played defense for Toronto and then Buffalo. He started this coffee and doughnut chain, you know?"

"No, I didn't. Must be pretty rich by now."

"Nope, he's dead. His wife got rich though. Good idea, this coffee and doughnut business!"

"How did he die?"

"Wrapped his Corvette around an overpass in St. Catharines in February 1974. He was speeding and had twice the legal limit of booze in his system. Should have been coffee!"

The ladies explained that they had another hour, hour and a half, of driving before they got home. They appreciated friendly Canadians and a chance to sit and relax. "Tim Horton's coffee shops are not popular in the States," said one of the ladies.

"Maybe they will be," riposted Klassen, "Burger King recently bought up the Timmy's franchise. Watch out America! You'll be overrun by Canada's coffee and doughnut imperialism before you know it!" Klassen thought that was clever. Wally kept his mouth shut, with an audible groan.

CHAPTER 76

> Two "despicable attacks" on Canadian soldiers this week will not weaken the country's resolve to fight terrorism at home and abroad, a somber Prime Minister Stephen Harper said Wednesday.
>
> [CTV NEWS ARTICLE BY SONJA PUZIC, WEDNESDAY, OCTOBER 22, 2014]

.....

WAKE-UP CALL FOR CANADA!
WEDNESDAY, OCTOBER 22, 2014

FOR THE SECOND TIME IN ONE WEEK, THE CANADIAN MILItary has been targeted by radicalized jihadists. On Monday, Patrice Vincent, a soldier, was run down and killed in Saint-Jean-sur-Richelieu, Quebec, 30 minutes south of Montreal on Monday morning. His partner was seriously injured. Police shot and killed Couture-Rouleau, 25, a self-proclaimed jihadist.

Today, Wednesday, October 22, Corporal Nathan Cirillo, 24 years old, was gunned down as he stood guard at the National War Monument in front of Canada's Parliament Building in Ottawa. The shooter then marched across the street to Parliament Hill; and was himself shot dead, in Parliament's Centre Block by Sergeant-at-Arms, Kevin Vickers, a former police officer.

The shooter was identified as Michael Zehaf-Bibeau, 32 years old, born in Canada. He had a history of runs-in with the law. His passport had been seized previously because the Canadian government considered him a "high-risk traveler," – the same circumstances surrounding the Martin Rouleau-Couture case.

Hind-sight is better than 20/20 vision. One expert said that safeguards needed to be beefed up, especially at the front entrance of Parliament Hill, not just with patrol cars, but with having "boots on the ground," ready to deal with any lone gunman who gets through regular security checks.

.....

Wally and his wife put their plates on their TV trays at 6:00 p.m., and settled themselves in for the news. He had just finished roasting veggies in the oven and barbecued two burgers. Wally was expecting the same old story about gas prices, tax hikes or ISIS overrunning Iraq and Syria, but not a shooting in our nation's capital, on Parliament Hill! Wally Guenter was amazed at the photographs which flashed across his TV screen, as he and his wife sat at supper time, watching the CBC News.

Wally noticed what a nice day it was in those photos, blue skies and sun. How could such chaos happen in Ottawa on this picture perfect day?

Photos of Cpl. Cirillo flashed across the screen from happier times, of him in a black T-shirt with the logo GoodLife Fitness on it. He loved the outdoors, loved dogs, had bulging muscles, and a big smile with gleaming white teeth. Wally thought those teeth were great. He wished he had them. He had paid a lot of bucks for three front implants, and now his back molars were going!

Craig Oliver, long-time reporter for CTV News on Parliament Hill, said this assault at the Nation's War Memorial meant "a loss of innocence" for Canada. Somebody else commented, "This just doesn't happen in Canada." Tom Clark, another CTV broadcaster cautioned, "The lone wolf is the hardest to catch and perhaps the most dangerous!"

At first, it was thought that there might have been accomplices, maybe two or three gunmen, but the police soon determined that it was Michael Zehaf-Bibeau who acted alone. He made it right into the Hall of Honour within the Parliament Building. Had he gone through a door to the left, he might have entered the room where the government was gathered in a caucus meeting. Prime Minister, Stephen Harper, was there. A member reported that they had barred the door with chairs when they heard the shooting. Had the shooter gone through a door on the right, there were about 100 Members of Parliament in there. This brash breach into the Hall of Honour within the Parliament Building could have been so, so much worse!

Wally thought of two ironies in the shoot-out in Canada's capital city. First that the hall through which the killer ran was known as "The Hall of Honour." "That's a twist on the idea of honour killing," thought Wally. Secondly, he found it interesting that Michael Zehaf-Bibeau's mother was reportedly a senior officer with Immigration Canada. "The poor lady," thought Wally, "she's going to suffer some fallout because of her son's act, especially with people who know the family."

The mother, like any mother, tried to find reasons for her son's act, saying it was mental illness, drugs and that her son's original intention for getting a passport was to study the Qur'an in Saudi Arabia. The RCMP insisted that the act was ideologically motivated, and that they had a video made by Zehaf-Bibeau to indicate as much.

"Whatever the truth," thought Wally, "the young shooter didn't think about consequences to other people." Cpl. Cirillo had a six year old son. Wally wondered if Zehaf-Bibeau had had different friends, and maybe a different upbringing, if the tragedy to Cpl. Cirillo might not ever have happened? "Nature versus nurture, with maybe just plain bad luck?"

.....

Wally watched the CBC News at 8 p.m. as Prime Minister Harper addressed the nation. *"My fellow Canadians: for the second time this week, there has been a brutal and violent attack on our soil."*

The P.M. acknowledged that Cpl. Nathan Cirillo was, "murdered in cold blood – as he provided a ceremonial honour guard at Canada's National War Memorial, that sacred place that pays tribute to those who gave their lives so that we can live in a free, democratic and safe society." He likewise acknowledged that Warrant Officer Patrice Vincent was run down two days earlier by a car driven by "an ISIL-inspired terrorist."

He praised the first responders who came to help Cpl. Cirillo, the City of Ottawa Police and the RCMP. He commented that this week's events were, "a grim reminder that Canada is not immune."

"We are also reminded that attacks on our security personnel and on our institutions of governance are by their very nature,

attacks on our country, on our values, on our society, on us Canadians, as a free and democratic people who embrace human dignity for all."

Prime Minister Harper assured Canadians, "We will not be intimidated." He said that the government is resolved to identify threats and to redouble its efforts to work with allies around the world against those who bring "savagery to our shores." The P.M.admitted, "today has been without question a difficult day."

"Together we will remain vigilant against those at home or abroad who wish to harm us. For now, Laureen and I and Ben and Rachel join all Canadians in praying for those touched by today's attack. May God bless them and keep our land glorious and free."

.....

Cpl. Nathan Cirillo arrived home to Hamilton, Ontario, along "The Highway of Heroes" on Friday, October 24. He received full regimental honours.

The 24-year-old's body was taken from the Ottawa funeral home shortly before 1:30 p.m. and was escorted by Ottawa Police. The Ontario Provincial Police [OPP] escorted the procession along different legs of the journey back to the young man's home town

The stretch of highway between Trenton and Toronto is known as the Highway of Heroes. When fallen soldiers pass along the route, it is a tradition of respect for mourners to gather on the overpasses to salute the fallen soldier and wave the Canadian flag.

A man in uniform saluted the motorcade as it passed below on the Highway. An Ottawa firefighter waved a huge Canadian flag as crowds waited on the overpass to show their respect. Overpasses at Pickering, Port Hope, Mississauga and finally Hamilton were all crowded with mourners. There was a steady stream of supporters who left flowers at the Hamilton Armory, the base of the Argyll and Sutherland Highlanders of Canada.

Wally wondered if Michael Zehaf-Bibeau received a salute in Jannah, the Muslim Paradise, or if he had 7 vestal virgins waiting for him? He chuckled sardonically, thinking, "I hear they're running out of vestal virgins up there. Does it sound right that a religion throws sex into heaven for martyrdom?" Wally checked himself. He shouldn't think that way about Muslims.

Prime Minister Harper mentioned Corporal Nathan Cirillo by name and acknowledged that the soldier was, "murdered in cold blood." The killer's name, however, was not mentioned, deliberately left out. It'll soon be forgotten anyway; but not the atrocity, and the cowardice of the act, killing Cirillo unarmed from behind!

Cpl. Cirillo was guarding the Tomb of the Unknown Soldier with a ceremonial rifle that was not loaded!

The National Hockey League postponed that night's game between the Toronto Maple Leafs and the Ottawa Senators at the Canadian Tire Centre in Kanata following the shootings in Ottawa that day.

In a statement, the NHL said it wished, "to express its sympathy and prayers to all affected by the tragic events in Ottawa."

CHAPTER 77

"More Americans may be motivated to travel to the Middle East to join ISIS or other terrorist groups. The online radicalization efforts could also encourage 'lone wolves' to undertake acts of terrorism within the U.S., similar to the two deadly terrorist attacks in Canada this week, both apparently motivated by ISIS's online communications."

[*The Wall Street Journal* ARTICLE BY JOSEPH LIEBERMAN AND CHRISTIAN BECKNER, THURS. OCT. 23, 2014]

. . . . .

FRIDAY, OCTOBER 24, 2014: NATIONAL POST

UPDATE BY MELANIE MARQUIS AND LINA DIB, CANADIAN PRESS

MICHAEL ZEHAF-BIBEAU WAS SHOT

NEARLY A DOZEN TIMES BEFORE KEVIN VICKERS FATALLY WOUNDED HIM

OTTAWA – The gunman who charged into Parliament after shooting a Canadian Forces reservist was struck by nearly a dozen bullets from security officers and finally was brought down by Sergeant-at-Arms Kevin Vickers.

Several sources, who have requested anonymity, have confirmed that Michael Zehaf-Bibeau was fatally wounded by Mr. Vickers near the door of the Parliamentary library.

Zehaf-Bibeau burst into the Parliament buildings after fleeing the National War Memorial, where he had shot Cpl. Nathan Cirillo and hijacked a ministerial car. He ran into Parliament's Centre Block through the main entrance with RCMP officers in hot pursuit.

A security service source says the gunman was intercepted by a House of Commons security guard who unsuccessfully tried to wrestle his gun away from him.

The guard yelled, "Gun!" to warn his colleagues and tried to yank the barrel of the weapon down but Zehaf-Bibeau managed to fire, wounding the man.

The gunman then bolted several meters down the Hall of Honour with police and guards chasing him. More shots were fired.

> Zehaf-Bibeau, his body riddled with bullets, huddled behind a column by the Parliamentary library. It was there that Mr. Vickers fired the fatal shots.
>
> Mr. Vickers then walked to a nearby room where the Conservative caucus was meeting, and told MPs the shooter was dead. Prime Minister Stephen Harper was rushed to safety.
>
> Mr. Harper had been speaking to his caucus when the gunfight erupted.
>
> "I had images of people hiding behind pillars and shooting," said Manitoba Conservative MP Steven Fletcher. "There were so many shots."

.....

Wally took a sleeping pill that night before bed. Karl de Jong suggested that pills might do the trick for a little while. Wally's mind soon floated into the dream-world, and he dreamed this dream, imagining the last thoughts of Michael Zehaf-Bibeau, as he lay dying, riddled with bullets, hiding behind a pillar in the Hall of Honour. What would he be thinking?

WALLY DREAMED A DREAM ZEHAF-BIBEAU: DYING THOUGHTS

"I'm shot and bleeding. This column will give me enough cover to get a few shots off of my own. Let them come and get me! This is Jihad!"

"I told them three years ago, I needed help. That psychiatrist 'deemed' me fit to stand trial for robbery in Vancouver. I needed to pay for my crack habit. I refused bail so I could stay in jail for my past mistakes and get clean. But no, I was fit to stand trial!"

"Deemed fit, what a joke. My crime was ludicrous. I held up a McDonald's with a sharp stick. They called police and I waited outside. I sat down on my backpack and waited for them."

"Yes, I said, to the psychiatrist in Surrey, I've been devoted to Islam for seven years. How could the prosecutors let me walk? I said I wanted to stay in jail to clean up and become a better man. Maybe jails were overcrowded, budget cuts?"

"I warned them, if you can't keep me in, I'm going to do something right now just to be put in. I'm a crack addict and a religious person. Maybe if I'm in jail, when I come out, I'd appreciate things more or maybe get therapy, like a detox."

"I spent all of 66 days in jail. I was sent to the Burnaby Hospital with an apparent mental disorder and what happened? They said I did not suffer from mental illness. I was driven to a detox centre in Vancouver and then what happened? They wouldn't take me because I was not intoxicated."

"That's when I blew my top and robbed McDonald's. My lawyer made me sound good. From a good family in Montreal, here in Vancouver for a fresh start, shouldn't be in these courts. The judge gave me one more day in jail and six months to pay a $100 fine. Said to me, 'good luck to you, sir' as he dismissed me!"

"I stayed at a shelter in Vancouver. Told a guy, the Middle East is going to take over the world. I hate the United States and Canada. I didn't care about living or dying. They thought I was nuts because I had a hair-trigger temper. If somebody bumped into me on the bus, I'd push back."

"When I came back to Ottawa, where did I end up? Another homeless shelter! Allah meant something better than this for me."

"I told them I'd do something. I warned them, didn't I?"

All of this flashed through Zehaf-Bibeau's mind in fleeting impressions which took seconds. No words in those thoughts, just pictures and feelings. The police cornered him by the door of the library behind a column, like a dog hiding behind a tree. Zehaf-Bibeau clutched his rifle. Kevin Vickers, Sergeant-At-Arms, wasted no time, firing the fatal shots which finally put the mad dog down.

.....

A picture later released by the National Post showed Zehaf-Bibeau's yearbook photo at Ecole Secondaire Saint Maxime in Laval, Quebec. He looked like a clean cut young man, with a part in the top of his hair, a hint of a youth's mustache, dressed in a white shirt and tie and dark sweater, beaming all smiles.

His mother insisted that her son was simply mentally ill. The RCMP countered that Zehaf-Bibeau was ideologically driven by Islam. He was allegedly a terrorist, pure and simple!

Wally pointed out the controversy between the mother's view and the police. "That's understandable," said Wally's wife. "It's a mother protecting her son."

Zehaf-Bibeau had applied to renew his Libyan passport on October 2, but was denied. He had travelled to Libya in 2007, but his passport had expired. The passport office was concerned that his appearance had changed, and did not match his passport photo. Officials questioned why the old Libyan passport gave his first name as Abdul, but his driver's license listed him as Michael.

CHAPTER 78

Good news and bad news are not absolutes. For instance, somebody's good news can be somebody else's bad news. Look at the D Day landing in Normandy, June 6, 1944. It depends on which side you're on, what politics you have, and sadly enough, often what religion!

[KARL DE JONG, PH.D.]

• • • • •

AAMIR IN ANKARA, TURKEY
TUESDAY, OCTOBER 21, 2014

AAMIR GLOATED OVER THE EXCELLENCE OF HIS PASSPORT. They did a great job making him into a young Turk by naming him Jorin Aslan. Money helped.

His false passport was not known to Canadian officials; and in Sofia, Bulgaria, he was apparently a young Turkish business man going home to family. He had no problem at customs, neither in Sofia, nor in Ankara.

When he registered at the *Hotel Capital* in Ankara, he handed over his Turkish passport, to be picked up the next morning when he left. That was customary in these countries.

Jorin had asked for a wake-up call on Wednesday morning at 9:00 a.m. He needed to catch up on his sleep. Flights were hard even on a 26 year old body. It was midnight in Toronto. Nothing had yet unfolded there which would go down as an infamous day in Canadian history.

JORIN STAYS AN EXTRA DAY
WEDNESDAY, OCTOBER 22, 2014

Jorin decided that he would spend another night in Ankara. He had breakfast at the hotel's buffet, and asked at the front desk for fun things to do in the capital city. He wanted a little perk before he went back to the front lines of ISIL.

"Well," said the desk clerk, "brothels are legal and licensed under health laws in Turkey as you know. But last summer there was a crack-down by the government, and they stopped issuing new licenses. We even had protesters with huge placards that read, Stop Sex Tourism."

Ankara prided itself for restricting the brothels inside the Bentderesi red light district. However, new government policy demolished much of that business the previous summer. HIV was on the increase since then. Jorin bought a condom in the Hotel washroom. He was confident if he walked around in that area, he'd find what he was looking for, government crack-down or no. You can't put a stop to the world's oldest profession!

Jorin was amused by the blog posts he had read on his iPad:

"Its a shame when a country develops backwards."

"I've had cars stop a few times when I'm walking somewhere!! [I do not look like a prostitute!] But if you are on your own at night, then they can think you are. I do live just round the corner from the red light district."

He thought it would be nice to meet that female who lived near the red light district, and really see if she did or did not look like a prostitute. He spent a leisurely afternoon in the area and eventually found what he was looking for. He came back to the Hotel Capital, minus one condom.

It was 4:00 p.m. He had a light supper at the buffet. He had also made contact with the ISIL cell in Ankara, feeling stupid with that password, "How 'bout them Leafs?" This wasn't Canada and the Turkish national game, if anything, was soccer!

He received a name of a second contact. All this done via Facebook, then a phone number, then a face-to-face encounter near the "Hotel Capital." The password was changed: "We will continue. Continue what?" "The Crusades that will never end." He let his cell know of his intention to take a bus to Gaziantep, population about 1 million. That would get him closer to the Syrian border. He was assured his road back to ISIL would be smooth.

CORPORAL NATHAN CIRILLO COLD-BLOODED MURDER

WEDNESDAY, OCTOBER 22, 2014

He shut off the lights and closed his eyes on the horrible wallpaper in his room until 8:00 p.m. The bus trip to Gaziantep would be an all-nighter, getting him closer to the Syrian border. That way he wouldn't have to put up with this outrageous wallpaper in Ankara.

Jorin checked Canadian News online once more before bedtime. It was noon, Wednesday, October 22, in Toronto. Jorin didn't think about the wallpaper any longer as he stared at his laptop screen. He clicked on the article written by Michele Mandel of the "Toronto Sun," first posted Wednesday, October 22, 2014 at 11:53 a.m.

"Toronto – Homegrown terror struck at the heart of Canada on a fall morning, leaving a soldier murdered, the shooter dead and a nation reeling in shock."

> "Cpl. Nathan Cirillo, a 24-year-old father of one and a reservist with The Argyll and Sutherland Highlanders of Canada was standing sentry at the Tomb of the Unknown Soldier when he was executed at 9:52 a.m. Wednesday by a masked man bearing a long-barreled rifle. One witness told reporters the young shooter with long black hair and a 'black and white Palestinian type head scarf over his face' raised his arms in triumph after shooting Cirillo twice at point blank range."

Jorin was happy he had stayed longer at the hotel with free Wi-Fi. He exulted in the news. "Allah is great." He retrieved his passport before 9:00 p.m. and asked for a taxi to take him to the bus station where he bought a ticket from the Süha Busline for Gaziantep. It was a 9 hour trip. Arrival time 6 a.m., another perfect part in his plan, in time for breakfast somewhere.

The bus made its pit-stops in convenient places for coffee breaks and free Wi-Fi, if you had a device. Jorin kept track of what was happening on this fateful Wednesday in Canada, a day to remember for Canadians and for jihadists alike. It was already early Thursday morning in Turkey.

He thought Prime Minister Harper's address to the nation was a polished delivery. It was put on "Youtube" shortly after it was delivered. Jorin listened to it when they made their 5:00 a.m. rest-stop Thursday morning. He resented the fact that the Prime Minister did not mention the assassin by name.

Jorin had to google other news items to confirm the jihadist's name: Michael Zehaf-Bibeau, his father was a Libyan. That was an astute oversight by the Prime Minister, a public relations coup, where the assassin's name was meant to be forgotten. The Prime Minister acknowledged the names of *Cpl. Nathan Cirillo and Warrant Officer Patrice Vincent. He also acknowledged that these acts were, "a grim reminder that Canada is not immune."*

"You got that right," thought Jorin. "It's only just begun."

Gaziantep was only one hour away. He would rent a car and drive toward Kobane [aka Ayn-al-Arab] within Kurdistan. His contact would get him to ISIL which was still fighting for control of Kobane. Kobane was smoking from all the air strikes inflicted by U.S. drones fixed on ISIL's cache of weapons.

CHAPTER 79

"A world with an infinite number of universes would virtually ensure that conditions in one universe would repeat in another, Greene said. In other words, there would almost certainly be another version of you reading this article, written by another version of me."

[*Live Science* ARTICLE BY TANYA LEWIS, JUNE 2, 2014 – INTERVIEW WITH BRIAN GREENE, PHYSICIST]

• • • • •

WHAT IF... ?
THURSDAY, OCTOBER 23, 2014

JORIN TOOK A LAST MINUTE SNOOZE AS THE BUS NEARED Gaziantep. He dreamt a dream of possibilities. He'd read *Star Trek* novels behind the counter at his father's Pioneer gas station in Hamilton. He dreamt of parallel universes.

Michael Zehaf-Bibeau ran past the left door where Prime Minister Stephen Harper was in caucus. A choice that could have been, might have been, should have been, opening a door to Universe A. To the right was the door where almost 100 Members of Parliament were gathered. Another choice not taken, in the panic of the moment, opening another desirable possibility, Universe B. The universe in which we live was or is Universe C, the one where Zehaf-Bibeau was shot and killed behind a column outside the door of the library.

Jorin liked A and B. He imagined Zehaf-Bibeau bursting through the left door with his long-barreled rifle. Zehaf-Bibeau spotted Harper almost immediately, the tell-tale glasses. His first bullet was for him, a clear shot through the glasses. Harper fell dead. His other bullets rent through the bodies of caucus members. Sergeant-at-Arms, Kevin Vickers, rushed through the door behind the man and emptied his revolver into Zehaf-Bibeau. Zehaf-Bibeau dropped dead to the carpet. He had done enough damage. The day's headlines listed the dead in the "Universe A" caucus meeting:

> Prime Minister Stephen Harper, Minister of Justice and Attorney General of Canada, Hon. Peter MacKay, Minister of National Defense, Hon. Rob Nicholson, Minister of Foreign Affairs, Hon. John Baird, Minister of Veteran Affairs, Hon. Julian Fantino, and Leader of the House, Hon. Peter Van Loan.
>
> The news reported this as, "a day which will live in infamy in Canadian History."

Jorin exulted in triumph as he dreamed about this universe A. To destroy the body of a country, snip its head!

He dreamt that Michael Zehaf-Bibeau chose to enter the right door, instead of running straight on down the Hall of Honour. Zehaf-Bibeau was faced with a horde of faces; and he just blasted away at anything and everybody, with his long-barreled rifle. He had reloaded on the run after killing Corporal Cirillo. He had seven bullets for seven lives. The Sergeant-at-Arms, Kevin Vickers rushed through the door behind Zehaf-Bibeau, and emptied his own gun into the crazed man's body. "I put him down," he yelled to the other officers rushing through the door.

Jorin did not exult as much in this universe B. He liked the scenario in Universe A much, much more. Maybe those universes were real? "All universes are possible realities," someone had once said. "Anything you can imagine, does and will happen!"

Jorin turned slightly in his seat and dreamed on. He remembered a fable he had read in Canada years ago in school: *The Lady or the Tiger*. He did not know how he made the connection. Maybe the left or right choice? He imagined that Harper was the youth who had to make the decision to choose the door, which the barbarous king had rigged in his amphitheatre of justice. Justice was blind and haphazard like the flip of a coin. Except that the king [Jorin] had put a tiger behind each of the doors! So whichever door Harper picked, it was loss/loss for him! Jorin had no idea why he remembered the tale. At the end of English class, the teacher had said, "Life is full of doors. You have to open different ones at different moments. You have to make the choice, sometimes for your life!"

Jorin awoke from his dream as the bus pulled into the station in Gaziantep. It was 6:00 a.m. exactly. He shook himself awake, grabbed his iPad and backpack. Stood up and passed through the door. He needed food and coffee.

He continued his thoughts. “My door has been decided before the beginning of time. The dye has been cast, the coin tossed. It’s East against West. But I will choose how the coin lands. I will make it so, or die trying.”

CHAPTER 80

"He has only forbidden to you dead animals, blood, the flesh of swine, and that which has been dedicated to other than Allah."

(An-Naĥl 16:115)

.....

KOBANE BURNING

THURSDAY, OCTOBER 23, 2014

HE ORDERED EGGS AND TOAST WITH JAM AT THE RESTAURANT. No bacon. That was the flesh of swine and not allowed by the Qur'an.

Jorin sipped his coffee and googled Kobane News for Thursday, October 23, 2014. Kobane had not yet been won. He noticed that articles now shortened the name of ISIL to IS, Islamic State. How typically Western to shorten names and become familiar!

The Turkish government had allowed Turkish and Syrian Kurds, under the name of Peshmerga, to join the fight against Islamic State militants. Jorin didn't like the sound of that. Thursday's headlines read:

> **US-led air strikes against Islamic State (IS) militants in Syria have killed 553 people since September, UK-based activists say.**
>
> The Syrian Observatory for Human Rights says 464 IS fighters, 57 other militants and 32 civilians have died.
>
> Meanwhile, the US has carried out more air strikes against IS positions near the besieged town of Kobane.
>
> Kurdish sources told BBC Arabic that IS had retaken a strategically important hilltop 4km west of the town.
>
> Kurdish forces fighting IS in Kobane took Tal Shair nine days ago.
>
> [BBC NEWS MIDDLE EAST, 23 OCTOBER, 2014]

A night photo showed part of Kobane burning in flames. The caption under the picture read: Intense fighting has resumed around Kobane after a relative lull. Another photo showed somebody with a victory sign in the foreground while a plume of smoke rose from a section of the bombarded town. That caption read: Air strikes are believed to have delayed the IS advance on Kobane, but may not stop the town from falling. Kurdish casualties have mounted as fighting with IS in and around Kobane in recent days has intensified.

The US military says that its fighters and bombers conducted six air strikes against IS positions in Syria on Wednesday and Thursday, including four attacks near Kobane which destroyed IS fighting positions, an IS vehicle and an IS command-and-control centre.

Jorin read that control of Tal Shair had flipped between Syrian Kurdish fighters and IS militants in recent days. Kurds last captured the hill - close to the border with Turkey - from IS on October 14. Tal Shair was a Syrian-Kurdish town right up against the border. Whoever had control of it, had a chance to control Kobane. Control of Kobane would give IS control of a long stretch of territory along the Syrian border.

The U.S. boasted the number of air-strikes: Iraq 334. Syria 247. "It was like a basketball score," thought Jorin. "Well, maybe not quite, the score was three times as high as any game." It was a see-saw battle from week to week, and Jorin definitely had to get back to it.

It was 7:00 o'clock and time to meet his contact. Jorin was on his second cup of coffee. A swarthy man with a full black beard approached him. He must somehow have gotten Jorin's picture.

The man immediately said, "We will continue."

"Continue what?" asked Jorin.

"The Crusades that will never end!" Jorin bowed and smiled.

He was led to a safe house for jihadists in Gaziantep nestled in southeast Turkey. Bribery and friends would get him back to IS militants. They always managed to arrange a time and a place to cross over to the other side.

CHAPTER 81

> "Every time you make a choice, you spawn a multitude of universes, leading to umpteen other yous – some of them living very different lives. This raises a myriad of moral conundrums, from what we owe our other selves to the death of hope."
>
> [*NewScientist* ARTICLE BY ROWAN HOOPER, SEPT. 25, 2014]

.....

CHORES AND CHOICES
FRIDAY, OCTOBER 24, 2014

WALLY HAD A LIST OF CHORES TO DO FRIDAY: CHECK HIS MasterCard balance, do Physio, buy a new keyboard for the computer [letters were worn off on the old one and crumbs from muffins blocked some of letters from typing], and check possible publishing companies for his novel. It was 7:30 a.m. and the first item which needed attention was getting the "Sloppy Joe" recipe into the slow cooker, a 6 hour process, which when readied, could be forgotten so Wally could focus on the other chores of the day.

Wally remembered a "Home Improvement" episode, about Tim the Toolman Taylor, where Jill had given specific instructions about getting the boys ready for school. A sequence had to be followed exactly to get things done right and on time. Tim, being Tim, just had the attitude, "It's as good as done," and mixed everything up with the result that the boys were late for school, had the wrong lunches and well, things did not go smoothly at all.

"I guess that was a maturing experience for Tim," thought Wally. "We all have to make our own mistakes to grow up."

Wally got the "Sloppy Joe" recipe ready. Lots of veggies to cut up. Gee that was busy work and took time, sweet time. He'd do it later.

He went to his morning Physio session to loosen up his bad back and shoulder. Then he walked around Heritage Village in Jordan; and he noticed that several owners of houses had flags lowered at half-mast, in honour of Cpl. Cirillo. Wally was wearing a poppy on his lapel ahead of November 11, Remembrance Day.

The funeral service for Cpl. Cirillo was to start at noon at Christ's Church Cathedral on James St. N. in Hamilton on Tuesday, October 28th. Wally had googled the event and time. An earlier photo popped up of Kathy Cirillo, the mother of Cpl. Nathan Cirillo, following her son's casket in tears. Wally thought, "She's probably looking for reasons for this killing. Why?"

Wally got his Physio done. Rode back to the house on his bicycle. Toque and gloves on. Sunshine had burst forth. Crisp leaves fluttered from the trees. He itched to be out with his camera, maybe on the Bruce Trail or Ball's Falls before the winds destroyed the leaves, and the snow blanketed everything. He preferred autumn colours to white snow.

He got back into the kitchen and took most of the morning just in the preparation of the "Sloppy Joe" recipe. Dice onions, carrots, sauté, dice zucchini, pepper. Mix chili powder, oil, salt. Good thing he had soaked the Pinto beans overnight in water. Okay turn to page 2 in the recipe; he followed instructions [in his own way], and put the mess into the slow cooker at 6 hours.

Years ago, when he left his teaching job because of stress, his wife had said to him: "I'm bringing home the big bucks, so you have to hold up your end of the apron string in house work." Wally figured, well, better a house-husband, than another nervous breakdown.

He finally went back to the computer to tackle his novel, chapter 81. He had the feeling he already had exceeded his 80,000 words to qualify for a good sized book. But you just don't stop when you get there. You have to tie loose ends up in a logical and non-hurried bundle, so the reader doesn't feel cheated. Wally figured that he needed to add whatever dabs were necessary to complete his verbal painting. "I'll finish when I finish," he thought, "I hope I've painted it with enough substance and art to make it all worthwhile. There's been weeks and weeks of obsessive work here and a pouring out of my soul."

He sat and stared. "If I could undo Cpl. Cirillo's death and make time go backwards, how would I rewrite the scenario? Maybe a Universe D or a Universe E?" thought Wally. He daydreamed in front of the computer screen.

UNIVERSE D:

"Michael Zehaf-Bibeau hasn't stopped the hijacked car yet and jumped out with his long-barreled rifle. He doesn't know that Canada has beefed up its security around the Parliament Buildings, a lesson learned from the recent breaches around the White House in the States. No budget cuts in Canada!"

"There are two armed guards in Mountie Uniforms at the entrance to the Parliament Building. They are armed and are wearing Kevlar vests. There are two rover agents walking aound the grounds between the War Memorial and the doors of the building. They too are armed. They are on half-day shifts to keep fresh."

"Cpl. Nathan Cirillo is doing sentry at the grave of the Unknown Soldier. Cpl. Branden Stevenson, Cirillo's best friend, is also on duty there at the War Memorial. Their ceremonial rifles are not loaded, as is tradition, but they have been given permission to wear loaded sidearms, and thereby, are a security reinforcement to Parliament Hill in case of real and present danger."

"Zehaf-Bibeau hijacks a car and jumps out with his rifle. He rushes by people who duck for cover. The roving guards spot the activity and yell, Halt. Unheeded, they shoot Zehaf-Bibeau several times. He's still moving. Cirillo and Branden turn to see the chaos. They draw their guns simultaneously while Zehaf-Bibeau aims at Cirillo and fires. Cirillo is shot in the hip. He fires back but Zehaf-Bibeau is not down and out. Sergeant-at-Arms, Kevin Vickers, comes out of the Parliament Building and puts the fatal last shots into the assailant. He then re-enters the Parliament Building to inform Prime Minister Harper, that it was a close call. The shooter is dead."

"Cpl. Brandon stays with Cpl. Cirillo until the ambulance arrives. That was some close call, he says to his buddy."

UNIVERSE E:

Fast reverse on that last universe! "Zehaf-Bibeau takes a bead on Cirillo. The rover agent shoots him in the shoulder. Zehaf-Bibeau drops the rifle. Cirillo and Brandon jump on him kicking the rifle away. They subdue him and call for backup. An ambulance is called. Zehaf-Bibeau is taken away in cuffs, one of the rover agents accompanying him"

"Sergeant-at-Arms, Kevin Vickers, comes out to check on the incident. He says, 'That was a close call. I'll go back and report to the Prime Minister that it's all over and calm the other members down'."

"The guy looked like he's on drugs. Probably mentally ill," says Cpl. Brandon.

"Who knows where his head was at?" says Cpl. Cirillo. "Might have been his way of calling out for help. Well, he'll get all the help he needs now!"

Wally only dreamed the incident could have been like that, but wishing didn't make it so.

Wally shook himself out of his reverie. He and his wife had to go vote for a new mayor and councillors in Jordan before supper time. There was one woman on the ballot for mayor, nice to see. Wally insisted on exercising their democratic right to vote. He read the brochures and hand-outs. Some of the candidates had come around personally, knocking at doors to explain their platforms for their campaigns.

Wally read the brochures to his wife. They discussed their preferences, and then, went to the Church to vote in their Ward. One ID and the yellow voting card were required.

Wally had to be told how to put the ballot sheet back into the sleeve, so nothing could be seen as to how he voted. He had trouble following directions on the sleeve [typical man!] "Why didn't they say, just put your Xs down and put the sheet back in the way you found it?"

They went home for supper. Vegetarian "Sloppy Joes!" His wife said, "Hmmm, interesting." Wally didn't like the sound of that. "I'll have to tweak the recipe a little," he said. His wife didn't say anything else about the meal.

"Well, at least we voted," Wally finally said, hiding his disappointment over the taste of his Vegetarian "Sloppy Joe."

CHAPTER 82

Where have all the flowers
gone, long time passing?

Where have all the flowers
gone, long time ago?

Where have all the flowers gone?

Young girls have picked them everyone.

Oh, when will they ever learn?

Oh, when will they ever learn?

[PETE SEGER 1962 ON THE CHARTS]

• • • • •

IN FLANDERS FIELDS AND POPPIES
WAR AND POETRY 1915
FRIDAY, OCTOBER 24, 2014

"GUELPH, ONTARIO, SEEMS SO FAR AWAY," THOUGHT Lieutenant John McCrae. "Sometimes I wonder what good I'm doing here in France as a Canadian surgeon?" McCrae had served in the Second Battle of Ypres during the First World War. His Scottish born grandfather would have been proud of him and his brother, both of them doctors. Thomas McCrae would become a professor of medicine at Johns Hopkins Medical School in Baltimore.

"Damned orders," said John McCrae to himself. He was ordered away from his artillery unit in June 1915, so he could set up three Canadian hospitals near Boulogne-sur-Mer in northern France. He expressed displeasure about his new assignment to a friend, "All the goddam doctors in the world will not win this bloody war. What we need are more and more fighting men." Nevertheless, he obeyed.

Lt. Alexis Helmer, was killed during the Second Battle of Ypres in 1915. Helmer was a friend and a former student. In McCrae's opinion, this was only one life and talent among so many, which were wasted in this "world war" equipped with new weapons invented to kill masses of people: air-planes, machine guns, tanks, hand grenades and chlorine gas. "All of them, insidious. Why can't nations get along?" asked McCrae.

"Damned killing!" McCrae cursed to no-one in particular. He looked up at the sky. He took a seat on the back of an ambulance, near an advance dressing post at Essex Farm, north of Ypres. During a lull in his duties, he pulled out a notepad and a pencil. He gazed toward the large numbers of poppies growing in the churned up earth of the recent battlefield. His mind wandered to the cemeteries which took up so much space in Flanders. Tears welled up in his eyes. His heart ached as he watched the poppies blow in the wind. It was May 3, 1915. "Alexis was buried only yesterday!" McCrae began to scratch a line into his notepad; shortly it would become a poem, a tribute to his friend, and to all those brave soldiers who died in this terrible war, this war to end all wars! It was later published in *Punch Magazine*.

In Flanders fields

In Flanders fields the poppies blow

Between the crosses, row on row,

That mark our place; and in the sky

The larks, still bravely singing, fly

Scarce heard amid the guns below.

We are the Dead. Short days ago

We lived, felt dawn, saw sunset glow,

Loved and were loved, and now we lie

In Flanders fields.

Take up our quarrel with the foe:

To you from failing hands we throw

The torch; be yours to hold it high.

If ye break faith with us who die

We shall not sleep, though poppies grow

IN FLANDERS FIELDS. [JOHN MCCRAE 1915]

John McCrae, poet, author, artist, doctor, became ill with pneumonia at his hospital in France during January 1918, which was some 10 months before the end of World War I. His illness was complicated shortly by meningitis.

He was honoured by being the first Canadian appointed as Consulting Physician to the First British Army, only four days before he died! Must have been something in how slow the paperwork was shuffled, never keeping up with real life. McCrae died on January 28, 1918. His burial included full military honours at Wimereaux Cemetery in France. Seventy-five nurses stood by to watch the procession. McCrae's horse, Bonfire, wore his master's boots backwards, as was the military custom, in those days. It was a cold winter day. The war was still going on until the following autumn, Armistice Day, November 11, 1918.

In another two decades, the world engaged in a new war to end all wars, World War II, which ended with the Atomic bomb being dropped on the Japanese cities of Hiroshima and Nagasaki. Then came the Korean War, the Vietnam War, and so on, and so on.

John McCrae would have been greatly disappointed in the world after his death. He would have had to write another poem or two or three perhaps, to get his message across about man's inhumanity to man.

If space aliens had dropped in on John McCrae one night beside his hospital bed in 1918, and asked him in a dream, "Is there intelligent life here on earth?" he would have had to say, "No. Not here! Look elsewhere!" If an angel would have asked him, "Why did you write this poem?" John McCrae would have said, "Because the world needs it!"

.....

Moina Michael was an American professor who taught at the University of Georgia when the First World War broke out. She took a leave of absence from her job and volunteered to train YWCA workers who were going overseas. When she read John McCrae's poem in 1915, she was inspired to write her own verse:

> We cherish too, the Poppy red
> That grows on fields where valor led,
> It seems to signal to the skies
> That blood of heroes never dies.

Ms. Michael had the idea to wear red poppies on Memorial Day in honour of those who died in the Great War serving their country. She was the first to wear one and sold poppies to friends and co-workers in Canada and the United States. The money went to charities which helped servicemen in need. A French woman, Madam Guerin thought the idea was splendid and promoted it in France and Belgium to help soldiers and war orphans alike. The U.S. Post Office honoured Ms. Michael by issuing a 3 cent stamp with her image on it in 1948. [Wikipedia]

.....

Wally heard that Canada's Governor General, David Johnston, and his wife, Sharon, were on a 4 day tour of Poland. On Sunday, October 26, 2014, they were scheduled to visit the former German Nazi Concentration Camp KL Auschwitz, in Oswiecim. They placed candles by a great stone wall at the foot of which lay wreaths commemorating the dead.

When Wally googled the event, he could see the day was overcast and misty. He could just make out the iron motto which spanned the gate of the old concentration camp: "Arbeit Macht Frei!" [Work Makes You Free!] "What irony!" thought Wally, "Not if it's forced labour. First, you burn people out, then you burn people up!" It is estimated that 1.1 million people were "exterminated" in that camp.

Wally thought, "Of course, war doesn't make any sense." Cynically, he thought, "I suppose it's population control in the bigger scheme of things, while making the captains of industry rich to keep churning out tanks, guns and planes."

November 11, *Remembrance Day*, was only 3 weeks away! What will we remember about the message in those poppies from so long ago?

"In Flanders fields the poppies blow
Between the crosses, row on row,"

.....

Wally remembered a line from an old Pete Seger song, "When will they ever learn?" If thousands of years had anything to say about it, maybe never! Or was there hope after the A-bomb was dropped on Hiroshima and Nagasaki? It took two punches to knock Japan out of World War II. The Japanese drafted a new constitution in February 1946, and put it into effect on May 3, 1947, with an amazing post war Article, which heralded good will.

> **Japanese Constitution 1947**
>
> ARTICLE 9. Aspiring sincerely to an international peace based on justice and order, the Japanese people forever renounce war as a sovereign right of the nation and the threat or use of force as means of settling international disputes. (2) To accomplish the aim of the preceding paragraph, land, sea, and air forces, as well as other war potential, will never be maintained. The right of ***belligerency*** of the state will not be recognized.

Was this something that Japan had learned the hard way as a nation? Or was it a subdued concession made by a defeated country? Some races never forget old grudges. History has been the witness to the poor character of nations. Writers and poets keep warning the human race to reform and to love one another. "Or," thought Wally, with a touch of cynicism, "was all that just sentimental schmaltz?" Just this past month, in October 2014, Japanese politicians had suggested that their constitution needed to be tweaked to include clauses about self-defense, especially in the light of the tension with China, over the sovereignty of certain islands off their coast.

Where have all the soldiers gone, long time passing?

> Where have all the soldiers gone, long time ago?
> Where have all the soldiers gone?
> Gone to graveyards, everyone.
> Oh, when will they ever learn?

Oh, when will they ever learn?

[PETE SEGER 1962, ON THE CHARTS]

CHAPTER 83

What the world needs now
is love, sweet love

It's the only thing that
there's just too little of

What the world needs now
is love, sweet love,

No not just for some but for everyone.

[SUNG BY JACKIE DESHANNON 1965]

.....

FIRST AIRED OCTOBER 23
TAVIS SMILEY AND ANNIE LENNOX
FRIDAY, OCTOBER 24, 2014 NOON

WALLY LOVED WATCHING THE TAVIS SMILEY TALK SHOW. Wally also liked the Charlie Rose Show. But he judged that Tavis edged Charlie out in his personal preference.

Tavis was engaging; he always leaned towards his guest in a friendly manner and exuded enthusiasm about his topics. It's great that he ended every program with the comment, "Keep the Faith!"

Wally sat down at the TV tray at Noon and watched the show, taped just two days prior. Tavis interviewed Annie Lennox, Scottish born singer of "The Eurythmics." She had a new CD coming out, entitled "Nostalgia," a collection of soul, jazz and blues. Quite a departure from her old rocker days in, "Sweet Dreams Are Made of This."

Wally admired Annie Lennox. She was globally aware, something he was working on, but then, she had, "travelled the world and seven seas." Tavis Smiley knew when to ask a question and when to let the guest talk.

Annie could talk and very well! She mentioned global issues, the Ebola outbreak. She saw how women and children died because of the disease, and as a mother, herself, she said, "that's just injustice. The women have no voice and I just wanted to make my contribution as a woman and I thought gender is a great leveler."

She observed, "Music is the great connector. It doesn't matter about skin color. It doesn't matter about culture. No, music will connect all of us. And the other thing is gender, my gender, the feminine gender."

She said that Billie Holiday's song, "Strange Fruit," was a protest song, written before Civil Rights. She considered "Strange Fruit" as the "darkest track in the whole album." She added, "because of what I've seen around the world, I know that this theme, this subject of violence, bigotry, hatred, violent acts of mankind against ourselves... .is a human theme that has gone on for time immemorial."

Annie Lennox asked why were racism, domestic violence, warfare and terrorism happening? "So I've always had that sense of empathy and kind of outrage that we behave in this way."

She pointed out that she and Billie Holiday have a lot in common. Tavis asked, "Like What for instance?" Annie wasn't stumped. "Like female empowerment, women's rights, bigotry, racism... there's so many things we could talk about. We could talk about lipstick too. We could talk about clothes." Then Annie got serious again, "But we could talk about the things that are still going on in this day and age that haven't changed one iota and the sort of pain that, you know, I feel because I would like to see a world that, you know, could transform."

Annie mentioned world poverty. Resources that are not distributed fairly. "I see huge disparity between the western world and the so-called developing countries. And I got to places where people are living as if they were in the medieval times... access to basic things like clean running water, sanitation, electricity, a safe home, education of young girls growing up, getting access to primary education, secondary education, maybe getting a college degree, future opportunities." She praised non-governmental organizations, NGOs, for working so hard on these very goals.

Leaving her topic of music way behind now, Annie launched into a comment about religion. "I don't have an issue with Christians," she said. "What I have an issue with is that people are so divisive and so polarized. How could you be Christian and then have another kind of Christianity?"

She really questioned a double standard. "So how can you follow one specific religion and say that, you know, this religion is supposed to be about love, peace, respect, honour of your brother and sister, and yet still find that you hate people of color? I've never understood that."

The main question for Annie was not which God was the right one. Her main question was, "Are you kind? Do you love or do you hate?"

Tavis added his own comment here. "When I said that you didn't have a problem with God, but a problem with Christians, somebody once told me that I love God, just save me from the Christians!"

Annie found labels interesting because they reduced human beings into a stereotype, into something simple. "I don't want to make any distinction between you as a human being. I don't care if you're Muslim, if you're Buddhist or Christian." She lived in Cape Town, South Africa, for a while. Although they didn't have Apartheid anymore, she still saw the same old poverty, same old violence, the same old struggle for survival, and people still didn't get out of that rut of poverty.

Annie got back to talking about her album, "Nostalgia." One of the songs that Billie Holiday sang spoke to an old, old disparity, the same old struggle, "God bless the Child That's Got His Own."

Wally loved the way Tavis Smiley ended his show, "And as always, Keep the Faith."

Wally considered himself lucky to have listened in on this interview. Tavis Smiley handled it just right. Wally was becoming globally aware, just sitting in front of the TV tray eating his lunch. An old black and white movie was coming up next at 1:00 p.m., as long as he made sure he'd start supper at 4 o'clock. "Slow down, you're movin' too fast, you gotta make the afternoon last." The movie was the 1937 version of *Lost Horizon*.

It was 12:30 p.m. Wally went to the computer to check his e-mails. An old pal had sent him a link with an intriguing title: "Pigs, Lipstick and Islam, Wild Bill for America."

Wally made himself an instant coffee, brought it back to the computer and clicked on the link.

CHAPTER 84

Cold hearted orb that rules the night,

Removes the colours from our sight.

Red is grey and yellow white.

But we decide which is right.

And which is an illusion?

[MOODY BLUES 1967]

.....

"PIGS LIPSTICK AND ISLAM"
LOST HORIZON, 1937 MOVIE
FRIDAY, OCTOBER 24, 2014

"PIGS, LIPSTICK AND ISLAM." WHAT WAS THAT ALL ABOUT? Wally accessed the YouTube video. He wasn't sure if it was just another "Islamaphobic" piece of propaganda or if there was some truth in it. He did not want to paint all Muslims with the same racist brush but with extremists infiltrating so many nations of the world and killing people... well, you never know, which attitude is right and which is an illusion?

Wild Bill wore a black cowboy hat, sported a grey mustache, leaned comfortably against a tree as he spoke. The tree gave him a look of solidity, maybe adding authority to his talk. Wild Bill opened with this comment, "Hi everybody, Wild Bill for America here, reminding you of an old saying, It doesn't matter how much lipstick you put on a pig, it's still a pig!"

His reference was to Islam and how Western countries were trying to put pretty makeup on a religion that was violent at its core and not peaceful. To Wild Bill, there was no such thing as a moderate Muslim. "This video is about ISIS, Islam and Muslims and their future plans for the U.S.A. and England and Norway, the Philippines, Spain and so on... "

Wild Bill said, unequivocally, "ISIS is Islam!" He spoke with conviction. Wally was not sure if the man was a bigot or a patriot.

Wikipedia said that "Wild Bill for America" was a pseudonym used by a Tea Party Video blogger who claimed to have been a Deputy Sheriff at one time. Another source said that his full name was "William Finlay." It was hard for Wally to label Wild Bill definitely, either a bigot or a patriot, or some of both?

Wally simply didn't know what to make of the man's comments. Maybe some of what he said was true. After all, the Spanish, French and English took North America away from "the Indians" and put them on reservations! What if Wild Bill was right about Islam spreading all over the world, and conquering it by conversion or by blood?

"The mass murders of ISIS are in the tradition of Muhammad himself and there is no amount of lipstick that can hide that fact. But Liberals in both the U.S.A. and England are still putting lipstick on that pig, still insisting that all Muslims should not be judged by the actions of a few... actually 100,000,000 of them that are active terrorists."

Obama allegedly said that ISIS is not Islamic. Wild Bill begged to differ, "One does not have to look far to see that the 'I' in ISIS stands for Islamic! Keep smearing that lipstick Mr. President!"

"People who do not understand Islam keep thinking that we can just let in the peaceful Muslims and keep the bad ones out. Islam does not work that way. Westerners must break out of that blindness. The entire Islamic religion channels every Muslim down the same path and it all hinges on the number of Muslims in any society."

Wild Bill went on to say that when they are less than 2% of the population, Muslims are friendly and kind and good neighbours, "following Muhammad's rule, Be a friend until you are strong enough to crush them."

"When they reach 4-6% of the population they begin demanding special rights: Halal food, no pork or alcohol in local stores."

"When they reach 8-10%, they become aggressive towards Jews and Christians. They begin forming Muslim neighbourhoods where only Muslims are welcome and begin setting up Shari'ah Law Courts. Street demonstrations with the signs, Islam Shall Rule the World, Freedom Go to Hell, Behead Those Who Insult the Prophet."

"And guess what happens when the Muslims reach 20% of the population? War comes to your town. Assassinations, burning synagogues and churches. Women who do not wear the burkha are raped. This pattern has been observed in every nation that has put out the welcome mat to Islam, every time."

"The evidence is indisputable and there is no excuse for ignorance. But amazingly, the Liberal Left, the U.S.A. and England keep doubling down on stupid. They keep smearing lipstick on that pig and chanting the mind-numbing mantra that Islam is a religion of peace."

Wild Bill pointed out that Muslims make up 4% of the population in the United States, allegedly with the feverish help of the Obama administration to bring more Muslims in.

"The March of Islam is the closest thing we have to the Star-Trek Borg! Resistance is futile! You will be assimilated!"

Wally didn't know what to make of this video. Was it just fear-mongering? Was Wild Bill a Prophet of sorts, a voice crying in the wilderness, who would one day be proven to be right and then, when it was all too late, say, "I told you so!" Wally thought of the old *Moody Blues* lament, "which is right and which is an illusion?" He hoped he wasn't one of those, "bed-sitter people," sitting on the sidelines, not knowing what was happening and not knowing what to do!

He also wondered if some North American Aboriginal Peoples were snickering over the fears that "the whites" were now having over Islam. Were "Aboriginal Peoples" finding the growing disquietude in the West a huge historic irony, and a sort of revenge? What races, what groups, what individuals had ever been safe on any continent or island, in any country or village, anywhere on earth in all of history... that were, truly safe?

Not a word was spoke between us, there was little risk involved

> Everything up to that point had been
> left unresolved

Try imagining a place where it's always safe
and warm

"Come in," she said, "I'll give you shelter from
the storm"

[BOB DYLAN – *Blood on the Tracks* ALBUM, 1975]

LOST HORIZON 1937 MOVIE

Look at the world today. Is there anything more pitiful? What madness there is! What blindness! What unintelligent leadership! A scurrying mass of bewildered humanity crashing headlong against each other, compelled by an orgy of greed and brutality.

[WORDS OF FATHER PERRAULT, "THE HIGH LAMA," BASED ON THE NOVEL BY JAMES HILTON 1933]

.....

The old black and white movie, *Lost Horizon*, starring Ronald Colman and Jane Wyatt [later of *Father Knows Best* fame] came on after lunch at 1:00 p.m. Wally had lots of time before he got the ingredients ready for tonight's supper, so he heated up his coffee in the microwave and settled down in front of the sitting room TV.

The plot was about a hidden society living within an idyllic valley sheltered from the bitter cold of the Himalayan Mountains. The valley is Shangri-La, a Paradise on Earth, where people live hundreds of years, in happiness and health.

The hero, Robert Conway and his companions, seek shelter in Shangri-La when their plane is hijacked and crashes into the snow-bound mountains. The survivors are led by Chang into the warm valley protected from the violent snows of the Himalayas. Most of the newcomers grow to love this Paradise. A few want to escape and get back to "civilization."

Conway, his younger brother George and Maria, a native to Shangri-La, escape from the valley. They take Maria with them despite being warned that she is very old. When they make it out of the valley, they are confronted with a harsh reality, because Maria falls exhausted, face down in the snow. They turn her over, and shockingly, discover she has become an extremely old woman and died. George loses his sanity and jumps to his death.

When a rescue party finally comes upon Conway, he has lost all memory of Shangri-La. On the ship back to England, he regains his memory; he jumps ship, and miraculously survives, and makes it back to Shangri-La. Searchers try to track him down but lose him in the Himalayas. Conway, somehow, through his insane determination, gets back to Shangri-La and this Paradise on Earth.

The movie was adapted from the 1933 novel by British author, James Hilton. The market was ripe for such an idea as *Lost Horizon*. The world's economy had slid into "The Great Depression of the Dirty Thirties." Lots of poverty, the 1930 Dust Bowl, farms wiped out in the Mid-West. The American movie which came along in 1937 was pure escapism for unemployed Americans who looked for a dream which would take them away from poverty and the real world. Hitler and World War II hadn't come along yet. Hitler's vision promised a different sort of "Utopia," but as they say, that's another story.

Wally pondered, "If only Shangri-La were real?" Would he be satisfied with the simplicity of Paradise? Or would he need something more? Was happiness and health enough? To him, Maria's fate was symbolic of the aging and death which all flesh is heir to. It's the human curse, perhaps of sin, as the Bible says. Wally wasn't sure. He thought there was some good advice in the Bible. "We reap the wages of sin." Yet, deep in his heart, he yearned for a place like Shangri-La, a Paradise on Earth.

Sondra: You see, it's not a dream.

> Robert: You know, I sometimes think that the other is the dream, the outside world.
>
> In 1713, a Belgian priest, Father Perrault, had stumbled upon the blissful valley of Shangri-La. The movie makes him much older than the novel does. The point in both is that he established a society founded on the simple rule, "Be kind." Wally recalled the TV interview which Tavis Smiley had with Annie Lennox, who said, "I don't have an issue with Christians." The main question is, "Are you kind?"

Wally was amused by Shangri-La's "religion," which seemed to be a hybrid of Tibetan Buddhism and Christianity. Father Perrault became known as the High Lama, and in fact, was still living, at the ripe old age of 250+ years in the movie, when Conway stumbled into the valley in the 1930s. Wally was disappointed, however, when the High Lama launched into what sounded like a Christian sermon, reminiscent of "The Great Commission":

For here, we shall be with their books and their music and the way of life based on one simple rule: Be kind. When that day comes, it is our hope that the brotherly love of Shangri-La will spread throughout the world. Yes, my son, when the strong have devoured each other, the Christian ethic may at last be fulfilled, and the meek shall inherit the Earth.

[MOVIE DIALOGUE DIFFERENT FROM THE BOOK P.165, *Lost Horizon*, COPYRIGHT 1933 JAMES HILTON, HARPER COLLINS PUBLISHERS, FIRST PERENNIAL EDITION 2004]

According to Wally, the script would have been more effective had it stopped the High Lama's speech at "Be kind," without going on to mention "the Christian ethic." Kindness, Wally figured, embraced, and probably appealed, to a wider audience than the mention of the Christian ethic. Wally found it ironic that the role of the High Lama in the old movie was also played by a New York Jew, Sam Jaffe!

However, the remake in 1973 of *Lost Horizon* was so different!! It was basically a Musical. The hero's name is changed to Richard, not Robert. [played by Peter Finch] He falls in love with Catharine, not Sonya. [played by Liv Ullman] The brother, played my Michael York, reprises the same role as the brother George, who is an irritating character, eager to escape from Shangri-La. His love interest is still Maria, played by Olivia Hussey. Chang is played by John Gielgud.

Just about everybody sings in the 1973 version, including Liv Ullman and Olivia Hussey. Wally felt this version was too fuzzy warm, without the solid drama packed in the old 1937 flick. It just lacked the suspense of the old black and white movie.

The newer 1973 version was more politically correct. The High Lama did not mention anything about "Christian ethic." He wanted humanity to "be kind" and show "brotherly love," so that "the meek shall inherit the earth." Nothing mentioned about Christianity.

It was also more fitting, in the newer version, that a Frenchman, Charles Boyer, played the part of Father Perrault [i.e. the High Lama]. One other detail struck Wally: the movie made the High Lama younger by about 130+ years, having him stumble into the green valley in 1847, later than 1713 in the old black and white movie. "Interesting changes!" thought Wally.

Wally asked himself, "Where does kindness come from?" Is there something innate in humanity, free from the Commands of a religion, which nudges people to be kind, same as hospitality? Does it issue from The Golden Rule, devoid of Biblical implications, "Treat others, as you yourself want to be treated." Is that the natural thing, an inborn instinct for everybody?

Wally had seen a documentary on monkeys. A mother, burdened with her own little one, stumbled upon a newly born orphan monkey. She looked upon the shaking infant, and passed it by to eat some leaves, then turned back, and cupped the new-born into herself, adopting the helpless infant. The infant stopped shaking. Now the mother was burdened with a twosome, not just her own. Nevertheless, she took on the job. Where does that impulse come from? Monkeys don't have a religion to take in orphans. Wally wondered about kindness, never mind religion.

Wally's mind flitted to other questions evoked by the movie. He could appreciate George Conway's view of Shangri-La. Robert Conway's brother felt claustrophobic within the confines of the Valley of the Blue Moon, from which he so desperately wanted to escape. His DNA was not satisfied with books, music and brotherly love. Some people simply are not wired that way; and have more of the greed, brutality, and need for stimulation in the world wired into their natures. The porters, for instance, never stayed within Shangri-La. They brought art, books and music in and took out bribes of gold.

In the 1937 movie, Conway, George and Maria, the three "escapees," cannot keep up with the porters as they get away from Shangri-La through the treacherous mountain paths. They are jeered at, and finally, the porters take pot shots at the trio with their revolvers, until they, themselves foolishly set off an avalanche which kills them. They ironically call to mind, the High Lama's very words judging the outside world:

"A scurrying mass of bewildered humanity crashing headlong against each other, compelled by an orgy of greed and brutality."

Wally had a wild thought. What if ISIS stumbled upon the rocky access in the Himalayas which led into the sheltered valley? Would there be a blood bathe? A couple of beheadings until the citizens of Shangri-La converted to Islam? Would ISIS be satisfied to remain there as an isolated Islamic State, hidden and protected from the rest of the world, happy with its own laws and traditions in their self-made Paradise?

Or would their leaders say, we cannot just remain hidden here within this secluded valley. We must spread our wings; and go forth, to show the entire world the Light of our Religion. We have our Great Commission to spread the word. The word Islam is defined as "submission," which if not done willingly, could mean bringing unbelievers to their knees by force. A thought flashed through Wally's mind. "Yikes! Muslims making Shangri-La submit! Muslims destroying Paradise? Shangri-La, a Paradise Lost!"

Wally could appreciate Father Perrault's assurance in the 1933 novel, "You see there is no need to fear invasion by an army. That will never be possible, owing to the nature and distances of the country." [p.150, *Lost Horizon*, copyright 1933 James Hilton, Harper Collins Publishers, First Perennial Edition 2004] However, with the technology ISIS had in hand in the year 2014, transgression into the secluded valley of the Blue Moon, by an army, could be possible. ISIS intended that no corner of the globe would be secluded from Islam. Wally also wondered how ISIS might regard the concept of religious freedom, and the comment in the book, made by Chang, "Must we hold that because one religion is true, all others are bound to be false?"

[p.76, *Lost Horizon*, copyright 1933 James Hilton, Harper Collins Publishers, First Perennial Edition 2004]

. . . . .

Wally connected ideas in *Lost Horizon* to lessons from *Gulliver's Travels*, written by Jonathan Swift, and published in 1726. He had read the book in university English, and watched the movie version, *The Three Worlds of Gulliver*, in 1960 when he was 14 years old. Kerwin Mathews starred as Gulliver, and he sang a beautiful song in it about lovers.

Wally discovered years later that Kerwin Mathews was gay. The actor lived with his partner for 46 years until his death at the age of 81. That marriage had a better track record than a lot of heterosexual marriages. Wally couldn't help but wonder, how his own world view had changed over the years, since the age of 14.

Wally recalled the big religious question, in Swift's tale, which cost 11,000 Lilliputians their lives because they rebelled against the royal edict to break their eggs at the little end. Big Endians either fled to Blefuscu or were put to death. A religious war raged between Lilliput and Blefuscu over the question, and neither side was willing to compromise. Yet, Lustrog, the prophet of the Lilliputian religion said, "All true believers shall break their eggs at the convenient end." Wally loved Jonathan Swift's illustration about how religious dogma could be reduced to strange absurdities, which cost lives!

In the movie, when Gulliver arrived in Lilliput, he saw how small-minded the Lilliputians were, and as a sort of giant-god, he could change the landscape, so that it could be transformed into a land of plenty, a land "of milk and honey," indeed a Paradise. Ironically, when Gulliver fled to Brobdingnag, the Brobdingnagians were the giants. They provided every need for Gulliver and his Elisabeth: food, clothes, shelter, as long as the two stayed in their play-castle, and entertained the giants. Their Paradise on earth was a gilded cage!

Jonathan Swift showed, in his original 1726 book, how greed and envy can snatch Paradise out of the grasp of humanity. James Hilton, in his 1933 novel, *Lost Horizon*, more than two centuries later, showed that things hadn't changed!

Wally shook himself free from his meandering thoughts. The old movie version of *Lost Horizon* was over at 3:00 p.m., and he had to get to his real-life chores. He'd just finished his mid-afternoon coffee and cookie [just one]. He walked into the kitchen to chop veggies, and to prepare the ingredients for that evening's supper. His wife would be hungry, and tired, after her usual tough day at school with needy, and sometimes, unruly kids.

CHAPTER 85

"Patriotism is a superstition, one far more injurious, brutal and inhumane than religion."

[GUSTAVE HERVÉ]

.....

REHANA "POSTER GIRL"
MONDAY, OCTOBER 27, 2014

WALLY KNEW THAT PATRIOTISM COULD MANIFEST ITSELF in fanaticism. When it was combined with religion, it was doubly crazy. Doubled-up, it could lead to genocide! The Holocaust kept repeating itself over and over again throughout history, different master races, different victims, different times, same old craziness!

Wally recalled God's intervention in the Old Testament, that the land of Canaan was the land promised to the Jews by God. If you had that belief, you could do almost anything!

It was also a "carte blanche" to move in on somebody else's real-estate. If God gave you the excuse, then do it, in the name of God! Jews did it to the Amalekites, Hittites and all the other "ites" in the Old Testament.

God was also a great excuse, used by the Muslims under Muhammad and later by the Christians under the Crusaders to just move in, kill and conquer and take the territory. Nothing like a promise backed up by God! "And now," Wally shook his head. "You have one type of Muslim moving in on another type of Muslim. It's all crazy, and people keep killing each other in the name of nationality and God."

The Kurds were always fighting somebody. If it wouldn't be the Islamic State, it would be Turkey or one of the other three countries that incorporated its people. Kurdistan refers to large parts of eastern Turkey, northern Iraq, northwestern Iran and northeastern Syria.

Now, that their battle was focused against an immediate threat from Islamic State militants, Kurdish men and women joined forces equally to fight for their "nationhood." It was estimated that the Kurdish army was made up of approximately 10,000 women, one-third of the army's Kurdish "man power."

Man is the only animal that robs his helpless fellow of his country - takes possession of it and drives him out of it or destroys him. Man has done this in all the ages. There is not an acre of ground on the globe that is in possession of its rightful owner, or that has not been taken away from owner after owner, cycle after cycle, by force and bloodshed.

[*The Lowest Animal* BY MARK TWAIN 1835-1910]

.....

Wally googled Kurdish women fighters and found this link: *Kobane "Poster Girl."* On Monday, October 27, rumors began to spread on social media that a *Kurdish female fighter,* known by the pseudonym of Rehana may have been beheaded by IS. The same gruesome photograph had apparently been circulating since at least October 5 on pro-IS accounts.

The Twitter photo where the girl was still alive, smiling shyly, and making the V-sign, must have been taken in soft light or possibly with a soft filter, showing a pretty young girl with long brown hair.

She was dressed in green and brown army fatigues. The camera caught her smile. The caption below the photo read, "A Kurdish female fighter named 'Rehana' has become an iconic figure in the fight against the Islamic State, ever since this picture was widely circulated on social media."

Wally remembered when he had made a "V-sign," actually a "Peace sign" in his day, driving to the West Coast to see Canada with two of his university buddies. Was it 1970? It seemed so long ago and yet like yesterday. A police cruiser came by, just outside of Dryden, Ontario. They hadn't even left the province yet, 3 days drive just to get out of the province and into Manitoba, half-way through Canada.

Wally made the peace sign at the cruiser, coming in the opposite direction. Dumb move. The police car turned around and followed Wally for quite a while. Stopped him on the other side of Dryden. Broken tail-light.

The policeman just wanted to make Wally sweat a little. For being a smartass! He gave him a warning to get the light fixed and let him go. Whew!

Winston Churchill's original "peace sign" meant Victory. The peace sign during the hippie era meant peace, make love not war. Rehana's peace sign again meant Victory. Things go in circles. What a pretty girl, just a kid.

Wally had an insatiable photographer's curiosity. That's why he always climbed a hill or slid down a slope to get closer to his subject. Kurdish resistance denied any and all ISIS claims that this was Rehana, the "*Poster Girl.*" Wally wanted to settle the question once and for all in his own mind.

He lifted two photos off the internet, and transferred them into his *Fireworks* program. The first photo was a cropped image of Rehana's alleged severed head. The second photo was of the famous Poster Girl where Rehana made the Victory sign. Wally oriented the severed head to face right as in the poster girl photo. Then he sized the head and gave it transparency to superimpose over the poster girl photo. He could adjust the transparency. The hairline, eyebrows, nose, slant of cheekbone and the distance to the lips seemed to match Rehana's face. There were too many similarities which could not be ignored, but then a lot of young girls looked similar in his eyes.

The severed head could indeed be Rehana's, maybe a 70% chance? There was always a difference between a dead face and an animated one, so Wally couldn't guarantee the comparison was a 100% match. "Too bad," he thought. "I hope it wasn't her. This kid was just as pretty as Rehana, but still a kid!"

Wally studied the photo of the ISIS fighter holding up Rehana's head. The militant beamed with a big happy smile, holding up her head in his right hand like a trophy. With his left hand, he held up his index finger, probably as a victory sign that ISIS was number One. The fellow wore green army fatigues. He had long scraggly hair, a beard and mustache. He wore his baseball cap backwards. Wally thought the elation in the man's smile was pure evil! The photo depicted not only man's inhumanity to man, but man's inhumanity to women! Was this a photo the young man could be proud of to send back home to family?

Wally had done a lot that day. Gotten all the way up to chapter 85 in his novel. He enjoyed mixing current events with fantasy, all wrapped in the package of a murder mystery. The storytelling seemed to flow by itself now, caught in an energy of its own. He remembered a time when he had writer's block. Well, it was more like recovering from a nervous breakdown. He didn't write or read anything for five whole years. His wife took out a *Star-Trek* novel for him one day and he was hooked. Then she suggested *The Hardy Boys* and when those were done, Robert Parker's Spenser novels, and a whole raft of murder mysteries followed suit.

CHAPTER 86

"Man's inhumanity to women issues from his fear of undoing tradition and his long history of male dominance."

[DET. JAKE KLASSEN]

.....

AAMIR BACK IN ACTION
MONDAY, OCTOBER 27, 2014

ABDUL ALI AL-SAYED WELCOMED AAMIR BACK TO CAMP with the standard greeting, "As salaam aleykum," [may peace be upon you] Jorin greeted him back, "***Wa alaykumu as-salaam***." There was no smile of welcome, however, on al-Sayed's face. He beckoned Aamir to sit. There was no offer of Turkish coffee.

"I have been briefed about your exploits in Toronto. Wahidi died in a useless hijacking of a minor airplane. Your explosion at the Union Station did nothing but blow a toilet apart! We are disappointed with this outcome of our money and time... At least, you returned, and now, you can redeem yourself."

Aamir kept his head bowed. Silence was golden in moments like this. Finally, al-Sayed said, "The Kurds say that we have not killed Rehana, their Poster Girl, whom many young Kurdish women rally around for their cause. You must determine if the head of that girl we killed on October 5th is indeed the head of Rehana. Our best software is at your disposal." Aamir made brief eye-contact with al-Sayed, and bowed again in compliance, "It will be done."

Unknown to Wally, Aamir went through the same process as Wally, using *Fireworks* and comparing the parameters of the heads in two pictures: the one with Rehana, the Poster Girl giving the peace sign, and the one of the militant holding up the severed head. Aamir wasn't quite sure, maybe 70%, but not absolutely, so he reported as much to his commander, al-Sayed.

Aamir explained, "The facial features are drained of blood, and a sunken face does not appear exactly the same as an animated person's face."

Al-Sayed ordered Aamir to go out with two militants, and capture another Kurdish female who looked like Rehana. "We must get her and deflate the hope of these young Kurdish women. Fighting against men in this Holy War is not natural for women! Capture Rehana this time, if the first one wasn't her!"

Aamir took his AK47 and picked two men, Daamin and Parvez. He hoped that the trio would have a guaranteed success this time, and if they were lucky, get some fun out of it too. The plan was to launch rockets into that quarter of Kobane defended by Kurdish women.

Shortly after the smoke settled, the Islamic State trio moved in to check on dead bodies, and to capture any laggards if they could. They found several. Aamir and his men shot the chubby ones. The order was to capture a skinny one, and drag her back across the Islamic State lines. Allah, it seemed, blessed their plan. They brought back "Rehana," at least one that looked like her. If it wasn't her, then she would have to do for their propaganda.

A dozen men surrounded her leering and jostling each other with elbows. She screamed and shook her head. Will Allah hear her plea?

The one who had said, "I'll see you later," stood above her. He ripped off her clothes while others held her down. He was going to rape her.

"My name is Aamir." he said. "You find your 'position' impossible?" he added, laughing at his own cleverness.

Rasha felt numb. It seemed like her mind had left her body. It was as if she were detached from everything, witnessing what was happening to her with no feeling at all. There was no Jihad John. No sword. No Allah, it seemed. She preferred a quick death.

.....

"My gun jammed. Three of them dragged me to the ground. They kicked and hit me over and over. They grabbed my hair, pulled me up and handcuffed me with FlexiCuffs. One of them pulled out his penis, and masturbated in front of me. 'I'll see you later,' he laughed."

"I'm glad Rehana shot over 100 of these jihadists over the past few months! I used to think I was lucky to look like her. Now I'm facing my own death, maybe a beheading? I wish they'd just shoot me now."

"How could I be so stupid to let them capture me? I should have run when my comrades ran. There were too many rushing our position... and then my rifle jammed!"

"Maybe I will become a Poster Girl too, if I get out of this? I heard Rehana's photo got over 5,000 tweets. Yes, I could picture myself as a Poster Girl too. But I'll be a dead one. I wanted no fame in my fight, only freedom for women!"

"More of my sisters-in-arms need to join the Kobane resistance. Jihadists don't like facing women soldiers. To get killed by one of us will send them to hell. So much for their 72 vestal virgins! What kind of heaven is that?"

"Will my sisters in the Women's Defense Unit miss me? I wish I had a bomb on me. Other women have used suicide bombings to take some of these ISIS thugs with them."

"I remember my dear friend, Deilar Kanj Khamis. She should have been a poster girl too. Her military name was beautiful, Arin Mirkan. Short and sweet. She blew herself up outside of the city. Killed 10 ISIS fighters who would never see Jannah, their Paradise."

"Haj Mansour reported that Kurdish fighters were forced to withdraw from that strategic hill south of the town. Khamis, another sweet sister in arms, stayed behind to the last moment; and attacked ISIS jihadists, with gunfire. She threw grenades as they moved in. Surrounded, she blew herself up with the explosives strapped to her body, her beautiful woman's body that is no more. I do not know if her sacrifice was worth it. We lost the hill again that Wednesday."

"ISIS likes beheading its captives. Soldiers or aid workers from the West. Doesn't matter. They make an example of anything that opposes them. Maybe it was 'Jihad John' hiding behind his mask, doing his proud deed for Allah. I've heard of reports that nine Kurdish fighters lost their heads this month, three of them women. Will I be the fourth?"

"Those damn Americans. They've left us with a mess. I'm not sure if their boots on the ground will even fix this."

"Rehana was said to be a phenomenon in the Muslim world. Maybe I will become one too, if I get out of this. I want freedom for women, with a chance to show our faces, and our choice to marry the men we want. My thoughts go out to my poor mother and father... and to the real Rehana, wherever she may be. May Allah bless her."

CHAPTER 87

> "I am with you: give firmness to the Believers: I will instill terror into the hearts of the Unbelievers: smite ye above their necks and smite all their finger-tips off them."
>
> [HOLY QUR'AN 8:12]

.....

COSMIC CONNECTEDNESS
MONDAY, OCTOBER 27, 2014

SO, WALLY WAS ON CHAPTER 87 IN HIS WRITING. HE WAS still taking sleeping pills under the supervision of his therapist, Karl de Jong. Tonight would be a sleeping pill night.

The beginning of his dream opened up in a field of poppies. Then the landscape changed to rocks, a town smoking in the background. A hand was raised and slapped a young girl hard. She was a Kurdish fighter captured by

Islamic militants. Wally was uneasy about this dream, but he could not escape it. He dreamed he was the girl.

WALLY'S DREAM
RASHA'S END

She wished she were Rehana but she wasn't. Maybe she'd be braver. Rasha felt like a young deer led to slaughter. Aamir grabbed her hair, pulled her head back, and whispered in her ear, "Amy." Rasha's last thoughts were, "We are all Rehanas. There will be others," as she faded into the void.

Aamir let his men do what they wanted. He did not care about consequences from his commander, whether this was Rehana or not. This one was just another fish in the sea, caught by Allah's grace in the ISIS net. She wouldn't be missed in the bigger scheme of things, and she wasn't Rehana anyway. When the men had done, Aamir grabbed her hair, pulled her head back, and cut her throat from behind. As she bled out, he whispered in her ear, "Amy."

He would plunge back into the fray with Daamin and Parvez, and catch another skinny female, one who might just turn out to be Rehana after all. Aamir was the supreme fisherman of females. There were lots of fish in the sea! He smiled with male superiority. Allah had made man that way!

CHAPTER 88

"Is it true that we Greeks are really dead and only seem alive? And in our fallen state we imagine that a dream is life? Or are we truly alive, and is life itself dead?"

— GREEK PASSERBY, WITNESSING THE DESTRUCTION OF THE LIBRARY OF ALEXANDRIA IN 391 A.D.

.....

WALLY WATCHES TV
TUESDAY, OCTOBER 28, 2014

WALLY WATCHED AN EXCELLENT DOCUMENTARY ON CTV, *Alexandria: The Greatest City*, narrated by historian, author and broadcaster Bettany Hughes. He was captivated by the documentary, so captivatingly done with intriguing historical detail.

Doctor Hughes related how Alexander the Great, in the fourth century B.C., conquered Egypt, and built the harbour in the mouth of the Nile, a harbour that attracted huge commerce from all corners of the Ancient World. It was there that his successor, Ptolemy 1 Soter built the famous library, which eventually stocked half a million volumes of great literature and science of that world.

In AD 391, Emperor Theodosius I, issued an edict that paganism was illegal. A crazed horde of Christians destroyed the pagan temples in Alexandria, including the Serapeum where many ancient books were stored.

The fourth century was not the only one in which the books and artifacts of the library were either burned or smashed. The Muslim army of Amr ibn al 'Aas captured Alexandria in AD 642. Arabic sources describe the destruction of the library by the order of the Caliph Omar. A 13th century historian, Bar-Hebraeus quotes Omar as saying, "If those books are in agreement with the Qur'an, we have no need of them; and if these are opposed to the Qur'an, destroy them." Apparently only 1% of Alexandria's library has survived into the modern world.

If the Islamic State should win the world, as they wish, will they burn all written knowledge, including the other 1%? Will there be a big burning spree of books, along with the bodies of Christians, Buddhists and Hindus? Will they also delete everything on the internet except the Qur'an and the Hadith, and will they deny that man ever walked on the moon? Or sent the Mariner to orbit around Mars? And deny that The Curiosity Rover ever landed on The Red Planet to look for microbial life and evidence of water? What would the new Islamic State allow on earth? Would they get rid of the internet and revert back to 7th century life? Every man enjoys 4 wives and makes them wear veils? Which direction will Time travel on a revised Planet of Earth?

. . . . .

"Agora" was a film about the history of the Library of Alexandria. "Hypatia and Alexandria" was another excellent documentary narrated by Doctor Bettany Hughes. Wally made a note to watch these, "if I have time and if I do not grow too old."

Doctor Bettany Hughes gave a brief account of the death of Hypatia. Hypatia was a philosopher and scientist who lived in Alexandria in the the 4th century CE. She was an expert in geometry, mathematics and algebra. She redesigned the navigational instrument, called the Astrolabe. Christopher Columbus had the Astrolabe on board, when he discovered America in 1492, [although he was not comfortable using it, because it failed when the sky was overcast at night].

It was a plain fact that Hypatia was easily 1,400 years ahead of her time, before anybody thought of the "Women's Liberation Movement." The intelligentsia respected her in Alexandria, until Cyril became Pope and Patriarch of Alexandria in 412. Cyril was also known as the city's new bishop, showing himself to be an ill-tempered, quarrelsome, hasty, and violent man. He had no tolerance for pagans, and that included Hypatia.

Any woman who had knowledge of the stars and could use instruments of calculation, like the Astrolabe was considered to practice witchcraft.

One day, in about 415, a mob of Christian zealots, led by Peter the Lector, stopped a woman's carriage and dragged her from it into a church. It was Hypatia. They stripped her naked and beat her to death with roofing tiles.

Then they tore her body apart and burned it. That was how they killed witches in those days! Enlightened people knew that Hypatia was one of the last great thinkers of ancient Alexandria; and one of the first women, to study and teach mathematics, astronomy and philosophy. A Women's Liberationist, centuries ahead of her time! [Wikipedia]

Wally was inspired by this documentary, narrated by Bettany Hughes. He deliberately missed his other favourite show, on at the same time, *The Big Bang Theory*.

He had to admire those women fighting alongside men in Kurdistan against ISIS. He was convinced that If there were a change in that part of the world, it would have to come from the women. "It's got to be done by Islamic women, themselves," he thought, "Men will not give up their power to let women be 'equal' there."

CHAPTER 89

"Inferiors revolt in order that they may be equal, and equals that they may be superior, and such is the state of mind which creates revolution."

[P.17, *Thale's Folly*, BY DOROTHY GILMAN, BALLANTINE PUBLISHING, 1999]

• • • • •

THE BIG SCHEME OF THINGS
TUESDAY, OCTOBER 28, 2014

VISIONARIES, ARTISTS, WRITERS AND PHILOSOPHERS HAVE had dreams which sparked change throughout the ages, through their writings, art and actions, and in the extreme their revolutions. Sometimes for good change, sometimes for bad, sometimes trading one bad change for another bad change.

Wally looked at historical fiction as a slice of life, a copy of what is real and needs to change. Charles Dickens aimed his writing skills at the social changes needed in Britain; Honouré de Balzac in France; John Steinbeck in America. Writers hold a mirror up to society, and say what's wrong with this picture? Surprisingly, some of them have succeeded in shaking the kaleidoscope of society, to make the colours change a little bit, sometimes a lot. Look at Abraham Lincoln, Martin Luther King, and that young Pakistani girl, Malala Yousafzai!

Wally thought of England's history, "The Magna Carta," The Great Charter of the Liberties of England, originally issued in Latin. It was sealed under oath by King John at Runnymede, beside the River Thames near Windsor, England, on the 15th of June 1215. That gave rise to English Common Law and democracy.

Sadly, the plight of the common man was not improved by the Magna Carta, but the idea of a Common Law was created, at least, a little seed for a later democracy. The Industrial Revolution gave rise to a middle class, though the commoner still did not fare too well during that time. Charles Dickens wrote about the shameful poverty in 19th century England. It looked like every century needed its own movers and shakers who could twist that social kaleidoscope a little bit more, to make the colours and patterns of the world change hopefully for the better.

The Reformation [1515], the American Revolution [1776], the French Revolution [1789], all were great turning points in society. But did they create a Just Society? For the most part, No! There was no just distribution of power and wealth through all those eras of "social change," even to the current day. But things got better as the centuries rolled along.

During the Renaissance and the Reformation Movement, Catholics still burned Anabaptists at the stake. As time went on, Americans freed themselves from the imperialism of Britain, only to create their own imperialism under the Monroe Doctrine and Manifest Destiny. European settlers originally looked for land and religious freedom in the New World, only to organize a new government which put American Indians on reservations. Then there was Slavery, all justified by the Bible. Later still, the Civil War was supposed to make black people equal, and to this day, it looks like that equality has slipped past the Constitution, despite a black President! But, it can be argued, things got better.

In France, Marie Antoinette was guillotined, so that the rabble could "eat cake." Even a century later, the coal miners of France did not have enough to eat and were enslaved by "Les Gras," the Fat Ones, the well-fed factory and mine owners. Emile Zola and Honouré de Balzac wrote about class disparity, and the "Comédie Humaine," which continued to plague their society a long time after the French Revolution. Even Revolutions don't seem to solve anything. But, it can be argued, things got better.

We can skim across history into the 20th century: the Russian Revolution, World War I, the Great Depression, World War II, the Korean War, the Cold War, the Vietnam War, the Hippie Movement, the Yuppie Movement, and in the huge Circle of History, Islam against Christians, and so on, and so on.

If Democracy is the best we can do, then heaven help us, we still have not achieved it, to make things right for the poorest of the poor and the blackest of the black. Look at Afro-American ghettos and the widening gap between those who have money and education, and those who have not!

Democracy is not democracy in a democracy! Not everybody can afford an education, healthcare and insurance.

Lots of folk are caught in a vicious circle of existence, like a guinea pig inside a wheel. Holding down several part-time jobs at minimum wage. Credit card bills, foreclosures. Living on the street. Food banks. Obesity. Now Americans are brainwashed by what the lawyers spout on TV, "getting you the money you deserve." Nothing but false entitlement and law suits!

Even Canada has shown signs of the "Just Society" crumbling, so hard won after World War II and the prosperity of the 1950s. "Universal Healthcare" for everybody slowly slipping out of our grasp, and the right to a University Education, just a pipe-dream from the 1960s. Pierre Elliot Trudeau called for a "Just Society." Was there ever one? Will we ever have one with food banks growing more numerous in our big cities, and homeless people sleeping on grates in the streets of Montreal, Toronto and Vancouver?

It's been pointed out that ISIS was attracting young men who were just plain angry and critical of the Western system. They were rife for recruitment in a group which said it could change the world. They wanted something they could understand in a clear way, and they needed to find a purpose in life. Many young men, both in the United States and in Canada, found themselves coming out of colleges with a diploma, a useless piece of paper, and no job. They got hooked on drugs and crime. They drifted into the streets and ended up in homeless shelters.

The cab driver in New York with a Ph.D. frustrated, that his intelligence was misused in the memorization of city streets. All the immigrants working at minimum wages, dreaming of "The American Dream," which was getting smaller and smaller, disappearing more and more into the past at the speed of light, ungraspable with a hope in a distant future which will never be!

Islam defines things in a strict world order. There is a place for everything: men, women, marriage, sex, clothes and food, all defined under the Holy Qur'an. It's all outlined in clear commands. An Islamic State would put order back into a crazy world! The West is decadent, full of infidels. Allah and the Prophet, may peace be upon him, would change all that.

.....

Wally could appreciate the accusations against "U.S. imperialism" and "U.S. interests" in the East. The underlying excuse was oil and not "weapons of mass destruction." Who knows what intricate justifications politicians used to butt into the affairs of other countries where raw materials and money were concerned?

There were those who argued that America should clean up its own mess at home before interfering with the affairs of Arab countries. "Let them handle their own mess," said Sam, a photographer friend of Wally's. "Otherwise we've got another Viet Nam on our hands. The ones who suffer are always the villagers." Sam criticized the huge poverty in the States, the ghettoes, the gangs and the continued racial issues. "Hospitals ask for your insurance or credit card first before you are cared for," he said. His friend was disgusted with the false American Dream. "And that's the country Americans want to fight for?"

Wally heard Sam often say that "we" should stay at home and let Islam deal with Islam. "Hey, I don't like what the Islamic State is doing anymore than anybody else; but all the Arab countries over there, who look to the Qur'an as the foundation of their Faith, have to have a vested interest in doing something against these extremists themselves, if Islam is really a religion of peace. Let them handle their own. We have enough trouble over here."

"You sound anti-Arab," objected Wally.

"No, I'm not," countered Sam. "I'm just anti-terrorist and anti-whatever ISIS is doing. I'm also not happy with what the United States has done in the past and with their sense of righteousness to butt into the affairs of other nations, when they've got real problems at home."

After all was said and done, there seemed to be justifications [and recriminations] for everybody all the way around. Wally didn't like what Big Brother was doing in the States either with tapping phone lines, justified by the Patriot Act of 2001, signed into law by President George Bush after 9/11. Things seemed to be swinging out of control "to the other side" with Big Government. His own country, Canada, seemed like it was on puppet strings pulled by Washington. Some countries laughed at Canada as being spineless and weak, a country without a real identity. Wally didn't know which was right and which was an illusion?

Wally was horrified when he forced himself to see the West through the eyes of an Islamic militant. What's the difference between the *Islamic State* and the world of George Orwell's *1984*? Wally saw no difference!

[Eric Clapton 1996]
[Chorus:]
That I can change the world
I would be the sunlight in your universe
You will think my love was really something good
Baby, if I could, change the world

CHAPTER 90

SOMEHOW, THE YOUNG PASTOR NEVER LIKED THE LINE IN the song by Sabine Baring-Gould: "Onward, Christian soldiers, marching as to *war*, with the cross of Jesus *going* on before." It reminded him too much of the Crusades.

.....

EVENING PRAYER MEETING
TUESDAY, OCTOBER 28, 2014

TWO DETECTIVES, JAKE KLASSEN AND HIS YOUNG PARTNER, Jonathan Evans, were present, as well as the usual two old ladies, who at times expressed very strong opinions about Scripture. The photographer, Wally Guenter, decided to join the group that evening. He figured it was a form of group therapy, for free, costing him less than his actual therapist, Karl de Jong.

Sunday's sermon had been on Ephesians 6:11-12, which always sparked lively debate about its applications in the world.

Put on the whole armour of God, that ye may be able to stand against the wiles of the devil. For we wrestle not against flesh and blood, but against principalities, against powers, against the rulers of the darkness of this world, against spiritual wickedness in high *places*. [Ephesians 6:11-12 King James]

Pastor Greg asked God to open their hearts, to be receptive to the guidance of the Holy Spirit. He commented that the imagery in the passage was warfare, which made him uncomfortable. He told the group, "There were a lot of atrocities committed by Crusaders in the name of Christ, against Saracens and Jews alike, in the Middle Ages."

"Now, I suppose," he said, "the Islamic State is looking at the West with a similar spirit by putting on the armour of Allah!"

"Kind of a reverse irony," said Olivia, always ready to add something. "But for us, the intent of the passage is what matters. We need to put on spiritual armour against the invisible wiles of the devil."

Mary, her friend joined in, "There are invisible forces at work which drag us down. I suppose at the extremes, we have to go to war, like we did against Adolf Hitler and the Nazis."

Klassen finally joined the verbal exchange. "And what's more," he said. "We have to be on guard for what's right and moral in our daily work place too. Do we become Sunday Christians only? What are we like during the week?"

Pastor Greg felt the answer lay in *The Golden Rule*. "Do unto others, as you would have them do unto you." He added, "In other words, be kind!"

The discussion inevitably went to the Islamic State militants, and the beheadings in Syria and Iraq, as acts carried out by, "the rulers of the darkness of the world." Henry, the 81 year old, adjusted his hearing aids. He found it amusing that Muslims and Christians considered each other "infidels."

Wally interjected that Mark Twain had something to say about Man having the one and only true religion.

Henry didn't see the humour in this. He was convinced that ISIS was the one which had the wrong religion. It was a sign of the end times. "The fight between Muslims and Christians is leading us to the Apocalypse and Armageddon!"

Henry declared that Ebola was obviously another sign of the end times. He found a passage in Revelations to back up his argument, probably already ear-marked in his Bible:

> I saw another sign in heaven, great and marvelous, seven angels holding the seven last plagues; for in them is filled up the wrath of God
>
> [REVELATION 15:1]

Since he was on a roll, Henry also thumbed through his *New Testament,* and picked out another fiery quote, a favourite from 2 Peter 3:10, "The heavens will disappear with a roar; the elements will be destroyed by fire, and the earth and everything in it will be laid bare."

"You just wait 'till them Arabs get the atomic bomb!" he prophesied.

Wally never understood the difference between Apocalypse and Armageddon, and actually didn't care, since it was not his favourite topic. Henry ended with a prophetic warning about ISIS, "I see black."

The pastor cut Henry off and said, "And on that note, let's all pray and go for coffee and cookies at the office."

But this discussion seemed to have gathered a full life of its own. Wally's mind wandered. He had watched Bettany Hughes's narration about the history of Alexandria the other night. What if Islam did take over the world? Would it rewrite history? Would it destroy all Western art and books? That's what Christians did with Greek art and books housed in the Library of Alexandria in 391 CE. Would Islam build a wall around themselves and keep the plague of Western civilization out? Like the gigantic Wall that separated West and East Berlin, or the armed border between North and South Korea?

Wally finally said to the group that he felt sorry for young radicals who looked for truth in an extreme interpretation of the Qur'an. He observed that the same happened throughout Christian history, and he was ashamed when Christian radicals burned so-called heretics at the stake, just for having different ideas. "Galileo had to be careful about what he professed," observed Wally, "the Inquisition was watching him."

Pastor Greg found an appropriate passage with which to end the prayer meeting:

> See to it that no one takes you captive by philosophy and empty deceit, according to human tradition, according to the elemental spirits of the world, and not according to Christ. [Col.2:8 ESV]

> He prayed for young radicals to see the truth that human life was sacred; and that people needed to accept other people's rights within their country, including different religions

> and cultures, as long as they did no harm. He prayed that Canada would remain a tolerant society; and a Mosaic which was uniquely multi-cultural, as an example to the world.

During coffee and cookie time, the group didn't talk sports or the weather. Henry told the others the news he'd seen on TV, that a mosque was defaced the previous week in Cold Lake, Alberta, where windows were smashed, and the building was spray-painted with the message, "Go Home."

When Wally finally went home, he googled, "mosque defaced in Cold Lake." He found that the town actually rallied around its Muslim community, and sent volunteers to clean up the mess. Wally could understand why it might have happened, only four days after Warrant Officer Patrice Vincent was struck down by a car driven by a terrorist in Quebec, and only two days after Cpl. Nathan Cirillo was gunned down in front of Ottawa's War Memorial.

Cold Lake also had a military base where Canadian CF-18 fighters flew out earlier in October to participate in airstrikes against the Islamic State in Iraq.

"Still," he thought, "for Canadians to incite hatred in a small town? How un-Canadian is that!"

Josh Elliott wrote a CTV article online about the incident. He quoted Mahmoud Elkadri, a mosque board member, as saying, "My kids saw it and they started crying and I said, 'Why are you crying?' They said, 'We were born here and raised here and this is our home'."

The reporter acknowledged that Muslim leaders in Canada have repeatedly condemned the radical Islamic State militants which seized territories in Iraq and Syria.

The president of the Cold Lake Islamic Society, Ajar Quraishi, told CTV Edmonton, that he was hopeful that the vandalism at the mosque was only an isolated incident.

CHAPTER 91

WALLY HAD BEEN FEELING WEAK AFTER HIS DESCENT TO the bottom of Ball's Falls for his photo shoot of the turbulent water cascading down to the Twenty Mile Creek below. "It's a good sun today," he had said to his companion, Sam Clemens. The air was fresh and the sky above the Falls was blue, mottled here and there with puffs of white clouds.

.....

PURPLE RIBBON ISSUE
WEDNESDAY, OCTOBER 29, 2014

WALLY RANG AT THE CHURCH THAT AFTERNOON. THE SECretary buzzed him in. "Pastor Greg, may I have a moment of your time?" Pastor Greg was more than willing to lend an ear.

"I've found out I've got pancreatic cancer," he told Pastor Greg. No preamble. Pastor Greg listened respectfully.

"I've written a novel. I told my wife to give you the memory stick with instructions about getting it published. One copy is to be donated to the local public library. My wife has instructions about the distribution of the other copies. I'd like Rimsky-Korsakov's *Scheherazade* to be played at my funeral."

"I'm on the last couple of chapters of my book. I hope to finish before I get too sick. I'm on morphine. My last chapter will finish with my recollection of my final climb down the gorge at Ball's Falls. I think I'll end my chapter with a poem. I want to do this while I still have the energy to write things down with a clear mind. Every day is a struggle."

Pastor Greg didn't know what to say. He prayed with Wally. He unpinned a note from his bulletin board.

"I've had this up here for years. It once encouraged another man with cancer. The story was about a father and son, paddling in a canoe, caught in a heavy rain. They were caught in the middle of the lake, trying to get to shore. The dad prayed and encouraged the boy, as they paddled hard towards the shore, wondering if they'd ever make it:

> "May the Creator of the Universe hold you tight and say that He loves you and that we're going to make it. I love you, buddy, we're almost there. I know the way."

During a lull in the conversation, Pastor Greg swallowed hard, and with open honesty asked a very private question.

"Have you already accepted your own death within your own mind?"

Wally fixed the young man with his eyes, and answered simply, "Yes." Wally got up and left.

When the door closed, a tear rolled down Pastor Greg's face.

Wally walked home with a quick deliberation in his step. He sat in front of his computer, booted it up, and gathered his thoughts, hands steepled in front of him. What was next? How would he say it? He felt driven. He would finish another chapter or two that very day.

CHAPTER 92

"Do not think that those who are killed in the way of Allah are dead, for indeed they are alive, even though you are not aware."

[HOLY QUR'AN SURA2:154]

.....

KURDISH WOMEN FIGHTERS
AAMIR'S FATAL END
WEDNESDAY, OCTOBER 29, 2014

IF LIFE IS BUT A DREAM, THEN WALLY'S DREAM CONTINUED with another sleeping pill on Wednesday night. He felt sorry for Rasha, and his mind was aware of Aamir in the aftermath of the man's vile action.

Aamir felt no remorse about what he did to Rasha. He and his two companions went back to attacking Kurdish women hiding in the rubble and rocks around Kobane. Daamin and Parvez believed the myth about losing Paradise if you were killed by a woman. Aamir scoffed at the idea. He relished the thought of catching another female fighter, to show his dominance.

.....

Asti and her sisters-in-arms had no explanation for the apparent disappearance of Rehana over the past three weeks. There was a picture circulated on the internet that she was allegedly beheaded. The gruesome photo made the rounds on Twitter. It may and may not have been of Rehana. There was no absolute proof! "We're not sure it's her," said the Kurdish resistance among themselves, "there may still be hope." In the media, they categorically denied the execution of their Poster Girl. Then, Rehana's friends came forward to put an end to the rumors, by claiming that Rehana made it out of Kobane, and was living in southern Turkey somewhere, alive and well!

Asti suggested a plan to hit back at ISIS. "War is deceit," she said. "They want women to rape? We'll give them one!" She devised a ruse whereby one of her sisters-in-arms, Elwa, would hide inside a blown-out hull of a truck, another sister, Jiyan, would hide on the other side behind a wall, a wall in which they'd knock a hole, the perfect size for pushing a rifle barrel through.

Asti, herself, would be the bait, propping herself against the back of a ruined building, pretending to have a jammed rifle. She thought Rehana would approve of such a clever plan.

"My helplessness will be too hard to resist," she said. "A perfect trap for a young lion whom we will declaw!"

She told her friend, Jiyan, "When he gets near me, shoot him in the head."

They used a chisel and sledge hammer to gouge a hole in the wall at eye level, and then, hid themselves. Asti crouched behind large pieces of rubble in front of the wall, in wait for any ISIS militants who patrolled that area. Make it believable!

Aamir was in the lead, looking for a stray Kurdish cat which he could bag. He loved to think of Kurdish women as stray cats. He spotted Asti. She stood up, apparently frustrated that her rifle didn't work. She struggled with it.

Aamir smiled. He approached slowly, sizing her up. He unzipped, aroused, "Hail The Conquering Hero Comes." He moved closer, all smiles, with his two buddies, Daamin and Parvez, lagging slightly behind.

A shot rang out from the hole in the wall to the left. Aamir clutched his crotch. "Impossible," he screamed. He wondered if his family jewels were still intact, and how ever would he pee... or have sex again?

Two more shots rang out from inside the blown-out vehicle. Daamin and Parvez fell in unison as their heads exploded robbing them of Paradise.

A fourth shot excavated Aamir's Adam's apple. He fell and emptied his life's blood onto the street in convulsions until he lay still. Above him, the city suffered another day of rocket fire from U.S. drones. In all the explosions and killings, Aamir himself lay defeated and dead while Kobane burned.

Asti was fuming at Jiyan. "I told you to shoot him in the head!"

Jiyan retorted, "I thought his crotch made a good target!" She added dryly, "I had a clear shot. It was a righteous kill!"

Elwa broke out in giggles, and so did Asti and Jiyan. Asti looked down upon the bodies in disgust. "None of these three were killed in the way of Allah, nor will they make it to Paradise. This one especially, I suspect, was the worst of these animals!" She prodded Aamir with her boot.

Asti had the idea to take a picture of their prize kill. She covered Aamir's neck with his head gear to hide the gaping wound, and lay the butt of his rifle across his crotch.

Asti took several pictures with her cell phone. "I know his face from somewhere but at the moment, I cannot place it. Maybe it will come to me later. Who knows?" She continued with the photos.

They posted the best one on Twitter, and then on their Kurdish website, showing that Kurdish women could kill, just as well as men, and defend their city and homeland! The photo went viral the next day; and soon, Western newspapers picked it up, all across the United States and Canada with the caption, "Kurdish women, defiant and deadly!"

It was shown on the front page of the *Hamilton Reporter* and *Hamilton Today*. Both Spencer and Abqurah saw the picture.

"That is my brother, Aamir," she said softly. She was saddened that he had destroyed the family and also sad that he had killed, Hazirah, his own sister. She was not sad, however, that he was dead! Of that, she was somehow... glad. She would not be the one to tell her parents. That part of her life was over.

"At least, Canada won't have to put out court costs," said Spencer off-handedly, as he looked at the picture. Then with an after-thought, he stared up at Abqurah, an apology evident in his eyes.

Spencer shut his mouth, faced Abqurah and held her. Finally, he said, "He had a choice. He could have made a contribution to society. He could have volunteered to help the shut-ins and the needy. He could have raised funds for Haiti or Africa. He could also have become a good computer programmer, making a decent living for himself, here in Canada. He could have gotten married, had children and lived a peaceful life. Instead he chose to hurt people."

Abqurah cried. It was a cleansing cry for the past.

.....

Asti fell asleep on her blanket. She dreamt of a café. Beler was next to her. A handsome Turk sidled up to them and spoke. "Is it true that the jihadists are afraid of being killed by a woman for fear of going to hell?" Everything faded away except Beler's face. She said, "He killed me. His blood for my blood. I am at peace."

Asti awoke. She shed a tear for her friend; and slowly, peacefully went back to sleep. Who knows what the next day of fighting will bring?

CHAPTER 93

> Said cynically. "It's a great life. You go in a circle and come right back to the beginning!"
>
> [HUMPHREY BOGART MOVIE, *Sirocco*, 1951]

.....

9:00 A.M. @THERAPY
BAD DREAMS AND FLASHBACKS
THURSDAY, OCTOBER 30, 2014

WALLY MET WITH KARL DE JONG. THEY SIPPED THEIR coffee. De Jong eyed Wally over the rim of his glasses. "So what's it going to be today?"

"Dreams," said Wally. I've had some doozies: First about the last thoughts of that gunman who broke into the Parliament Building, as he lay dying. Second, about a Kurdish girl, Rasha, on her last day of captivity before they beheaded her. Wally explained the dreams, how real they seemed, and how tired he was when he woke from his restless sleep.

"Everything is connected, Wally," said de Jong. "Maybe those experiences were real emanations sent out to you by the Universe. Some people say, by God." De Jong believed that certain human beings had super sensitive souls which acted like receivers to other people's thoughts and feelings. "But be that as it may, let's talk about what these dreams meant to you."

Wally said he felt sorry that Zehaf-Bibeau did not receive professional help when he first asked for it. The signs were there. De Jong commented that courts wanted to clear their agenda as fast as they could, because they were so backlogged. "Then there's budget cuts!"

"Maybe we need more bailouts," de Jong added off-handedly. "The U.S. government printed new money, a couple of years ago, to bail out the auto industry."

"I don't think bailouts would have helped somebody like Zehaf-Bibeau," remarked Wally.

De Jong asked, "What about the dream about that Kurdish girl, Rasha?"

"It made me sad. How could IS militants justify beheading anybody, in the name of a just God?"

He sipped his coffee and said, "In my dream, her last words were, 'We are all Rehanas. There will be others!"

Wally added, "I can identify with what people go through during wartime. I understand more about Post Traumatic Stress Disorder now." He told de Jong that this was the condition which retired him from the teaching profession. He felt the classroom was like a war zone, at times, and that wasn't what teaching was supposed to be at all!

"I never was good at disciplining when I taught highschool. Believe me, sometimes the behaviour in my class got outrageous. Maybe Sidney Poitier, in *To Sir With Love,* could have settled things down… but I was frazzled when somebody scratched the blackboard with their fingernails and pencils started dropping. Teaching what was in a book was beside the point!"

One day, Wally sent the whole class to the principal's office. "Little things, I can handle. But it's the whole class and it's happening day after day. I've asked for help before." The principal insisted that the students had a right to learn; and that if Wally couldn't handle the discipline, he wouldn't be employed at the school the next year. Wally had to earn their respect!

Wally had no office support. He talked to a misbehaving kid and if that didn't work, he'd send the kid out into the hall, or to the principal. The principal would send the kid right back in. "He's got a right to learn."

Wally thought, "Yeah, he's got a right to learn, but if he doesn't want to? What about the other kids' right to learn?… and my right to teach?"

By Christmas, Wally walked into the doctor's office, sat down on the floor and cried. His doctor referred him to a psychiatrist who said, "You're on holidays now, Wally." He was on sick leave for three years. Wally underwent a regimen of therapy, dosages of Imipramine and lots of walking. He never went back to teaching.

"Well," said Wally, "that was my nervous breakdown… the first one and I hope, the last one!"

When Wally met his wife, he was still recovering from the after-shock of his nervous breakdown. He could see how soldiers became incapacitated through the stress of war, actually how anybody cracked through repeated harassment and stress even in civilian life.

"One of the side-effects, and it lasted five years," Wally told de Jong, "was that I didn't read one single book through that entire time... and having always been a writer, I found I couldn't write."

It was his wife who told Wally about *The Hardy Boys* and *Mrs. Pollifax*. He especially enjoyed Dorothy Gilman's writing. When he read *Thale's Folly*, he identified with Andrew who had writer's block, who used to have the hunger to create with words and lost it after a scary plane crash. Wally was amused by Miss L'Hommedieu, the old lady who writes... "but her stories have neither middles nor endings." [p57] Tarragon explains to Andrew that she makes up her beginnings, and leaves the rest out, because she doesn't like reality. Wally understood the feeling.

When Wally made a last ditch effort to redirect his career into public relations, away from teaching, he knew he had made another mistake there too. In the year 2000, he enrolled in Corporate Communications at Sheridan College. He was convinced he would come out of the course with a diploma in "spin-doctoring," no matter what the professors said about professional ethics.

One of them, a former senior reporter for the Kitchener-Waterloo Record, said she became a professor at Sheridan College because she enjoyed the status. "There's a sense of urgency to achieve something at a certain age," she said. "You got that right," thought Wally. He was the oldest student in the class, just learning how to use the computer.

.....

But at my back I always hear
Time's winged chariot hurrying near;
And yonder all before us lie
Deserts of vast eternity.
[Andrew Marvell 1621–1678]

.....

Wally was offered a job writing biographies for the research doctors at Sunnybrook Hospital in their "Institute for Clinical Evaluative Sciences," ICES, but declined. Wally's wife did not find the big city, Toronto, attractive. She liked Jordan, the Niagara farm area, and the fact that she landed a contract with the Niagara District School Board. It didn't make sense to move to an expensive city.

Wally became a "house-husband" and had to make psychological adjustments to accommodate the marriage and his role in the world as a "liberated" man.

Karl de Jong and Wally had a good long gab fest about dreams and changes. Wally put the past behind and talked a bit about current events. He was convinced that change, if it would ever come in Muslim countries, would have to come from Muslim women themselves.

Maybe the internet would help spark the change. Otherwise an Islamic State would quarantine the internet and create its own world, isolated from any outside influences which might corrupt their women.

Wally thought of the old movie with Charles Boyer, *Algiers*, 1938 with Sigrid Gurie and Hedy Lamarr.

Pepe Le Moko, a thief who escaped from France with a fortune in jewels, has for two years lived in, and virtually ruled, the maze-like, impenetrable Casbah, "native quarter" of Algiers. A French official insists that he be captured, but sly Inspector Slimane [Joseph Calleia] knows he need only bide his time. The suave Pepe increasingly regards his stronghold as his prison, especially when he meets the beautiful Parisian visitor Gaby [Hedy Lamarr], who reminds him of the boulevards to which he dare not return. This arouses the mad jealousy of Ines [Sigrid Gurie], his Algerian mistress. [www.imdb.com]

Pepe has a deep insight about the human condition, while reclining on a top bunk in a room, as Mme Tania and he wait for news. They banter back and forth:

> Pepe le Moko: Same old story
>
> MmeTania: Well, life is like that.
>
> Pepe: And we're dumb enough to hang on because we don't want the story to end... smart!

Wally saw the Islamic State as the Casbah ruled by its own laws. But more than that, he saw Pepe's comment ring true, that we are curious and want to hang on to life to the bitter end. Wally, like Pepe, considered the urge to hang on to life, at all costs, as being dumb.

"Maybe there's a case for doctor assisted suicide," Wally finally said to de Jong. "We want to go on with our own life's story... although if the pain gets too much... ?"

Charles Boyer lost his son to suicide in 1965 when the boy was 21 years old. He lost his wife, Pat Paterson, to cancer in 1978. Two days afterwards and two days before his 79th birthday, Charles Boyer took an overdose of Seconal and died. He is interred along side his wife and son in the Holy Cross Cemetery in Culver City, California.

Wally found Charles Boyer's life and death poignant.

Like Wally, Karl de Jong loved old black and white movies. "Imagine, 1938!" said de Jong, "before Hitler invaded Poland, before World War II. Ann Franck was still alive. Six million Jews were not in concentration camps, still working and loving, and unwary of the storm which would sweep them underground." Being a music lover, de Jong added, "Glen Miller was still alive and jazz was going strong."

Wally said he really enjoyed Charles Boyer singing, "C'est La Vie" at the beginning of the 1938 flick. What a multi-talented man he was! What a waste! "Life is simple if you try to enjoy it before you die." Boyer was singing about the same sentiment that Frank Sinatra sang, years later in his version of, *That's Life.* Wally thought, "It is the same old story!"

And as funny as it may seem
Some people get their kicks stomping on a dream
But I don't let it, let it get me down
'Cause this fine old world, it keeps spinnin' around

[FRANK SINATRA-RELEASED 1966]

CHAPTER 94

You know the day destroys the night
Night divides the day
Tried to run
Tried to hide
Break on through to the other side
Break on through to the other side
Break on through to the other side, yeah
[*The Doors* 1967]

.....

3:00 P.M. @CHURCH
A HEART TO HEART
THURSDAY, OCTOBER 30, 2014

WALLY HAD SET UP A MEETING WITH PASTOR GREG. IT WAS like getting a double dose of therapy each week, first from

Karl de Jong and now Pastor Greg. He liked the young man who had a sincere heart for the Bible and for people. His door was always open.

Pastor Greg was offered the senior pastor position at the church but had declined it, in favour of remaining Youth Pastor of the church. He said he wasn't quite ready to assume a senior position, but he agreed to take over the Tuesday evening prayer meetings.

Pastor Greg had recently married. His wife played the harp. They were suited to each other in temperament and in talent. She in music and he in speaking.

"About the novel I'm writing," Wally said. "It touches on sensitive issues for Muslims. I'm concerned."

"How so?"

"Well, it's not exactly *The Satanic Verses* of Salman Rushdie but you know a *fatwā* was issued by the supreme leader of Iran, Ayatollah Ruhollah Khomeini, in 1989. I just don't want anything like that to happen to me from ISIS for writing my novel."

Wally continued, "In a way it's lucky I'll avoid all that because of my cancer. Doctors expect me to be gone in about a month or so." He paused. "My wife plans on selling the house and moving to Arizona. She always liked the hot climate there. I won't be around to enjoy it."

"I've instructed her to give you the memory stick with the novel on it, including the last chapter which I've just written."

Pastor Greg said that he would be glad to do it, and with Wally's wife, handle anything that needed doing from the publisher.

"You know," said Wally. "I'd appreciate it if you accompanied my wife to the top of Ball's Falls. I've always said I'd like to be sprinkled over the Falls and just become part of Nature back there. Wait until it's a sunny day though. I hope we still get those in November. I hate rain."

The secretary asked them if they could use a coffee; she was making some. They both said, yes. Wally and Pastor Greg settled in for a lighter discussion. Usually it was about music or books, sometimes music and books. This time it was music.

Wally asked if Pastor Greg had ever heard of the *Doors*, Jim Morrison.

"Can't say that I have. I've heard of *Madonna* and *Bruce Springsteen*."

Wally couldn't really blame Pastor Greg. He was only 30 years old.

"This was before them."

Wally wondered if Pastor Greg had ever heard of Woodstock. He went on to explain that Jim Morrison was a poet, a singer and a rebel. He was addicted to drugs and sex and abused himself, so that by the time he was 27, he was found dead in 1971, in a hotel room in Paris allegedly overdosed on heroine. He was buried in the Père Lachaise Cemetery.

"My wife and I visited that grave back in 1989," said Wally. "We had lunch near Chopin's statue and then we just followed the graffiti which said, 'Jim This Way.' When we got there, we noticed that his gravestone was moved sideways. Did someone try to dig under? There was a peace sign spray painted in red on the stone. Hippie types bowed in sadness over the grave."

"I said to my wife, Okay now I've seen it, done it, let's get out of here. We took in the Louvre and the Eiffel Tower before we left Paris. It was springtime."

Wally recalled, "I guess I liked Morrison's lyrics when I was in my 20s and a bit of a rebel myself. I was attracted to the dark nihilism in Morrison's songs during my university days."

"Pretty negative stuff," judged Wally, not quite recalling all the lyrics. "I'll refrain from singing them to you," said Wally.
"Thank you," replied Pastor Greg.

Riders on the storm
Riders on the storm
Into this house we're born
Into this world we're thrown
Like a dog without a bone
An actor out on loan
Riders on the storm

[THE DOORS 1971]

Wally added, "I guess that's what you get when you read too much Friedrich Nietzsche when you're young. Morrison adored Nietzsche."

Wally enjoyed the fact that this was turning into a learning session for Pastor Greg. There was still an old teacher in Wally, wanting to come out.

"I wonder," he said, "instead of Paradise, if Islamic militants will face a big, black Nothing? If we reap what we sow? It'll be a surprise to them, if they don't end up in Heaven on the other side."

.....

We chased our pleasures here
Dug our treasures there
But can you still recall
The time we cried?
Break on through to the other side
Break on through to the other side
[The Doors 1967]

.....

In real life, negatives often seem to outweigh the positives. At least, it was something positive to watch the golden glow of the afternoon sun outside the office window at the church. Wally and Pastor Greg soaked it in, and then focused back on their coffees. Wally was refueled with his second cup; and so, he talked about Life versus Death. He had heard on the News that 13,000 cases of Ebola had been reported world-wide. And there were 5,000 deaths!

"Ever hear of Albert Camus?"

"Can't really say that I have."

Wally took a sip of coffee. "Albert Camus [1913-1960] was an existentialist and you might say, had a nihilistic view on life, like Morrison."

"He wrote a book, *La Peste*... you think Ebola is bad?" commented Wally. *La Peste [The Plague],* was published in 1947. It tells the story of medical workers trying to contain and find a cure for a plague which sweeps the Algerian city of Oran.

"Sound familiar?" questioned Wally.

"I'll have to read the book," affirmed Pastor Greg. Wally finished his coffee and let himself out the door. Pastor Greg went back to preparing his Sunday's message. He thought, "I've got to say something positive in my sermon!"

CHAPTER 95

"Western civilization is an abomination," Abbud said. "Its influence on our society is like an infectious disease that needs to be wiped out."

[P.178, ROBERT LUDLUM'S, *Bourne Betrayal*, NOVEL BY ERIC VAN LUSTBADER, WARNER BOOKS, 2007]

.....

A LITTLE BIT OF THIS...
STEREOTYPES IN A NUTSHELL

EVERYBODY DOES IT. STEREOTYPING AND PROFILING. Governments and individuals do it. One country against another, one culture against another. People in general. It simplifies things. Makes things easier to understand, whether it's another race, another colour, all neatly categorized and simplified. You can accept, condemn, become tolerant with one big paintbrush. The mind looks for simplicity, right or wrong.

Over a century ago, the American Humorist, Mark Twain, said some interesting things about the Chinese and about missionaries, which bore a certain application to the lynch mobs rising up in the United States at the time.

The Chinese are universally conceded to be excellent people, honest, honourable, industrious, trustworthy, kind-hearted, and all that - leave them alone, they are plenty good enough just as they are; and besides, almost every convert runs a risk of catching our civilization... O kind missionary, O compassionate missionary, leave China! Come home and convert these Christians!

[HTTP://PEOPLE.VIRGINIA.EDU/~SFR/ENAM482E/LYNCHERDOM.HTML]

Wally wondered how the Chinese looked at Americans. What do we look like from the other side?

There are so many barriers when it comes to stereotyping and profiling. You look at nations, skin colours, cultures and religions. There are so many pigeon-holes into which people put people. Handsome or ugly, fat or skinny, ectomorph, endomorph, mesomorph. Which is better and which is right? And then there is the brain and mind which is stamped with a particular culture and religion. Even atheists have a pigeon-hole and are usually not tolerant of everybody else because everybody else is stupid. Oh, what a world we live in! The melting pot is already boiling over, as we create an even smaller global village with jet planes and the internet. Of course we could erect more Berlin walls!

"But there must be some legitimacy to stereotyping," thought Wally. "There must be a grain of truth in simplicity." Wally's father-in-law had e-mailed a funny piece recently, allegedly written by John Cleese, of *Faulty Towers* and *Monty Python* fame. Wally recognized the "traits" of certain nationalities immediately and chuckled at Cleese's British wit in capsulizing national stereotypes.

From: John Cleese, (English writer and actor)

The English are feeling the pinch in relation to recent events in Syria and have therefore raised their security level from "Miffed" to "Peeved." Soon, though, security levels may be raised yet again to "Irritated" or even "A Bit Cross." The English have not been "A Bit Cross" since the blitz in 1940 when tea supplies nearly ran out. Terrorists have been re-categorized from "Tiresome" to "A Bloody Nuisance." The last time the British issued a "Bloody Nuisance" warning level was in 1588, when threatened by the Spanish Armada.

The Scots have raised their threat level from "Pissed Off" to "Let's get the Bastards." They don't have any other levels. This is the reason they have been used on the front line of the British army for the last 300 years.

The French government announced yesterday that it has raised its terror alert level from "Run" to "Hide." The only two higher levels in France are "Collaborate" and "Surrender." The rise was precipitated by a recent fire that destroyed France's white flag factory, effectively paralyzing the country's military capability.

Italy has increased the alert level from "Shout Loudly and Excitedly" to "Elaborate Military Posturing." Two more levels remain: "Ineffective Combat Operations" and "Change Sides."

The Germans have increased their alert state from "Disdainful Arrogance" to "Dress in Uniform and Sing Marching Songs." They also have two higher levels: "Invade a Neighbour" and "Lose."

Belgians, on the other hand, are all on holiday as usual; the only threat they are worried about is NATO pulling out of Brussels .

The Spanish are all excited to see their new submarines ready to deploy. These beautifully designed subs have glass bottoms so the new Spanish navy can get a really good look at the old Spanish navy.

Australia, meanwhile, has raised its security level from "No worries" to "She'll be right, Mate." Two more escalation levels remain: "Crikey! I think we'll need to cancel the barbie this weekend!" and "The barbie is cancelled." So far no situation has ever warranted use of the last final escalation level.

Regards,

John Cleese ,

British writer, actor and tall person

And as a final thought - Greece is collapsing, the Iranians are getting aggressive, and Rome is in disarray. Welcome back to 430 BC.

Life is too short...

CHAPTER 96

"*Man* is a Religious *Animal.* He is the *only* Religious *Animal.* He is the *only animal that has the True Religion--several of them.*"

[MARK TWAIN 1835-1910]

.....

A LITTLE BIT OF THAT...
ANIMOSITY IN A NUTSHELL

CHRISTIANS SAY THAT THE WORLD'S TROUBLES WENT BACK to Adam and Eve. Others say, it began with Father Abraham when he left Ur, in Mesopotamia, to immigrate into a land already inhabited by somebody else, i.e. Canaan. Moses faced the same problem, way later, trying to re-inherit the Promised Land. The two themes which caused big problems in the Book of Genesis were always, posterity and the land.

Wally tried to understand why Jews, Muslims and Christians squared off against each other, even into the modern day. Where was the start of all this enmity? He went to the computer to google, "origin of Jews and Arabs."

According to the Jewish and Christian view, the animosity goes all the way back to Father Abraham, previously known as Abram. When God shuffles people around, it seems there's a name change which goes with the move. It's like having a new start or being reborn. Abram became known as Abraham, *"for I have made you the father of many nations." [Gen.17:5] Father Abraham* was the tenth generation from Noah through Shem. It is estimated that he was born 352 years after the Deluge, in 2018 B.C.E, according to one historical source.

But before the name change, there was a problem in Genesis 16:1-2, which recounts that Abram's wife couldn't conceive a child. How would the family line continue? It seemed like it was a more open society in the old days, despite them being the old days! A wife would have to be pretty "understanding" to tell the husband to pass his sperm on to the housemaid to preserve his line of descendants.

> Now Sarai, Abram's wife, had borne him no children. But she had an Egyptian slave named Hagar; **2** so she said to Abram, "The Lord has kept me from having children. Go, sleep with my slave; perhaps I can build a family through her."

Hagar got pregnant and her son was named Ishmael. Animosity grew between the two women when Hagar rubbed it in that she was with child, whereas Sarai was still barren. [Genesis 16:1-16]

Only later, Sarai herself became pregnant with her own son whom she named Isaac, meaning "laughter." One account claims that the Jews are descendants of Abraham's son, Isaac. The Arabs are descendants of Abraham's other son, Ishmael. According to the Jews, Isaac was the promised son who would inherit the blessings of Abraham. [Genesis 21:1-3]

Family jealousies became worse when Ishmael mocked Isaac. [Genesis 21:9] Therefore, Sarah talked Abraham into sending Hagar and Ishmael away. [Genesis 21:11-18] It is interesting that Genesis 16:12 describes Ishmael as, "a wild donkey of a man; his hand will be against everyone and everyone's hand against him, and he will live in hostility toward all his brothers."

Wally's interest got really piqued as he read on about the origin of Jews and Arabs. The gap widened between Jews and Arabs by the time the 7th century Christian Era rolled along. [http://www.gotquestions.org/Jews-Arabs.html]

The Muslim Bible, *The Holy Qur'an* was written in approximately 23 years, beginning December 22, 609 CE, when Muhammad was 40 years old, and finished in 632 CE, the year of his death, at the age of 62. It is said that Muhammad dictated the Qur'an to scribes during trances at various intervals inspired by the Angel Gabriel [Jibril].

Wally never liked the idea of Jibril putting Muhammad into trances to link up to what God had to say through him. The communication reminded him of the Urim and Thummim or "seer stones," which the angel Moroni provided to translate the plates holding the words of God, namely the Mormon Bible. Trances and scribes, Urim and Thummim... these conduits to God just didn't sit right with Wally.

At any rate, Wally's immediate goal was to read up on what caused the widening gap between Arabs and Jews in the 7th century. The Qur'an says, at one point, Muslims need to treat Jews as brothers and at another point, commands Muslims to attack Jews who refuse to convert to Islam. The Qur'an also raises the question of blessing, which of Abraham's sons was truly the son of promise? The Jewish Tanakh's "Genesis" says it was Isaac. The Qur'an says it was Ishmael! The Qur'an teaches that it was Ishmael whom Abraham almost sacrificed to God, not Isaac, in contradiction to Genesis 22. This debate is carried through to the modern day, contributing to continued hostility between Jews and Arabs in the 21st century.

Islam also had a claim on Jerusalem when Muhammad was taken by the angel, Gabriel, on his miraculous night journey to the Dome of the Rock, from which he ascended through the seven spheres to heaven to speak with God. That story gave Islamists a good excuse to take over Jerusalem at some future point, to the warranted worry of Jews and Israel.

Wally questioned in his own mind, the miracle of Muhammad's flying, one night, from Mecca to Jerusalem's Dome of the Rock. First of all, he didn't think that Muhammad was "the unlettered Prophet," claimed by the Qur'an. [Sura 7:158] Muhammad travelled extensively in his first wife's business, Kadijah, and so, not only was it reasonable that he dealt with other cultures, but he must also have been trained in record keeping, as a merchant. Furthermore, his successful dealings would have given him enough money to hire teachers for a special education and self-betterment. In this regard, he probably read the *Old Testament* of the Jews and the *New Testament* of the Christians, being a genius, and a man with an ambitious and lively mind. Wally knew he couldn't prove any of this, except that other scholars had surmised as much, that Muhammad was indeed, not unlettered!

[http://www.radicaltruth.net/index.php/learn/muhammad/32-was-muhammad-illiterate]

Wally found it a point of interest that the angel, Gabriel, was common to both the Christian and Islamic traditions, first playing the role of messenger to the Virgin Mary, and six hundred years later, inspiring the words of Allah to Muhammad in a trance, making him the final prophet of God, and the Qur'an the last and final word from the Almighty. There's nothing like divine inspiration, because, well, inherently, you're not supposed to question it!

Now, if Muhammad was indeed "lettered," then his night journey might have been more metaphorical, than real, serving the Prophet's own purpose of inspiring a new religion, which could unify the various tribes in the Arabian Peninsula. Wally felt that Muhammad's night journey smacked a lot of Revelations from *The New Testament*: "And he carried me away in the Spirit to a great and high mountain, and showed me the holy city, Jerusalem, coming down out of heaven from God." [Rev. 21:10 NIV]

The Prophet's Night Journey laid a spiritual and territorial claim on Jerusalem because it could mean future wars between the people of the *Qur'an* and the people of *The Book*, namely, the Jews. Wally shook his head over this convoluted history. No wonder, intelligent atheists like Richard Dawkins, felt that religions caused nothing but trouble throughout history, and will continue to do so. Wally could see where John Lennon in his song, "Imagine," and Dawkins in his book, "The God Delusion," had legitimate reasons for criticizing, if not hating religion(s).

CHAPTER 97

"There are *more* things in heaven and earth, Horatio, *Than* are *dreamt of in your philosophy.*"

[HAMLET TO HORATIO, 1.5.167-8]

.....

... AND THE OTHER THING
THE 95 THESES AND QUANTUM PHYSICS

WALLY WAS HOOKED ON WEEKLY DOCUMENTARIES PUT ON by PBS, the "Public Broadcasting Service." He was particularly interested by one entitled, *Martin Luther*, narrated by the movie actor, Liam Neeson. The biography traced Luther's spiritual journey from an obedient Augustinian friar to an enlightened Reformer with the 95 Theses, which he nailed to the Castle Church door in Wittenberg. Pope Leo X was selling "indulgences," which were certificates, guaranteeing to reduce the time spent in Purgatory, depending on how much money you paid to the church. Pope Leo X needed to come up with a scheme to raise funds, because he had run out of money for finishing the construction of St. Peter's Cathedral, and "indulgences" seemed to be the perfect "religious fundraiser."

Luther preached that indulgences were not what Jesus taught about Salvation! Rather, one's Salvation was a free gift from God, through grace, and not through achievement. This meant that the Believer did not need the Pope and his indulgences, and in fact, did not need The Church. "It's not about you and the Church; it's about you and God!" [PBS documentary]

Wally couldn't help but think, "Wasn't Muhammad like the Pope in some ways?" The tax on non-Muslims, the "jizya," to raise money for a growing Islam? What about the 72 virgins promised to jihadists in Paradise as rewards? Whose idea was that? He could see a connection to the Roman Catholic Church from half a millennium ago, and its mistaken notion about Salvation.

Wally had also been uneasy about that dictum plastered on the outside of Mosques, "There is no god but Allah, Muhammad is His Prophet." Why were Allah and Muhammad conjoined so closely in one sentence, separated by a comma? Muslims should think, "It's not about you and the Prophet; it's about you and Allah!" Wally felt that the Prophet was idolized by extremists, even though his face was veiled in paintings for that very reason, to prevent idolatry.

The Medieval Church could be accused of that very sin, in the statues it made of the Virgin Mary for its great cathedrals, to whom the faithful prayed, as an intercessor between God and Man. Martin Luther would disagree with that notion, saying again, that prayer should go directly to God.

What about Jesus then? The Qur'an recognized him as a Prophet, in the past tradition of Prophets. According to the

Catholic Church, Jesus was more than that. He claimed he was God incarnate, and that Salvation only came through him. So to pray to him, was indeed, praying directly to God, according to the Catholic Church. Wally, to tell the truth, never thought about praying to Jesus, as a conduit to God. When he prayed, he prayed to God directly!

Shakespeare had written, "*What's in a name*? That which we call a rose by any other name would smell as sweet." [Romeo and Juliet, Act 2, Scene 2, 1-2] However, the young lovers in the play are sadly mistaken. There's a lot in a name. If you declared yourself an Anabaptist in 1569, you could be burnt at the stake. If you declared yourself a Christian amidst ISIS militants in 2014, you could lose your head!

The Israelites sensed the significance of the spoken Word, because the universe was created by the word of God. [Genesis 1, "God said, let there be…"] Wally agreed that the Israelites came up with the most sensible name for God, if they had to name Him, "YHWH."

> "In the *Tanakh*, YHVH is the personal name of God and his most frequent designation, occurring over 6,800 times. This is the Ineffable Name or Unutterable Name of the God of Israel."
>
> [HTTP://WWW.HEBREW4CHRISTIANS.COM/NAMES_OF_G-D/YHVH/YHVH.HTML]

Wally figured that Christians had trouble praying to an ineffable God, so that the person of Jesus, as God incarnate, Immanuel, God with us, made praying a lot easier. They had a better picture of someone to whom or through whom they could pray. Jesus came to earth to offer himself as a blood sacrifice to bring mankind back to God. He also claimed the name of Messiah, the chosen one. The Muslim word, Allah, for God, held reverent meaning too, apparently sharing the same root as Elohim, another word for God in Hebrew. He figured the reverence, or even worship, extended to the Prophet, Muhammad, may peace be upon him, served the same mental imaging for the divine, that Christians had for Jesus.

It would take a lifetime to scratch into any inkling of understanding for the origins and cultures of world religions, and he didn't have that time! He disdained the idea of conversion by force like ISIS pursued to make non-believers submit to Islam "to see the light" or "off with your head!"

Wally wanted to know about Josephus, the Jewish historian, about the Qumran Dead Sea Scrolls, about the Nag Hammadi "Gnostic Gospels," and the Jesus Movement in the First Century CE. Wally also wanted an understanding of the creation of the Universe, the Big Bang Theory, how multiverses might be possible, the wonderful world of particle physics. But he had to bow his head to the limit of his own intelligence, and most of all, to his failing health, and to the years he had already lived. With all the spheres of possible knowledge whirling around him, Wally also had to bow his head to his secret admission, that there was a certain comfort in ignorance. He was comfortable going to church every Sunday and to prayer meetings every Tuesday evening. He read Scripture with coffee and cookies in the security of his own home. He remembered a warning from Paul in his letter to the Thessalonians.

> When people say, "There is peace and security," destruction will strike them as suddenly as labor pains come to a pregnant woman, and they will not be able to escape.
>
> [1THESSALONIANS 5:3, ISV]

Wally liked Paul because he had great insights into ethics, how to lead a good life, and how you can't take anything for granted. Wally would describe himself as a Christian, despite the doubts he had in some parts of his own Faith. He identified with the humanity of "doubting Thomas," and forgave him for his lack of Faith in what he could not see.

He did not understand the concept of the Holy Trinity, but he accepted it, because he was raised with the concept as a boy. As he grew older, he applied that concept to the laws, or lack of laws, in Quantum Physics. Maybe the Father, Son and Holy Spirit were a "subatomic consciousness," which could be in all places, at all times. Maybe they were tinier than the Higgs boson, three elementary particles, stretched throughout Existence, forming a kind of collective awareness of all time and space? But why then, should that cosmic consciousness care about the fall of a little sparrow? He even wondered if Heaven was not "up there," but rather, in a parallel universe, a parallel dimension which had different laws of physics? Wally had just finished reading Professor Brian Green's *The Hidden Reality* [publ.2011], which seeded these thoughts in his mind for an explainable Heaven, as a reality in an invisible world.

In the security of his own study, in the 21st century, Wally realized the transgression of such thinking as "heretical." He'd be burnt at the stake during Martin Luther's time, if he expressed such ideas to his friends! Though he entertained and enjoyed this line of thinking, he dismissed the thoughts, and refocused on the amorphous concept of God within his heart, to whom he prayed each night. He had to believe that God had a personal interest in him. He didn't always think in terms of Jesus, when he thought about "God"... but it helped.

Was he wrong in reading both his Bible and books on Physics? He felt the whole business was beyond his intelligence, but sometimes he couldn't help but wonder? Maybe Nirvana is the state of consciousness which taps into the cosmic collective awareness which is God? Wally entertained the idea that Quantum Physics explained the miracle of Jesus appearing out of nowhere in the Upper Room to his Apostles after his Crucifixion. Maybe if Wally were young enough or had another lifetime to live or maybe were a genius, he might have a running chance at understanding all these questions.

At night, alone, Wally had to pray to Something, for help in daily living. It was tough enough getting by! He had to hang onto something. Samuel Taylor Coleridge coined the phrase, "willing suspension of disbelief," in 1817, which Wally applied to his Holy Bible, especially *The New Testament*, and premises of his Christian Faith. If certain things were beyond his Understanding, then he'd have to accept certain things "on Faith." Life was easier for him as a Believer, than as a Godless man.

However, he did have certain rules for his own Faith, and for those which co-existed in the world around him. Be kind! Do no harm! And if asked, explain your Faith with gentleness, but do not force your view upon others! "Live and let live," thought Wally. He appreciated the diverse colours of all races, most cultures and most religions in the world, as long as they behaved with kindness and gentility. He felt they added to the enrichment of the planet. "Hmm," thought Wally, "like the Vulcan philosophy in Star Trek, IDIC, Infinite Diversity in Infinite Combinations!"

Along that line, religions, or at least the dogmatic ones, didn't agree with Wally. He admired Martin Luther, the Augustinian friar, and the Anabaptists who followed him, giving rise to the Protestant Reformation which stood up to a corrupt Roman Catholic Church at the time. He thought there was still a need for Reformers in both Christianity

and Islam. Who knows, maybe in Buddhis
as well? It would be nice to have a pleasant cha
Dalai Lama.

> There's a wideness in God's mercy
> like the wideness of the sea;
> there's a kindness in his justice,
> which is more than liberty...
> For the love of God is broader
> than the measure of man's mind;
> and the heart of the Eternal
> is most wonderfully kind.
> [Words: Frederick William Faber, 1862]

CHAPTER 98

"By the authority invested in me, I now pronounce you man and wives!"

[Islam and Mormonism – sweet deal for the man!]

.....

"... marry such women as seem good to you, two and three and four; but if you fear that you will not do justice (between them), then (marry) only one..."

[Qur'an 4:3]

HISTORIANS ACCEPT POLYGAMY IN ANCIENT CIVILIZATIONS as a cultural fact of life in those Old Testament days. Even in Muhammad's day, in the 7th century CE, a man was allowed to take four wives. Muhammad had eleven, by some accounts. After the Battle of Uhud, many Muslim men were killed, leaving widows and orphans. Therefore, interpreters of the Qur'an see this Sura 4:3 as a compassionate revelation which allowed men to be guardians and providers for several wives, because too many men were killed. Some Islamic traditions carry on the polygamous practice into modern times when there is no need for it.

[HTTP://EN.WIKIPEDIA.ORG/WIKI/POLYGYNY_IN_ISLAM]

Wally was convinced that jealousy had to rear its ugly head in a polygamous relationship, even though the Qur'an says not to enter one if the man could not treat all his wives equally. Muhammad, himself, had his favourite, Aisha. Father Abraham sent Hagar and Ishmael away by Sarai's request. So polygamy had inherent problems, due to human nature!

The founder of Mormonism, in 1829, Joseph Smith, accumulated as many as 40 wives, with the claim that the woman earned a ticket to heaven if the man "sealed" her in matrimony. Joseph Smith had 10 wives who were under the age of 20. He probably had his favourites, and also had various tensions develop within the Smith household due to natural, human dynamics among people, the big one involving, jealousy!

The Shafia marriage in 2012 in Montreal had its own tensions within a polygamous arrangement. Rona Amir, the first wife of Mohammad Shafia became "auntie" to the Shafia children. She was treated, "like a servant to the preferred wife." Along with the daughters, the first wife fell victim to drowning in a car set up as an "honour killing," allegedly concocted by the father, son and the second wife. [Melinda Dalton CBC news article, Jan. 29, 2012]

Ancient times, modern times. Wally saw the whole business as, "the same old story." He compared Islam and Mormonism. "A sweet deal for men!" Wally thought. "That's real chauvinism. No wonder Feminists are upset!" He had questions. Did the archangel, Gabriel, and the angel,

Moroni, misrepresent God? Weren't both sexes equal in the eyes of the Lord? Was God a misogynist who had an axe to grind against all women because Eve tempted Adam in the Garden? Why didn't God speak to Muhammad personally? Why send Gabriel? Sort of second hand messenger service, wasn't it? Wait, in the Christian tradition, God also sent Gabriel to Mary with the greeting, "Hail, O favored one, the Lord is with you." Was Gabriel both Christian and Muslim?

Wally wondered if God was too busy keeping Everything together, so He delegated authority to His underlings. Seemed to be a whole hierarchy, a whole society up there in Heaven, from the top down. Well, why not? God was King! Wally couldn't help but feel disappointed in that view of the Cosmos, as God, the top dog in the Heavenly Realm, sending out messengers to do His bidding. Was the idea of God as King and angels hallalujahing Him in the Heavenly Realm merely a human fabrication, for describing something beyond human understanding?

Wally still considered himself a Christian, cradling Jesus to his bosom, rather than Muhammad or Joseph Smith. He knew there was some speculation that Jesus had sexual relations with Mary Magdalene, but Wally figured historians were more qualified to investigate that likelihood, than he was. The gospels do not touch on Jesus' sexuality or marital status. There was enough written about Muhammad and Joseph Smith though, in Wally's mind, to disincline him toward those religions, and rather go with Christianity, the religion of his upbringing.

CHAPTER 99

From the day we arrive on the planet
And blinking, step into the sun
There's more to see than can ever be seen
More to do than can ever be done
There's far too much to take in here
More to find than can ever be found
But the sun rolling high
Through the sapphire sky
Keeps great and small on the endless round

[1994 ANIMATED FILM *The Lion King*
"CIRCLE OF LIFE" BY ELTON JOHN]

. . . . .

WALLY WRITES A TRIBUTE "UNPOSTED"
FRIDAY, OCTOBER 31, 2014

WALLY FOUND THE FOLLOWING WEEK BUSY. IT ENDED WITH his mother's death on Saturday. He dropped in to see Pastor Greg. "I'd like an announcement in Sunday's service during Prayer and Share."

Wally intended to include a chapter on his mother, Rosemarine, in his novel too. Why not? She was 92 and lived through World War II. She could speak 5 languages, having been born in Serbia close to the banks of the Danube River.

She moved to Canada with her husband and three children in 1954. Became a Canadian citizen, took the oath of allegiance and made a new life in Canada with her broken English.

What a mixed history and what a life, both blessed and cursed! In her old life, in Austria, she lived in Lager Wegsheid, which was a collection of army barracks which sheltered refugees of various nationalities after 1945. It had been a camp for the Nazis during the war, with anti-aircraft guns positioned all around its perimeter in case Allied aircraft flew overhead.

Wally told Pastor Greg that he would include a chapter in his novel about his mother because she was what one might describe as, "a real original." Every time he thought of her, he was reminded of Franz Lehar's beautiful violin piece, *Schöne Rosemarine.* Lehar was an Austro-Hungarian composer who also lived through World War II. Both mom and he spoke German and Hungarian as easily as eating Wiener Schnitzel and Goulash. Too bad they never met. An exchange in different languages might have been like watching an international verbal tennis match. Words batted back and forth with swift repartée to score the winning point in a game of multi-lingual banter. Mom was good at arguing! You don't argue with a woman, especially her!

When Wally recalled the week in which his mother died, he wrote it up like an entry into a Blog. He never posted it, but kept it hidden in a secret folder on his computer, a secret he shared between God and his own heart of hearts.

.....

ON MOM'S DEATH, "UNPOSTED":

Another chapter of my life is closed. My mother is dead. Mom died just shortly before 1:00 p.m. at the Trinity Home in Kitchener, on Saturday, just two days ago. I've been meaning to write something because that's how I usually, "let things out." These are my Monday morning ramblings, my Monday morning blues, in words.

My brother phoned on Saturday at 1 p.m. to tell me the news. "Mom passed away." She was 92. I had no tears, maybe that would come later at the Funeral Home on Tuesday evening or at the church on Wednesday morning. I just felt a gentle sadness.

At about 6 p.m. on Saturday, I was thinking, it's been 4 hours now. Mom was still alive today! I didn›t want to roll back the time; I wouldn't want to freeze time at a quarter to 1:00 to prolong the tiny life she had left at that point. Mom was skin and bone. She had not spoken for over a year. She refused to eat anything in the last month. I wouldn't want her to continue in such a state, just to have her keep breathing. I don't think she'd want that for herself; I know I wouldn't.

I remembered mom, three years ago, at my sister's 60th birthday party celebrated at the Concordia Club in

Kitchener. She was up and dancing, whistling to the music as she danced. Mom loved whistling. She still recognized us then. Well, that all disappeared a year ago. My brother said she drifted in and out of awareness; and often didn't recognize him, even though he and his wife visited regularly every week.

I was so glad that I drove to Kitchener before she died, a couple of days ago, on a Wednesday. I stayed all morning and most of the afternoon. The weather was nice and the sun was out! Lovely drive to Kitchener.

The noise of the trucks on the highway was still buzzing through my head when I walked to my sister's room at the Trinity Home. My sister is in the same Home as my mother because she's handicapped with Multiple Sclerosis. The law of the universe did not hand her a blessing. We're all dealt something difficult, I guess, at different times.

In a way, it was a blessing that I made it to Kitchener on Wednesday and not Friday. On Friday, it rained heavily, so there were dangerous road conditions. Also the doctor had given mom a needle to sedate her, so she would not feel any pain through her last hours.

I didn't feel guilty that I brought my Star Trek novel, *The Better Man*, and read while I sat with mom on Wednesday morning. I broke off the reading to look out the window from mom's third floor room at the green plants in the garden below. The sun would occasionally peep through the clouds. I spoke to mom intermittently: "The sun is shining outside the window, mom. I'm glad I visited you today. It's Wednesday morning. Everything still looks green. I'm glad you're my mother." Of course, all that was said in simple German.

I occasionally raised my face from my novel and told mom about the weather or about the old family photos which hung on the walls around her little room. The nurse brought in a glass of cranberry juice.

I've always found the staff at the Trinity Home very caring and thoughtful. It can't be an easy job. The nurse let me put the straw in mom's mouth. Mom took forever to suck the juice up. It moved up the straw, and then fell down again, up the straw and down. Finally, there was enough suction to get the juice into her mouth. Success in little things! By the time she was through, the glass was mostly empty and the nurse was pleased. They record these things.

I had a bowl of soup downstairs in the tiny cafeteria, which was also the entrance to the home and the foyer. I sat down beside the resident pastor. I visited my sister once more and told her I'd go up to mom's room and probably stay until about 2:30 p.m., so I could get on the highway before the huge onslaught of traffic.

Mom opened her eyes twice during this visit. Once in the morning when I talked "at her" and once in the afternoon. Her left eye was clear and it glowed with recognition. Her right eye was blind due to macular degeneration. She said no word, but I know she recognized me during those two times when she opened her eyes.

Well, it's a chapter closed now in our family history. How glad I was that I had visited mom last Wednesday. I told her that I was glad she was my mother.

I didn't tell anyone that I, myself, wasn't long for this old world.

It started with complaints in my back a few weeks ago. Now the reason was clear, pancreatic cancer. Everybody seems to be dying of cancer these days. Well, there is Ebola and War, I guess. Makes one cynical, doesn't it? And yet, you have to have hope in something, and well, you just have to keep on going!

It's the Circle of Life

And it moves us all
Through despair and hope
Through faith and love
Till we find our place
On the path unwinding
In the Circle
The Circle of Life

[1994 ANIMATED FILM *The Lion King*
"CIRCLE OF LIFE" BY ELTON JOHN]

CHAPTER 100

Mark Twain [1835-1910]: "Of all the animals, man is the only one that is cruel. He is the only one that inflicts pain for the pleasure of doing it."

.....

THE NIGHT OWL

SATURDAY, NOVEMBER 1, 2014

FOR NOW, WALLY KEPT CHAPTER 99, "TRIBUTE TO MOM, Unposted," in a separate document within his computer, hidden within a larger folder entitled, "The New Crusades Revised." Later that night, shortly after midnight, he found he couldn't sleep, so he quietly closed the door to the bedroom, hoping not to disturb his wife. She breathed steadily in sleep. He heated up half a glass of milk in the microwave, and booted up the computer, making sure the speakers were turned off, so the electronic signal of the computer booting up would not give Wally away, signalling that "the night owl" was on the loose.

Wally sipped his warm milk and googled "Islamic State atrocities." He was curious about what the Islamists were doing in the villages and towns "over there." He was amazed at what could be viewed on the internet, pretty close to anything and everything, very little censored. Wally read the reports of children being beheaded, crucifixions and amputations being carried out. He saw a picture of crucifixions taking place of victims stretched across metal poles, while a crowd cordoned off by barricades, snapped photos with digital pocket cameras or cell phones. He read that women were raped in villages while husbands were made to watch. He saw a photo of a decapitated nude woman held sideways by two men, while a third held a basin to catch the blood flowing from her neck. How could anybody's God condone such things?

One photo showed a line of bodies in a ditch where masked jihadists stood triumphantly above shooting down at their captives with AK-47 rifles. If anyone was still alive, a jihadist jumped into the ditch to slash the victim's throat, an act which was partially blocked out in the photo by digital manipulation by some "sensitive censor."

BLOODY FLASHBACK:

Years earlier, before Wally's nervous breakdown, when he was still a high-school teacher, he had used a colleague's gym shorts to take his students for a run around the gym. Anyway, after the class, the shorts went missing.

"I know how you can make up for it," said his colleague, Geoff, who ran a hobby farm just outside of Crooked Creek,

Alberta. "We're slaughtering a pig this Saturday. You can come and scrape the bristles off the hide with a knife," he said, "ahhh, I can almost smell the bacon!" Wally wondered what his Jewish grandmother would have thought about this "penance."

It was the middle of February. He was told to wear a toque, coveralls and boots. It was going to be a cold morning.

When he drove into the yard, he could see the sow grunting in an enclosure. Freshly fallen snow made everything white, except where the pig dug the earth up with its hooves along a muddy trail inside the corral. A huge tripod on poles stood nearby, with a cauldron of boiling water suspended with a chain over a blazing bonfire. The boiling water would soften the pig's hide so the knife could easily scrape off the bristles. Wally wondered what he had gotten himself into? This for a pair of missing gym shorts? A .22 rifle lay propped up against the corral.

His colleague, Geoff, had taken on a different identity that morning. No longer a fellow teacher professionally attired, but a farmer in dirty coveralls out to get his bacon! A few other teachers were there volunteering their time, dressed down for the occasion with toques, coveralls and boots, ready to pitch in. What article of clothing of Geoff's had they lost?

Geoff took the rifle and opened the gate to the corral. He cornered the pig and put a slug behind the right ear. The pig squealed but did not go down. It waddled off grunting. Geoff approached again from behind placing a second round behind the ear. The pig still did not go down. Geoff got a huge knife and straddled himself over the pig. "Good thing, he's wearing those coveralls," thought Wally. Geoff's coveralls were already speckled with blood. The pig now seemed dazed and did not protest against the rider who finished the pig off by slitting its throat. The white snow became soaked with red blood.

Wally had vague memories of the pig being opened up from stem to stern and the dogs sniffing at the steaming entrails. The pig was hoisted up with a hook on the chain and then lowered into the steaming cauldron. When it got lifted out, Wally set to work scraping the bristles off its hide. Geoff got a lot out of Wally that morning for a cheap pair of shorts! Wally felt "short changed!"

He couldn't help but think of the passage in Deuteronomy where the pig was listed as unclean, not to be eaten. He promised himself it would be a long time before he thought about tasty bacon again.

Wally had seen men overpowering that pig with superior force. He had seen the letting of blood, but that situation was of an animal slaughtered for food, not for sport. He shook his head over the photos he had seen that night on the internet of bloody men, women and children butchered in the Middle East, human beings who were killed simply for having different ideas and beliefs than those held by the Islamist militants.

Wally shut the computer down quietly. He still could not sleep, so he stole over to the TV in the sitting room, far away from the closed door to the bedroom. He found an old movie on "getTV." He slipped a "memo" into the back of his mind that he might yet make another entry into the computer about his bloody experience in Crooked Creek, if he wasn't too drowsy once the movie was done.

"MR. WINKLE GOES TO WAR"

Edward G. Robinson starred in a 1944 black and white film, "Mr. Winkle Goes to War." The main character was

Wilbert G. Winkle, a middle-aged bank clerk, who, in the movie, is not happy with his job. He is happiest in the little machine shop he built out back of his house, and does not like keeping books at the bank! His wife, on the other hand, likes the security and status which comes with the bank job. He's been at it for 14 years, and Mr. Winkle has marked June 1, 1942 as the day of reckoning, the day he would gather enough courage to quit, "Today or Never!" He wants to create a little fix-it business in his shop, because he loves working with his hands.

Wally liked the words in Mr. Winkle's newspaper ad, "The whole world needs fixing! Whatever it is, don't throw it away. It can be fixed." Mr. Winkle was such an optimistic soul, looking for a job where he could fulfill himself with his gift as a "Mr. Fix-It." Mr. Winkle was also a soft soul, with a large streak of kindness, and in a way, innocence of heart.

Wally was convinced that some things couldn't be fixed. He thought about Aamir's mean streak, where he killed people in the name of Islam and took pleasure in it. Mr. Winkle's boot camp buddy, Joe Tinker, had a brother who was killed by a "Jap," so he was in the war for revenge, wanting to grab a Jap by the throat with his bare hands. And in fact, before he gets shot at the front, he does just that, gets a hold of a Japanese soldier and strangles him.

But movies are simple, like many novels, where the action moves straight ahead without too many hang-ups. Who knows what life-story the Japanese soldier had, who shot Tinker's brother? Who knows what life-story the Japanese soldier had, who was strangled by Tinker? And who knows what type of person it was, who finally shot Tinker, himself?

Wally's own Onkel Johann was drafted into the German army right off the farm, and if he didn't serve, he'd be shot. Onkel Johann had a plate in his skull from a head wound, and suffered terrible migraines in later years, luckily or unluckily surviving World War II. He was a decent sort. But as for Aamir? Wally was convinced, Aamir needed killing!

How ironic that Onkel Johann fought for the Germans. He was part Jewish, but that heritage never surfaced when he was drafted into the military. Oma Guenter had written "Schwartz" on the wedding certificate, for her maiden name, when she married Opa Guenter. It had been Schwartzmann. She wanted to erase any evidence of her Jewish heritage, not because of anti-Semitism in Romania during the depression years between the two Great Wars, but rather because her father, a strict Rabbi, was a wife and child beater. Oma Guenter thought if her father was a man of God, she wanted nothing to do either with him or with God. She became a non-practicing Jew, which stood her in good stead because nobody knew, not even Opa, until they got married. Opa still loved her, and remained committed to her when he found out. She did not have her sons circumcised, and then the war came. Wally felt that Onkel Johann could be forgiven for being on the wrong side in World War II, but as for Aamir? Yes, Aamir needed killing! Wally had heard the news from Detectives Spencer and Klassen, and seen the internet picture of Aamir shot dead. Wally wasn't sorry.

As it turns out, in the 1944 movie, Mr. Winkle never places the ad for his Fix-It Shop. He gets a draft notice from the army, to report to boot camp. Long story short, Mr. Winkle gets a job in the army fixing bulldozers and heavy machinery. The Japanese attack, and only because Mr. Winkle is able to drive a bulldozer into the Japanese machine gun nest, is his troop saved. He's a hero when he comes home, and the wife sees the error of her ways, never again telling him what to do with his life. Happy Ending!

Wally had another half glass of warm milk before the end of the movie. He enjoyed the black and white film immensely, especially the episode of Mr. Winkle grinding it through boot camp. Wally thought about 1944 and the rise of Nazi Germany. Mr. Winkle's war was a different sort of war than the jihadists now fought in the Middle East seventy years later... or was it?

Edward G. Robinson died of bladder cancer in 1973, at the age of 79. His middle initial, 'G', stood for his Jewish heritage and his original surname of Goldenberg. Wally liked how Edward G. Robinson portrayed Wilbert G. Winkle in the old movie. An older guy, huffing and puffing through boot camp, but gritting it out despite everything, and then becoming a hero, despite being a little unassuming guy in a big World War. Wally hoped that Robinson's portrayal of Mr. Winkle in the 1944 movie would be permanently preserved in the American Archives. Wally thought to himself, "That's a gift to you, from Edward G. himself!" A wonderful record on celluloid of the man and his talent. Wally washed out his cup, and went back to bed. He'd write something in his book... later.

CHAPTER 101

WALLY HAD BEEN FEELING OUT OF SORTS FOR A MONTH... and that was already one month ago. He had made an appointment with his family physician and told him the symptoms: losing a bit of weight, the wife thought it was great! Having abdominal pains, they thought is was indigestion! The doctor scheduled an MRI. Wally had pancreatic cancer.

.....

"THAT'S LIFE... " [FRANK SINATRA]

MONDAY, NOVEMBER 3, 2014

AN APPOINTMENT WAS MADE WITH AN ONCOLOGIST AT THE Juravinski Clinic in Hamilton. "You'll get treatment from one of the best," said his doctor. Wally was not comforted. He found it ironic after his brother-in-law, Leonard, had died of cancer not too long ago. "What in the hell are they feeding us these days?" Wally thought.

He didn't tell his wife. Just like he didn't tell her that he was writing a novel. He booted up the computer every day, when she headed out for work at 7:30 in the morning. He found he just couldn't write the more "delicate" parts of his murder mystery when she was in the house. All this secrecy, not saying anything. Must be coded into the male DNA!

Wally couldn't sleep. The secret was killing him. At 3:00 a.m., in the dark, he told his wife, "I have something to tell you." She listened quietly, "It's late. I have school in the morning. What?"

"I have cancer." A pause.

"How do you know?"

"An MRI test. Showed dark spots on my pancreas. I might have two months."

His wife cried. "Impossible! This can't be happening!" He held her close. She settled down, "We'll deal with it together."

They didn't sleep the rest of the night.

She whispered over to him, "I love you."

He said, "Me... you... too!"

She booked off sick that morning, "due to a family medical emergency."

Wally and his wife ate a silent breakfast. They went through the motions. The sun came up. "Thank goodness it's not raining," thought Wally. They sat on the couch and stared into empty space, two zombies. Everything seemed unreal.

"Hey, how about a picnic at Port Dalhousie?" asked Wally. "We'll buy a roasted chicken at Superstore. I'll bring a can of Pepsi, you bring your water; and we'll pack a few buns in a bag, and head out."

They took their books. His wife used the iPad. She was re-reading Dorothy Gilman's *The Unexpected Mrs. Pollifax.* Wally brought two books, *The Clairvoyant Countess* and *Thale's Folly,* thanks to the influence of his wife, "to broaden his scope." He hadn't started either one. He wasn't sure which one would get the toss of the coin.

They settled themselves on a bench at Port Dalhousie. Sailboats were still skimming across the water with their sails billowing out full and white in the breeze. The sun shone brighter now but Wally and his wife wore jackets, head bands and gloves. The wind was nippy but they were determined to make a picnic of it.

"We've had a good 26 years," he said.

"I don't want it to end."

"All stories come to an end," he said. "It depends on how you end them. We have a choice."

"Yes, we do. I'm glad I decided to make that choice with you."

They leaned against each other and watched the boats. White seagulls squawked and floated overhead hoping for a crumb or two from the picnic.

"I'm so close to finishing my novel," he observed. The work was no longer a secret. "There's some good stuff in it."

"How do you know," she teased.

"Cause I say so. Final answer!" They chuckled. He tore off a leg from the chicken, skimmed off the fatty tissue and gave her the rest.

"I agreed with Pastor Greg that I'd hand him a copy of the novel on a memory stick. You'll have to arrange it with him to handle the publisher, and square away the red-tape on getting the book into print."

She hated to hear this, like a last will and testament! She bucked up.

"Yes, dear."

They decided that he would not go through chemotherapy and radiation but rather do pain management for his last few weeks. "We can't avoid the inevitable," he said. "And I don't want my last days spent in misery from chemo and radiation."

They glanced out at the waves rolling over Lake Ontario, and their eyes locked onto the timeless sea, dark green water below and blue sky above. The morning sun was behind them now, warm against their necks. They both stared mesmerized, not wanting this second, this minute, and this hour to end. Time moved on relentlessly. They knew it.

Wally thought, "At least we will still have the rest of October and all of November... and" as an afterthought from an old movie, he thought, "We'll always have Paris." He remembered their springtime there in 1989 touring the Louvre and walking under the Eiffel Tower. What a ratty little two star hotel they had! The *Hotel Oriental*! But it was like a honeymoon!

.....

BROADWAY MUSICAL RENT

SEASONS OF LOVE [JONATHAN LARSON]

Five hundred twenty five thousand six hundred minutes
Five hundred twenty five thousand moments so dear
Five hundred twenty five thousand six hundred minutes
How do you measure, measure a year?
In daylights, in sunsets
In midnights, in cups of coffee
In inches, in miles, in laughter, in strife
In five hundred twenty five thousand six hundred minutes
How do you measure, a year in the life?

.....

Wally thought, how do I measure two months? So little time, but I guess it's the quality. I've been lucky. "If I could save time in a bottle."

CHAPTER 102

"When I die I hope to be

A better man than you thought I'd be"

[CANADIAN BAND, *Motherlode*, 1969]

.....

WALLY'S LAST TREK...
FRIDAY, OCTOBER 24, 2014

IN RETROSPECT, IT WAS A PERFECT MORNING! GREAT OUTING with a camera to Ball's Falls. Wally was still feeling energetic enough to walk and maybe even climb. He had his pal, Sam Clemens, with him who said he'd come along to get a few pointers on picture taking. Both camera buffs trekked down the Bruce Trail towards the embankment which would lead them down to the gorge.

Sam was a spitting image of Mark Twain, whom Wally greatly admired. A bush of wavy brown hair, a handle-bar moustache. Maybe he was the spitting image of Wyatt Earp? He wore a green turtle neck and a heavy red chequered jacket, like the kind lumberjacks wear. His camera bag was slung around his shoulder.

Wally had recently donated more copies of his Photobooks to the local libraries. He felt content that things were in the works for the publication of his novel! He planned ahead so that his last chapter 102 would be written ahead of time and slipped into the back of the book for a "warm" closing. He was amused that his novel was most often written in the third person, as if Wally were not himself, but someone else, who might carry the brunt of the crosses he had to bear over the past three years. Well, what the heck, maybe his writing, excised from the personal pronoun, had given him the strength to keep on going with all the things he had to say. His name would be remembered!

"It's a good sun today," thought Wally, as he took in a deep breath of fresh autumn air. He gazed at the sky. Azure blue, white puffs of cloud floating across the wide canvass. Not too nippy for the end of October. The leaves were delightful in their splashes of reds, oranges, browns and yellows, mostly in their prime. Earthy colours from a crazy painter's brush!

"The leaves are prime enough to get some great pictures," thought Wally. "Nature gives the photographer what it gives! It's a gift and a blessing." The leaves rustled under their footsteps. They wore boots for their trek. They had sandwiches and water bottles in their backpacks.

Wally still didn't have a cell phone. Sam had one. They wouldn't be stranded down in the gorge if somebody broke a leg! He had a trip planned to Kitchener the following week to visit his mom and he wouldn't want to miss that! It was only right that Wally finish his novel with something positive, a walk in the woods at Ball's Falls with a camera in hand, the way it should be. Wally and Sam followed the "Blazes."

"Yep, sure a good sun today and sure smells like autumn!" Wally eyed grey squirrels scampering up the trees and hurling themselves from branch to branch in search of acorns for the winter. A brown chipmunk zipped across his path. Was it Chip or Dale? "Hey there little guy!" said Wally to the disappearing tail. A hawk circled lazily above, like a little black glider without direction in the vastness of the sky.

Wally had bought a 30 foot length of rope at Canadian Tire for $30. It would make the climb down the embankment easier, once he tied it to a stump at the top. They strapped their cameras behind their backs and slid down the slope. Just 20 feet below, a little path grew wider, and led them down to the bottom of the gorge where Twenty Mile Creek splashed noisily by.

The sun blazed hot at 10 o'clock that morning. Wally and Sam were in good time and in good light to get some fantastic shots. Wally looked back up the steep slope down which they had come. The cliff was sheer and rocky, trees spread here and there upwards to the top. Huge boulders were covered in moss, and green shrubs grew across the face of the cliff. Blue, blue sky and white clouds hovered over everything. Everything indeed felt blessed!

They waded through the scraggly brush to get closer to the Falls. Spray already whipped their faces. They'd have to be careful about keeping their lenses clean and dry, so their pictures would stay in focus. Wally had clean hankies. Sam had a shammy.

They lifted their cameras to the open air only when they'd get a good shot. Wally was pleased with what he got. His pictures would make nice enlargements. Maybe he'd donate some of them to the local senior's home. They could plaque them if they wished. Old folks might enjoy looking at the great outdoors, from their warm indoors.

As they trekked, Wally stopped and kept penciling something into a black notebook. This was driving Sam crazy. He finally asked, "What the hell are you writing in there?" Wally confessed, "Just some ideas for a poem. Some of the lines are already written in my head, but I'm scratching down other ideas, which I'll weave into my poem when I get home."

"So, I'm in company of a photographer and a poet?" queried Sam.

"Yep," joked Wally. "You can tell your grand-kids about this someday."

They both had a chuckle.

"You'll have to let me read the finished poem when you're done," commented Sam.

"Maybe you can read it in my novel, once it's published," returned Wally.

"So, what's it about?"

"Oh, a little of this and a little of that."

They concentrated on their pictures. Wally never went snap happy. He framed his shots carefully, made sure his lens was dry, and focused only on what he wanted in the frame of his picture. Sam, on the other hand, took more photos, and decided that it was better to get more, than too few. He could always delete the less impressive images later in his computer.

Wally wondered how much time he had left to live. He felt a pang of pain in his belly. The exertion or the cancer? Life, at least his life, was too short! Still, he considered it a blessed day down here at the Falls. During the last couple of weeks, when people asked him how he was doing, he refused to say, "Fine." That was such a standard, and glib answer. Basically, a lie. Lately, he'd been saying, "Every day I'm vertical, is a good day!"

While down there in the midst of the noise of the rushing water, in the midst of the massive rocks, the majesty of the trees, the bright leaves, and the blue sky, he wondered what he'd put into his last chapter?

What does one put into the last chapter of one's life? He hoped there was an afterlife, and that his atoms would someday join the stardust in the universe, and become one with God, whatever He or She was? He prayed that there was a personal God who cared about him.

Wally thought about his 27 years with his wife. And what he had learned. He knew he had found love and how he was lucky to have found her. A life together, not always easy, not always hard. "It's been a good ride," he thought. With his 68 years, he was convinced he had actually lived Life, and not just floated through it, like a sleep walker. He liked Bach's song, "Sleepers Awake!" He felt he was truly alive down here in the gorge, looking up at Ball's Falls, with the blue sky canopying everything above.

Wally felt a jab in his abdomen again. It dissipated. He wondered about death. "Maybe this is the start of mine. Can you imagine what Leonard went through?"

What would Wally put into his novel, half fiction, half reality, half dream, and half night-mare? Death was, of course, a natural human process. Each one of us has to come to terms with it sometime in our own way. Is there a grown up way to face it? Too bad, when you figured some things out, you have to give it all up and go back to Nothing. He figured Alzheimer's was a cruel joke on humanity. The Universe played that trick on Dorothy Gilman in her last days, after all the wisdom she'd gleaned, either as "Mrs. Pollifax" or as "The Clairvoyant Countess." But she had a good life, almost to the end. Wally thought of his own life, all his years rolled into a ball. He had his chance to pick the colour, to make the ball as tight or loose as he wanted, and now he was close to throwing the ball back into the basket.

Wally thought of his life, and the ending of his days, "Well, you've had your say!"

Maybe the Hindus had it right, you come back in a life form you deserve and have to start all over again each time. The idea didn't appeal to him. Though maybe for Aamir it might just be the right thing. Wally pictured Aamir as coming back as a rat. Or maybe a virus of the Ebola kind. Doctors were busy now finding a vaccine which would wipe the disease out. There were all kinds of Ebolas in society. Not just the disease itself. Racism, poverty and militarism. Viruses in the social fabric of different cultures which needed to find a cure, and a wiping out, eradicating centuries of evils and injustices. Maybe the top religious leaders or heads of state are the infection?

"Will the populations of this Blue Planet ever become more humane before we all blow ourselves to Kingdom Come?" thought Wally to himself. "Before the microbes take over as The Supreme Life Form of what used to be this Earth, this Eden?

Wally was happy with this morning's outing and his picture-taking. He signaled to Sam that he had had enough. They retreated from the loud roar of Ball's Falls and trekked back into a quieter shelter along Twenty Mile Creek, near the path which led back up the gorge.

"That was great," said Sam. "How many photos did you get?"

"32," said Wally.

"I got 72," replied Sam, self-satisfied.

They opened their backpacks and lit into their sandwiches. Wally sipped his Pepsi, and eyed the sky, the trees, the fast torrent in the Creek, and the noisy water cascading down from Ball's Falls. "Ah, this is living," he said.

He asked himself again, what would he put into the last chapter of his novel, his life? Wally was determined to go out with a poem and not a whimper. He glanced at his pal, Sam, and said, "It is a good day for the camera." He added to himself silently, "It is a good day to die." Where did that line come from, maybe an old movie somewhere?

"A poem, not a whimper." He had to remember that line. "To end with a poem, not a whimper... seems like a courageous intent, more than I can handle in real life?"

He asked himself, "At the point of death, what will be my last words, crossing over to the other side?" He thought, "I've tried to do no harm... maybe, I'll hear, 'Well done, good and faithful servant'!" [Matt 25:23 NIV]

Wally and Sam chatted about current events. Kobane burning. It hadn't been good lately. October was a cruel month. They could see November being cruel, as well. Actually, every month was a cruel one!

"So, what do you expect from next month?" queried Sam.

"Same old story!" said Wally.

"Do you think ISIS will take Kobane?"

"Who knows? It's in Allah's hands," Wally said tongue-in-cheek.

"Will that part of the world ever change?"

"Not unless the women get fed up being raped and wearing burkhas. It's the women who have to change the society?" Wally added cynically, "The Islamic State could always pass a law against women looking at the internet. They could gouge out their eyes just for looking!"

Wally checked himself, "I don't want to think about those things. Right now, it's us and our cameras. Who knows where we'll be in 50 years, or next month?"

They enjoyed the fact that their cameras were not guns. They enjoyed being so far away, ensconced here at Ball's Falls, safe from the Middle East. Here in Canada, they could still walk along the Bruce Trail; smell the autumn leaves, and enjoy the climb down to Twenty Mile Creek, to take in all this beauty with their cameras.

"We've still got it good here," judged Wally.

"Yep," agreed Sam.

Wally put his black notepad away. They gathered their cans, and wrapping paper, put their garbage into their backpacks, and then faced the arduous task of climbing back up the cliff. Thank goodness for boots. Wally looked forward to finishing and polishing the lines in his poem. The photos he took would help him remember.

He had a good memory but not eidetic. In his heyday, he had a decent brain, the synapses of which fired regularly, but now-a-days, misfirings occurred more and more frequently in his 68 year-old cranium. Wally used to joke with his wife about why he married her.

"I needed a memory," he joked, "because I don't have one."

Both he and his wife didn't age well. His wife had premature osteoporosis, and they each suffered from their own aches and pains at night.

"We've aged before our prime," he said glibly to his wife one day. "We used to talk of love and now we talk about plumbing!" She thought this was clever but not funny.

Sam had used his mint-green Hyundai Accent with the hatchback to drive up to Ball's Falls. He dropped Wally off in his driveway, and said, "We'll have to compare pictures. I'll post mine on Facebook."

Wally quit Facebook some time ago under his wife's strong suggestion. He told Sam to bring over a memory stick with his photos on it. They'd compare them on his computer. Wally didn't like comparing, but if Sam insisted! Well, maybe they actually could learn something from each other's approaches?

Wally created a folder named, "Holding Dock," in his computer. He'd taken all his photos in the RAW format and he transferred everything into that folder. He then created a new catalogue in Lightroom and imported the images into that software. He intended to go over them with a discerning eye before he tackled his poem. He breathed deep as he eyed his images one by one; yes, it was a good sun that morning!

He opened a blank page in Word and stared at it. He had two menus open on his computer, each minimized to half the screen. Thumbnail images of Ball's Falls on the left half, and a blank Word Document opened on the right half, where he would write his poem, yet unwritten.

As he stared at the emptiness of that half of the screen, he thought of the poet, Robert Frost. Wally decided to take a different tack. He typed out the title, *The Road Taken*. He stared some more at the blank page, and then the first line of his poem crept unbidden into his mind. "Something to find... " As he typed, the rest of the poem took shape, word by word, floating down like autumn leaves,

THE ROAD TAKEN

Something to find leads me away
to woods and lonely trails unseen,
to question the road I've taken...
and the different future
that might have been.
Some trail leads me
to waterfalls that crash.
My eyes see sparkles
in a single splash...
tiny drops, like people,
that tumble and toss,
and teem and toil,

and run... oh, where?
Like love, like life, so fleeting,
like things, not always fair!
I imagine a droplet is the sun,
a splash - the galaxy,
our existence - a miracle,
our universe - you and me!
Seeing is more than eyes alone,
and more than merely looking.
We have a mind, a heart and soul,
to see the wonder in the whole!

.....

HISTORICAL NOTES

Jews, The Great Commission: Genesis 22:17 …indeed I will greatly bless you, and I will greatly multiply your seed as the stars of the heavens and as the sand which is on the seashore; and your seed shall possess the gate of their enemies. "In your seed all the nations of the earth shall be blessed, because you have obeyed My voice."

Christians, The Great Commission: Matthew 28:19 **19** Therefore go and make disciples of all nations, baptizing them in the name of the Father and of the Son and of the Holy Spirit...

Muslims, The Great Commission: "Invite to the Way of your Lord (i.e. Islam) with wisdom and fair preaching, and argue with them in a way that is better. Truly, your Lord knows best who has gone astray from His Path, and He is the Best Aware of those who are guided." [The Holy Quran, an-Nahl: 125]

1 Peter 3:15 But in your hearts revere Christ as Lord. Always be prepared to give an answer to everyone who asks you to give the reason for the hope that you have. But do this with gentleness and respect. [NIV]

Crusades: 1095-1291: There were 7 crusades. The crusades were a series of Holy Wars called by popes with the promise of indulgences for Christians who fought in them.

Joan of Arc: burned at the stake in 1431 for heresy.

Galileo Galilei (1564-1642): in 1633 Galileo was found "vehemently suspect of heresy," namely of having held the opinions that the Sun lies motionless at the centre of the universe, that the Earth is not at its centre and moves, and that one may hold and defend an opinion as probable after it has been declared contrary to Holy Scripture. He was required to "abjure, curse and detest" those opinions. He was sentenced to formal imprisonment at the pleasure of the Inquisition. On the following day this was commuted to house arrest, which he remained under for the rest of his life.

.....

Muhammad [570-632]: considered by Muslims as the last prophet to mankind. Primarily worked as a merchant. Took retreats in a cave in the mountains and at the age of 40, reported that he had been visited by the angel, Gabriel, and received his first revelation from God. At age 43, he started preaching that God is One and that complete surrender to Him is the only way acceptable to God. Muhammad gathered an army of 10,000 converts and marched on the city of Medina. He united most of the Arabian Peninsula converting the various tribes to Islam. The revelations. each known as *Ayah,* lit. "Sign [of God]," which Muhammad received until his death form the verses of the Qur'an, regarded by Muslims as the inspired "Word of God."

Islam split into two main factions shortly after Muhammad's death in 632 with two different views on succession.

Sunni: Abu Bakr was Muhammad's friend and became the first Caliph after the prophet's death. They became known as the people of tradition and unification. Sunnis are a majority in most Muslim communities.

Shiites: Others felt that the successor should come from within the prophet's own family, i.e. Ali ibn Abi Talib, his cousin and son-in-law. Fierce rivalry has waged between the two factions throughout the centuries to the point of violence.

"Do not take my enemy and your enemy as friends and show them no sympathy!" [Sura al-Mumtahana 60:1]

The most extreme Islamists seek to impose the totalitarian Shari'ah Law on the entire world. The Shari'ah can only be enforced in an Islamic state.

.....

This novel is dedicated to all children and civilians who have been killed in all wars throughout this planet's history by militants and terrorists, of any religion or race, who have no conscience and no loving God.

BY ALEXANDER KUCHARSKI

Waldemar Guenter died on November 29, 2014, after a short battle with pancreatic cancer. Wally wasn't just a photographer. He was also a writer who used that talent as a sort of therapy, against the bad nightmares he was having after discovering Hazirah's body in the woods. Wally's book, "The New Crusades," came out of that traumatic experience.

Wally is best described in his own words:

I've been a reporter, editor, electrical apprentice, teacher, Bible student, web designer and most recently wedding photographer. I've knocked around the block a few times, and hopefully am wiser for it! Where did the time go?

For relaxation, I watch old black and white movies, and love the old crime shows, like "Peter Gunn."

Even though I'm computer savvy, I don't have a cell phone. I don't Facebook, nor Twitter. I don't even like e-mails.

I was born in Austria, and my wife and I love traveling. We lived in France for a year, and have fond memories of tenting, and driving through Europe with our rent-a-car.

Wally told me, before he died, that he wished all guns in the world could turn into flowers or cameras. Like John Lennon, he wished there were no wars, although he felt there was a need for religion, or at least some faith in a power beyond this world. Thank you, Wally, for your tenacity in finishing "*The New Crusades.*"

R.I.P.

AUTHOR: WALDEMAR GUENTER -

NOW DECEASED
NOV.29, 2014

CPSIA information can be obtained at www.ICGtesting.com
Printed in the USA
LVOW06*0856260915

455778LV00007B/11/P

9 780994 775313